An Uncommon Dialogue

Debra J. Drake lives in Wellington, New Zealand,
where she is working on her second book.

Debra J. Drake

An Uncommon Dialogue

Wakefield Press

Wakefield Press
1 The Parade West
Kent Town
South Australia 5067
www.wakefieldpress.com.au

First published, 2005

Designed by Liz Nicholson, designBITE
Typeset by Ryan Paine, Wakefield Press
Printed and bound by Hyde Park Press

National Library of Australia
Cataloguing-in-publication entry

Drake, Debra J., 1958–   .
An uncommon dialogue.

ISBN 1 86254 679 7.

1. Drake, Debra J., 1958–   . 2. Mentally ill – Australia – Biography.
I. Title.

305.9084

I'd like to dedicate this book to Ty,
a continual reminder that miracles exist.

Chapter One

'I hate this fucking planet!'

Phil, my psychiatrist, laughed. 'You and a million others.'

I gazed out of his window, looking for the hundredth time at the huge oak tree in the back garden. In summer we held our sessions outside, under its canopy, cool in the shade and miles away from the noise of the world.

'What are you thinking?'

I sighed. 'I'm wondering when my spaceship will turn up.'

'Where is it going to take you?'

'Somewhere normal, with people like me. They're going to realise that they made an awful mistake and dropped me off on the wrong planet. Any time now and they'll be back, full of apologies.'

'Nice fantasy.'

'Beats reality.'

We sat there quietly. I knew that I was avoiding things, looking for a diversion. The past sat in my lap like a dirty great blob. I was forty-one and felt a million years old.

'Have you seen your mother lately?'

'Yep. I spent the weekend there.'

'How was that?'

'Okay, I guess. The usual.'

I didn't want to talk about her.

'You really believe,' I asked him, changing the subject, 'that I'll end up okay?'

'I know you will,' he answered with confidence.

'How can you say that? I'm obviously totally fucked-up.'

'This works. You'll just have to take my word for it.'

'What if you're wrong, though? What if I'm one of your failures? When do you eventually concede defeat and tell me that it's time to leave?'

'I'm not going to abandon you. It will be you that leaves me.'

'Sure. And pigs will fly.'

'You're going to have to trust me, aren't you?' he replied, for the thousandth time. And I wondered, what does trust feel like? What does it even mean? I thought back to our first meeting, six months ago. It had seemed easier then, a simple matter of questions and answers.

'Hello, I'm Phil. Take a seat please.'

I had prayed for an infirm eighty-year-old, and he certainly wasn't *that*. I handed him the letter from my doctor and sat down at his desk. 'That's my referral.'

'Thank you, I won't take a moment.' Bloody attractive, too. About forty, I guessed. I watched him reading the letter, my nervousness increasing. He's a psychiatrist. Would he want to commit me, or put me on drugs?

'Your doctor says that you've been depressed lately, is that correct?' he asked, folding the letter and taking out a pad and pen.

'Yes, that and a lot of other things.'

He smiled. 'Would you mind telling me about it?'

I took a deep breath. I had decided in the waiting room that I would tell him everything, even the shameful bits. But that was when I thought I'd be talking to a geriatric. 'I have pretty severe mood swings and I've been spacing out a lot more, especially just lately.'

'Spacing out? Can you describe what that feels like?'

'I've done it for most of my life. Anything can trigger it, sudden change, confusion or just being in an awkward situation. I sort of "zap out". It's like being miles above my body and floating in the ether. I used to be able to handle it, but recently it's got a lot worse and it's happening more often.'

'And these mood swings, what are they like?'

Here we go, tell him everything now, don't sweeten it up. 'Bizarre. I've always had them too, but like the spaciness, they're becoming more intense and harder to control. I go manic for about a fortnight. Everything speeds up, especially my thoughts. I can hardly sit still, the energy is so relentless.' My pulse rate was increasing with the memory.

'Do you have trouble sleeping during these episodes?'

I nodded. 'I can't lie down, I have to keep moving, keep doing things. The last time this happened I started three businesses in two weeks. It was nonstop from morning to night. Ideas kept flashing into my head at a thousand miles an hour.'

'Do you ever feel as though you know what people are thinking or feeling?'

I looked at him in surprise, how did he know that? 'Yes. It drives them crazy, but it's as though I know absolutely everything that's going on inside them, and for some reason they're keeping it from me. I can't seem to leave them be.'

'Do you ever get violent?'

I shook my head. 'No, but I certainly become irritated very easily. I can't understand why people won't keep up with me. They seem so slow.'

He was taking notes and looking up every once in a while. I allowed myself to take in his body; so solid and strong. Could he really help me? Would he have the answers that I so desperately needed?

'Do you ever think you're God when you're experiencing this?'

Was it safe to tell him? But I was just so bloody tired of hiding. 'Not exactly God,' I started nervously, 'but I do feel as though I'm attached to everything and I know all the answers. It's pretty intoxicating.'

'So you feel euphoric?'

'Yep. Sometimes I feel as though I should be able to fly. I want to share it with somebody, to take them to the fantastic heights that I'm in, but I just end up frustrated.'

'Do you become promiscuous?'

Ugh, the awkward stuff. 'I guess ... I get a little wild.'

His face softened. 'Would you mind explaining that to me?'

I looked down at his desk, unable to make eye contact. 'I get involved in all sorts of messy situations.'

'With men?'

'Yep.'

'What usually happens?'

I stole a quick glance at him, wishing again that he wasn't so nice; it was making everything that much more uncomfortable. I took a slow, deep breath. 'I'll make a phone call to a man; suggest that we get together with a bottle of wine. It's usually somebody that I stay well away from.'

'And you'll have sex?'

'Yep.'

'Is there one particular man?'

'Nope, there are quite a few on the sidelines.'

'And you just make a call and they come running?'

I looked up in annoyance. 'It's not *that* bad.'

He smiled gently. 'I'm only repeating what you said.'

I sighed. 'Okay, yes, I guess it is a bit like that. Only a few days later I wake up and can't understand for the life of me why I ever made that phone call. I think that's why I eventually stopped having sex altogether.'

'When was that?'

'Over four years ago. I just got sick of it, and all the problems that came with it.'

'Do you masturbate?'

Good Lord, how personal was that? How could he even *ask* it? I suddenly became absorbed in my fingernails. But I was aware that he was waiting for an answer. 'On and off,' I muttered quickly, scowling with disapproval.

'Did you have difficulty with sex?'

'I guess so, it's always been disappointing.'

'Do you have orgasms?'

I felt my insides heave. Surely these questions weren't right? What sort of a doctor would ask something like that? But yet again, I could feel him waiting. I kept my eyes glued to the floor. 'Yes, I do.'

'We'll go over this in more detail later, right now I need to get some more history. After these manic periods, what happens next?'

'I crash. I'll wake up one morning barely able to get out of bed. It's only then that I become aware of the mess that I've got myself into. I usually have to make phone calls to repair the damage. Sometimes I've started a job that I wouldn't normally go near, or I've resigned from one that I'd really wanted to keep. It all looks like a giant mess.'

'And how often do you have these episodes?'

'They used to be maybe twice a year, but just lately it's like the whole process is speeding up. I've had three already and it's only May.'

'Do you remember your first one?'

I nodded. 'I was eleven and living in Ireland.'

'Do you know if there was any sexual abuse in your childhood?'

'Plenty.'

He looked up from his notes. 'Would you mind elaborating on that for me, if that's okay?'

'Sure. Mum's boyfriend, Roger, molested my bigger sister and me for three years. The other men were just friends of Mum's who visited our house. Three of them were in England, but Frank was in Ireland.'

'How old were you when this started?' he asked gently.

'I'm not sure, but it finished when I was twelve, when we moved to Australia.'

He frowned. 'You say this as though you're reading it from a book.'

I shrugged. 'I guess it feels a bit like that, as if it happened to somebody else.'

'But that must have been very traumatic for you?' he insisted softly, his eyes full of concern.

'It happened. What can you do?'

'Yes, it happened. But it shouldn't have.'

I didn't know where he was coming from. 'But it did. There you go.'

He kept eye contact with me, which was starting to make me feel uncomfortable. 'We'll discuss this further in our later sessions, okay?'

'Sure.' It wouldn't get him anywhere; I had dealt with all that stuff years ago.

'Do you ever hear voices or believe that the television is sending you messages?' he asked, returning to his notes.

'No.'

'How much alcohol do you drink?'

'Hardly any, it goes to my head too quickly. I usually only

have wine when I'm in one of those manic periods, but even then it's rarely more than three glasses.'

He jotted everything down. 'Do you take any illicit drugs?'

'No.'

'Ever had an eating disorder, like anorexia or bulimia?'

'No.'

'Do you smoke?'

'Yep, about a packet a day.'

'Have you ever been hospitalised?'

'No.' I answered warily. Did he think I should be?

'Have you sought psychiatric help before?'

'No.'

He looked up from his notes, surprised. 'Never?'

'No,' I said defensively. 'It's not as though I'm out of control or anything.'

He arched his eyebrows. 'That's not what it sounds like from what you've been saying.'

I was starting to feel nervous. 'Well, I don't like medical things, or drugs, I keep well away from them.'

'So you've never been prescribed medication?'

'No.'

'Ever had a psychotic episode?'

'What is that like?'

'Feelings of euphoria, inappropriate behaviour like running naked through the street, a sense of being invincible?'

I didn't like the sound of any of this. 'Do you think there's something really wrong with me?'

Once again, his face softened. 'I know some of these questions may be a little unsettling, but they're standard, I ask them of all of my patients.'

I nodded slowly. 'Then no, I don't think I've had a psychotic episode.'

'Ever had feelings of paranoia?'

Other than right now, did he mean? 'No.'

'Have you ever attempted suicide or had suicidal thoughts?'

'I've never tried to kill myself, but I've certainly thought about it, especially just lately. I'm so tired of this, you know? I keep trying things to sort it all out but nothing works for more than a week or two. I'm beginning to think that it's always going to be like this.'

Phil looked up from his notes, his eyes full of concern. 'I do understand, you know? We can make things easier, though. You did the right thing by coming here.'

I slumped back in my chair, feeling lost and defeated. 'I'm *so* tired.'

'I imagine you must be. How long have you been feeling depressed?'

'I'm not sure, it gets interrupted by those manic moods, you know?'

'I understand. It must be very trying for you?'

He was so gentle, and had such a warm, soft voice. I wanted to believe with all my heart that he could help. 'I used to be able to control it, but not anymore. I'm afraid that maybe I really am crazy, you know, maybe it's not just my personality.'

'Is that what you've believed up to now?'

I nodded.

'Does anyone else in your family suffer from a mental illness?'

Anyone *else*? 'I don't have a mental illness,' I answered indignantly.

'I see,' he said, looking up from his notepad and smiling, 'so why are you coming to see me?'

'Because,' I said slowly, 'obviously something is not quite right. I've just got to sort a few things out.'

And I haven't even told him about *her*, I realised with horror.

What if *she* turns up to an appointment? Would he be so keen to see me then?

'Okay. That's probably enough for now. I'll need to gather some family history, but I can do that in our next session.' Phil put down the pen and leant back in his chair. 'Are there any questions you'd like to ask?'

Only about a million. 'What's wrong with me?'

'I'm afraid I can't answer that right now,' he said gently. 'I'll need to get to know you a bit better first, and gather more history. But obviously there are a few problems we'll need to address. These mood swings must make life pretty difficult for you?'

I nodded. 'They're starting to scare me. Why are they getting more intense?'

'It's hard to say, but you're in your forties, that's often the time when these things erupt. I think we're much more resilient when we're younger; you were probably able to cover it up a lot easier. But I really can't say much more until I have more information.'

'Can it be fixed?'

He smiled. 'Yes, it can.'

'Without drugs, though?'

'There's medication that would make your life a lot easier. You don't have to suffer like this, you know.'

I shook my head firmly. 'I don't want drugs, it's scary enough already.'

'Let's see how we go with that, will we? I do know of a support group that may help you gain a little more understanding of what's going on for you?'

'What? Sit and talk with a bunch of depressives?' What a gruesome thought.

He paused, his eyes lit with humour. 'Well, they do have their manic moments too.'

I was starting to like him. 'No, thank you,' I answered, able to smile for the first time, 'I think I'll pass on that.'

'Your choice, of course. Any other questions?'

'How long will this actually take?'

'I usually like to allow about two years.'

My mouth fell open. 'Two years? You're joking?'

He smiled. 'No, not at all. What were you expecting?'

'I don't know,' I stammered, 'two, three months, tops.'

He arched his eyebrows again, something that I would soon become familiar with. 'It takes a lot of time to create this much damage, it can't be repaired over night.'

But two bloody years?

'Did you have other plans for that time?' he asked, his eyes still smiling.

So, he's a funny bugger too, huh? 'No,' I answered slowly. 'I guess I was just hoping I could start some sort of a life.'

'I think we need to stabilise you first, wouldn't you agree?'

I sighed. 'I guess so.' But I was still uncertain. It was fine right now, while I was in charge, but what about later, when she turns up? I decided to play it safe. 'Are there any rules, you know, like do's and don'ts?'

'Not really. Obviously there's no sex and no violence, all very Freudian, but other than that I'm very flexible.'

No sex? I felt myself bristling. Did he think I was about to throw myself at him? Did I look that out of control? Bloody cheek. 'I don't think,' I told him, in my best clipped tones, 'that you'll have any problems like that from me.'

He smiled warmly but didn't say a word.

I rolled my eyes. 'So what happens next?'

'I'd like you to have a blood and urine sample. Then we'll get together again next week, if that's what you'd like?'

'Okay, it's not as if I've got much to lose.'

He was starting to get up from his seat, so I figured the session must be over. I collected the notes for the clinic and made my way to the door. To my surprise I felt his hand upon my shoulder.

'We'll work this out together,' he said gently.

It was the nicest thing I'd heard in a long time.

'What's he like, darling?' my mother asked as I climbed into the car.

'Bloody attractive, unfortunately. Really friendly too. Heaps of personal questions though.'

'I don't think I'd like that.'

I didn't doubt that for a moment.

'What does he look like?'

'Hard to say, really. He's fair-haired, gorgeous eyes, about five ten, and a very solid body, you know, stocky. Not quite sure of his age, though, maybe about thirty-eight.'

'Married?'

'Yep, he wears a wedding ring.'

'Hmm, and when will you see him again?'

'Next week.'

'Well, who knows, dear, maybe he only asks questions in the first session?'

'I don't know how it works, but I guess it's all necessary.' I was remembering his enquiry about orgasms. My stomach did a belly flop. 'Can you just drop me off, Mum? My head's in a bit of a spin.'

'But I was looking forward to you staying the night at my place, dear. I thought we could go out for a play on the pokies and I've prepared your favourite meal.'

'I know, Mum,' I answered, feeling guilty as hell, 'but I need to think, and Ty may come back early. I think I'll just go home.'

My mother went quiet and didn't speak to me for the remainder of the trip.

I busied myself in the kitchen, trying to slow down the racing thoughts. Had I done the right thing? Was it safe to have told him so much? I had heard that it took two psychiatrists to have you committed, but maybe that was years ago? Maybe it was only one, these days? I started to feel scared. How much had I said to him? Was he already preparing a hospital space? I noticed with annoyance that I had peeled a dozen potatoes at least, far more than I would need. I had to slow down somehow; energy was starting to pour through my veins.

Concentrate on the dinner. Finish that and we can go for a walk.

I hastily wrote a note for Ty, my seventeen-year-old son. He had planned to stay overnight with a friend, but was known to change his mind at the last minute. My body was starting to shake, a sure sign of trouble.

I threw on a jacket, locked up the house and headed down the road at a fast steady pace.

Don't think, don't think. Just see the pavement, feel your feet on the ground and count your steps. One, two, three, four.

I let the numbers fill my brain, blocking out the confusion and fear.

That's right, fifty-seven, fifty-eight.

I could feel my pulse going down. I walked till I felt it was safe enough to go home.

Chapter Two

'More questions, I'm afraid,' he apologised.

'That's okay, fire away.'

'All right, I want to know a bit about your family. How many of you were there?'

'Initially we were seven. Mum, Dad, Mark, Cheryl, Jo, Kim and myself. I was the second youngest. When I was six years old, Mum left my father and the two eldest. That reduced my family to four.'

'So there was your mother and . . . ?'

'Jo, eighteen months older than me, Kim, two-and-a-half years younger, and myself. Oh,' I added, 'and Roger. He was one of Mum's boarders. She'd been having an affair with him. Not that we knew that, of course. But that's why we left my dad.'

Phil was writing it all down. 'Tell me how it happened? Do you have recall of the events?'

I nodded. 'Yep. Mum had told Jo and I to come home for lunch that day. Mark and Cheryl, the two eldest, were to eat at the school canteen as usual. Kim was only four, so she was already at home with Mum. When Jo and I got home at lunchtime, there was a taxi outside the house. We left in a hurry. I didn't see them again for twenty-five years.'

Phil looked up from his pad. 'Where did you go?'

'The taxi took us to Sheila's, one of Mum's friends. I can only remember playing in the garden with Jo and Kim, while they stayed inside, talking. Eventually a man showed up and we all piled into his car. We drove for hours, till it was dark, I think. Then I remember a caravan park, with Roger waiting. He'd been expecting us. The driver had been a friend of his.'

'How long did Roger stay with your mother?'

'About four years all up. We stayed in England for three months, but were constantly on the move because Mum found out that Dad had the authorities looking for us. Finally we sailed to Ireland and caught a train to County Cork. We lived there for three years.'

'How was that for you?'

I grimaced. 'Our home was a single room on the top floor of an office block. My sisters and I shared a double bed. Mum and Roger slept about ten feet away from us. Roger was ... I don't know, weird.'

'Weird?' Phil asked. 'How so?'

I felt uncomfortable. It was too embarrassing to discuss. I shrugged my shoulders. 'Just weird. Anyway, after three years we went back to England, to Southampton this time. Mum worked in a pub and Roger found a job on a building site. We shifted quite a lot; I think we changed school about three times in the space of a year. There were lots of arguments. Roger had a violent temper. Mum finally did a midnight flit and we returned to Ireland without him.'

'How old were you at this time?'

I did the sums. 'Eleven, I think. Jo was twelve and Kim, nine. Mum put the three of us in an orphanage while she looked for work and somewhere for us to live.'

'How long did that take?'

'I can't remember how long we stayed there. Neither can Jo. I know I hated it though. Mum would visit us on the weekends and each time we convinced ourselves that she'd be taking us home with her. But weeks passed. We even started school somewhere. Jo eventually stopped talking to Mum altogether, she was so angry with her. It was an odd time, my memory seems to have lost quite a bit of it.'

Phil nodded and turned the page on his pad.

'And Roger was one of the men who sexually abused you?'

'Yep. Me and my big sister, Jo.'

'And how old were you when this started?'

I shook my head. 'I really can't remember when it began, but my first clear recollections of it were when we moved to Southampton. I was eight or nine then.'

'And there were other men?'

'Terry, Ray and Frank. The stuff with Frank happened in Ireland.'

'Were these your mother's boyfriends?'

'No, just men she knew from working at the pub. There were always plenty of men around our house.'

'I see. And did your mother know about the abuse?'

I sighed. 'I'm not sure how much she knew. There was one occasion when it took place in their bed, but I'm not certain that she knew what was going on.'

Phil looked up from his notes. 'Roger was molesting you while your mother was in the same bed?'

I nodded quickly, wanting him to move on.

'And you've never discussed this with your mother?'

'I brought it up once, about ten years ago. But she acted weird.'

Phil nodded. 'That's something we'll need to go over in our future sessions, okay?'

'Sure.'

'Are you all right with this?' he asked gently.

'I think so. I'm just feeling a bit spacey, you know.'

15

'I understand. It's called dissociating, by the way. It's a common coping mechanism for people who've been sexually abused.'

I nodded, desperately trying to pull him into focus. I was starting to fade away.

'From the sounds of it, you've had a very traumatic childhood.'

I shrugged, not comfortable with his concern. 'I got through it, I guess. What else can you do?'

'Yes, you got through it,' he said quietly, looking into my eyes, 'but it shouldn't have happened. No little girl should have had to put up with that. It must have been awful for you.'

I shrugged again, his tender manner disconcerting me. 'You survive these things, don't you? Not much point in wallowing in it.'

Phil returned to his writing. 'Where was your mother during all this?'

'How do you mean?'

'When the sexual abuse was taking place, where was your mother?'

'I'm not sure. The stuff with Roger began when she was taking night classes at a secretarial school. That's when he started with Jo and me.'

Once again Phil looked up from his paper. 'Do you mind telling me what eventuated?'

Yuk. Such personal stuff. Why were the details necessary, what difference would they make?

'We can cover this later if you'd prefer?'

'I think so, if you don't mind.'

He was such a nice man. And patient, too. But how long would that last?

'How did these men have access to you girls?'

'Mum worked in a pub. They were her friends, so they got to know when we were at home alone.'

'Was she aware of this? That they were visiting your house?'

I nodded. 'Oh yes, often it was her idea.'

Phil frowned. 'Okay, we'll have to cover that later as well. I still need some history. You were twelve, you say, when you arrived in Australia, did you have any problem making friends at school?'

'I stuck pretty close to Jo. I did have some friends, but we went to about eight schools by the time I was twelve. I was used to leaving suddenly.'

'Why so many moves?'

'My mum would get restless. Or there'd be a violent boyfriend who she needed to get away from. It was generally midnight flits. We would often arrive home and find Mum standing there with a suitcase packed.'

'How old were you when you left school?'

'Fifteen.'

'Did you like school?'

'I loved it. I was going to be a journalist.' I looked out of the window, surprised that I was still so bitter.

'So what happened?'

'It was three months before exams, one of Mum's boyfriends had threatened to shoot her. We left Melbourne that night, took a train to Adelaide. By the time we got back, the exams were over. I got a job in an office.'

Phil was busily writing it all down. I sat there awash in memories, what a bloody mess it all was.

'How old were you when you first had consensual sex?'

'Fifteen.'

'How was that?'

I shrugged. 'Pretty spacey. But he was a nice guy, my first real boyfriend. We had to take off again though, because of that bloke who had said he'd kill Mum. But this time we went to Sydney. I didn't see my boyfriend again.'

'Have you ever married?'

'Yep. I met my ex-husband when I was seventeen. Stayed with him for eleven years, in New Zealand. He was a Kiwi.'

'Any children?'

'A son, Ty, he's seventeen.'

'Has your son always lived with you?'

'Yep, although he has spent time with his father. He was four when we left Auckland and came back to Australia.'

Phil took a deep breath and put the notes into my folder. 'That's enough for today. Now tell me,' he asked, looking into my eyes and smiling warmly, 'what are you hoping I can do for you?'

God, now there was a big question. I thought about it for a few moments, trying to clear my befuddled brain. 'I guess I need to make sense of everything that went on back then. And I'm tired of feeling so out of control. I'd like to get a hold on things, live a normal life, you know?'

'I understand. You've had a very tough time of it,' he answered softly. 'And this is never easy, wading through the questions. Would you like to set up a regular appointment?'

I nodded, still uncertain about what we were actually going to *do*.

'You can make arrangements with my secretary on your way out. I'll see you next week, Deb. Okay?'

He was being so *nice*. I was already starting to feel edgy.

Ty was due home in an hour. I slipped into mother-mode and started to prepare dinner. But I was excited. I had found some-one who was going to help. Did that mean that after all of these years, I could let go now?

I could feel my energy level increasing by the moment; I was spinning too fast. I put the radio on but couldn't find a station with the right speed of music.

Calm down, Ty will be home soon. Focus on the dinner.

I peeled the potatoes and prepared the stew, trying to stop my mind from racing and my energy from going off the Richter scale.

I had almost completed everything when the telephone rang.

'Hey, Mum.'

'Hey, Ty. Where are you?'

'I'm at Adam's, we're going for a surf and I'll have dinner at his place. I'll be home about eight, okay?'

'Okay, you be careful, though. It's pretty rough out there today.' I could almost hear his eyes roll.

'Yes, Mum. See you then.'

I turned everything off; the stew would keep till tomorrow. Sitting in my lounge room I let the thoughts flood in. Everything Phil had said during our session was whirling around my brain. His smiles, his shrugs, the questions; all were dancing about and vying for attention. My insides were knotted with conflicting emotions. Would Phil provide the answers that I had been searching for? He had said that he would need to get to know me. What did that mean? Once again, my stomach heaved at the mere thought of him. After half an hour I decided to go out for a walk, I was starting to spin out again and needed to keep focus. I walked and walked, trying to slow myself down, but there was so much to think about. It was such a relief to have finally told someone, but I was aware of the attraction too, and the dangers that lay within it. And what about everything that I hadn't told him yet? My thoughts took me back to Ireland, and Roger, the tiny room that we had all shared for three years. Could I tell Phil everything that had gone on in that room? Would he believe me? There were so many things he didn't know. Which ones were important? How would I know?

I arrived home exhausted but a little more grounded. As soon as I climbed into bed though, my mind resumed its frantic activity. Events from my past were flickering through my head like a movie reel out of control. There were strong emotions inside that were starting to unsettle me. I kept picturing Phil's solid body and thick woollen jumper.

I wondered what he thought of me. Was I just another loopy female? Was he waiting for the right time to suggest medication again? Fear started surging through my body. Why had I told him so much? He was a psychiatrist, for God's sake. He had power. I leapt out of bed, got dressed and hurried out into the night.

Just walk. Just keep walking and everything will be okay. He won't put you away because you don't have to go back to see him. He's not going to send someone over. You'll be all right. Just calm down.

The week between sessions was tumultuous. By the time I found myself sitting in Phil's office again I was so spaced out that I could barely see him.

'More note-taking, I'm afraid,' he started, with a pad and paper in readiness.

I nodded. I was miles and miles away, drifting in the ether.

'I'm not so sure that this is a good idea.'

'Why's that?' he asked gently. 'Having second thoughts?'

'Yep.' I stared fixedly at the desk, trying desperately to pull something into focus.

'You're feeling spacey?'

I looked up in surprise. People couldn't usually spot it. I nodded; talking was too hard.

'It's pretty natural for you to feel like this, we're digging into the past, and it's bound to bring a lot of uncomfortable feelings up.'

I nodded again. I didn't want to talk. Words felt like sludge, thick and slow.

'Maybe I should leave?' I managed.

'You can if you want to. But it's all right if you stay, you don't have to do anything. We'll just be taking notes today.'

'Okay.' I was too tired to resist.

'I'd like to go over these moods swings of yours in a little more detail. How long have you been having them?'

I thought back to when it first started. It seemed centuries ago. 'I was twelve. We were living in Ireland ...'

Mum had sent me out to buy meat from the markets. It was a fantastic winter's day. The moment I stepped out onto the pavement I was hit by the crispness in the air. There wasn't a cloud in the sky. It was bitterly cold and the sun was shining. The atmosphere transfixed me.

Something inside me started to soar. My pulse was racing. I stood stock still in the middle of the busy street, absorbing everything, feeling everything. Soon I was a part of it. I *was* the crisp air, the biting cold. My mind was shot-through with clarity. I knew all there was to know. It was intoxicating. I wanted to grab the people passing by. To tell them that everything was fine. Nothing mattered. We were living in a dream; it wasn't real at all. Reality was something way, way out there, where we truly belonged. We were the air, the sky, and the coldness. We were everything, not these tiny, pathetic, frail bodies that we believed were our identity. I got so excited that I had to just walk and walk and try to calm down.

Phil was busily taking notes. 'How long did this last?'

'I can't remember.' I answered truthfully. 'I don't even recall going to the market.'

'Are you aware of any specific events that trigger these episodes?'

'Not really, often I just wake up with it, although I do get a little wary as it gets closer to winter. Those crisp days seem to do something to me.'

'Manic episodes are sometimes triggered by seasonal changes.'

'Really?'

'Yep.'

'Do you think I'm a manic-depressive?'

'I still can't say yet. Sometimes these things can be behavioural, I'll need to get to know you a little better before I can make that assessment.'

Get to know me? Which bit was he talking about? And what did 'getting to know me' entail?

'What are you thinking?' he asked gently.

I shook my head. 'There's so much stuff, it's hard to know what's relevant, you know?'

'I understand, it always looks a little overwhelming to begin with.'

I was still avoiding his eyes, unsettled by his presence. It was as if his maleness filled the entire room. I could feel my stomach churning. She was already being drawn towards him, feeling that familiar desire to get inside him and find his weakness. What would he want? What was missing from his life? There was always something. I pushed her thoughts aside, wanting to stay focussed and present. 'What do we actually *do* here?' I finally asked, breaking the silence.

'That's a good question. I guess I like to think of it like a journey that you and I take together. I'll be there to navigate, but generally it will be you that guides us. We'll go wherever you lead.'

I grimaced. 'I don't know whether that will be a good idea. I'll probably take us round in circles.'

'Circles are fine,' he answered, smiling warmly. 'They can be quite enlightening.'

'Will you give me homework?'

'No. No homework.'

'So what do I actually do?'

'You don't have to do anything. This time we spend together will be all yours, it's up to you how we use it.'

I had no idea what he was talking about. 'And there are no tasks or anything?'

'Nope.'

'I don't get it, then. How does this work?'

'It's a spooky sort of process, I guess. Basically we allow it to unfold, but the main thing is that you do it in your own time, when you're ready.'

'But will you let me know if I'm being too slow?'

Once again, he smiled warmly, causing my insides to bellyflop. 'No, I doubt whether I would,' he answered softly. 'Whatever speed you go at will be the right pace for you. There's no right or wrong here.'

'But what if I'm going off on some weird sidetrack; you'll let me know, won't you?'

'I think wherever you take us is where we need to be.'

God, wasn't he going to take any control? How crazy would this be? 'I still can't believe that you're going to leave this up to me. I haven't a clue about what's going on. There must come a time when you step in?'

He shook his head. 'As I said, this is your time.'

Jesus, this was going to be some weird trip. 'I think you'll eventually have to change your mind on that.'

'Why's that?'

'Because although I seem quite stable now, things can get pretty bizarre.'

'In what way?'

I thought of her again. How long could I keep her at bay?

She was already biting at the bit, longing to ask him questions and find that little edge that they always gave her. I knew my stomach was churning because of *her*. She was fantasising already. I suddenly realised that Phil was waiting for an answer. 'I'm sorry,' I stammered, 'would you mind repeating that?'

'That's all right. I was asking in what way do things get bizarre?'

'Oh, I don't know, you know, things . . . change.'

'I guess we'll just have to wait and see what happens, won't we?'

I nodded. *Yep. And I hope that I can keep control.*

'And you say your mother doesn't suffer from mood swings?'

'Not really. She gets pretty depressed at times. That's about it.'

'What about your sister, Jo is it?'

'Yep, she has a lot of problems too, with relationships and things. I think we've tried nearly everything to fix them, but so far nothing has worked. She gets spacey as well, but in a different sort of way, you know, sort of airy fairy.'

'I understand. Did you and she talk much about the abuse?'

'When it was going on, we didn't. But just lately, ever since I brought it up with Mum, she and I have been going over it.'

'Does that help, having someone you can talk to about it?'

I shrugged. 'Yes and no. We have so many unanswered questions. We tend to lead each other round in circles.'

'Were you close to her?'

'We fought a lot when we were younger. Mum always left Jo in charge of us when she worked at nights. We'd often end up in screaming rows, pulling each other's hair out, that sort of stuff.'

'So what did you children do in the evenings, when your mother was at work?'

'Sometimes we just went out onto the streets. We had roller skates, we used to race all over the city. It was fun.'

'This was in Ireland?'

'Yep. There were some good times there.'

He smiled. 'You had quite a lot of freedom then?'

'Too much, I think. We could basically come and go whenever we pleased. But not when Roger was there, of course.'

'You lived in Ireland twice, is that right?'

'Yep, first time was with Roger, when I was between the ages of six to nine. Then we went there a second time, after Mum had left him in England. I was eleven then.' So many moves, I wondered if Phil would ever be able to keep track. He was still taking the odd note or two, so I could only hope that he'd somehow manage to put the pieces together. 'It's a bit messy, isn't it?' I offered.

'I'll become more familiar with it, in time. But I wonder how it must have been for you.'

I shrugged. 'I got used to shifting suddenly. Sometimes it was fun.'

'And the moves were always sudden?'

'Yep. We'd only take a suitcase or two.'

'And everything else got left behind?'

'Yep.'

'Hmmm.'

What was he thinking? Should I be feeling something about all this? But I wasn't, they were simply the facts. What was the point in making them out to be more meaningful than they were? I glanced up from my fingernails and was disarmed to find Phil looking directly at me. It sent a shiver though my entire being. Quickly I returned my gaze to my lap.

'That's about all we have time for now,' he said quietly.

'Oh, sure, sorry, I . . . hadn't even noticed the time.'

'That's okay, I can keep an eye on it. I'll see you again next week?'

I nodded, eager to get away.

I didn't feel like going straight home, there was too much going on inside me, so I stopped off at my local pub, cashed in a twenty-dollar note, and sat down to play the pokies. As I mindlessly pushed the buttons I wondered whether I ought to tell Phil about the gambling. I didn't imagine he would be too impressed, but it was the only escape that I knew. I loved walking into the familiar setting, ordering a coffee, getting a cup full of coins and settling in for as long as possible. It calmed down my mind.

Two hours later and sixty dollars poorer, I arrived home and started preparing dinner for Ty. I enjoyed being in mother-mode; it was my most stable role. As I pottered around the kitchen, I let the thoughts play around in my head. There were so many doubts and fears. His questions about orgasms and masturbation kept reverberating through me, bringing with it a surge of sexual desire. He was so attractive. And so gentle. Why couldn't he have been an ugly, shrivelled-up old man? Or better still, a woman? I doubted there were more than three or four years between our ages. How uncomfortable was this going to be? In the last twelve months I had started three separate jobs, only to flip out and resign. I had enrolled for university then changed my mind. And my mood swings were becoming harder to control. The only moments of sanity were with my son; it was like my mind flicked into a different space, allowing me to focus and to take care of whatever needed to be done. Once Ty left for school though, or when he'd gone to bed, all hell would break loose again. It was starting to frighten me.

My thoughts were interrupted by the screen door flying open and Ty racing into the toilet; his usual mode of entrance after a day at school. I put the chicken into the oven and started on my sweet-and-sour sauce.

'Hey Mum, how's it going?'

I smiled at him. 'Good, I had my appointment with Phil today.'

'How was it?' he asked, opening the fridge door and searching for a snack.

'Okay, I guess. Mostly background stuff. How was your day?'

'Not bad, I've got Adam coming over; we're going for a surf.'

I looked out the window at the cold, grey day. 'It's freezing, Ty.'

He rolled his eyes. 'Yeah right, Mum.'

I laughed. 'Is Adam staying for dinner?'

'Doubt it. He's got band practice tonight, I'll probably join him.'

Ty was heavily into electric guitar and keen to form a band of his own. Luckily his bedroom was a granny flat at the back of our garden so the noise was kept to a reasonable level. 'So when do you think you'll be home?'

'Not sure, but not later than ten.'

That gave me about four hours alone. Maybe I'd be okay if I stayed focussed on the television. Adam arrived and the two of them donned their wetsuits and headed down to the beach at the end of our road. I turned the oven down low, knowing they could be gone for quite a while. After switching on the television and flicking through the stations, I found a documentary. Bit by bit I allowed myself to become absorbed, ignoring the growing furore inside my head.

For the rest of the week I tried to keep my mind calm by not focussing on Phil or the upcoming session. I was spacing out badly though, even at home, and at one stage couldn't bring my kitchen into focus. I held on to the bench and closed my eyes.

It's okay, just feel your feet on the ground, you'll be all right. Think of normal things like cooking the dinner and doing the washing.

I opened my eyes and busied myself around the house, but the floating sensation was sickening. My thoughts were interrupted by the telephone. I knew it was Mum.

'Hello, dear, I'm just calling to see how you are?'

'Not bad. I think this stuff with Phil is stirring the cauldron up a little, though.'

'Are you sure it's a good idea, seeing him?'

'I've got to do something, Mum. I'm tired of having something wrong with me.'

'There's nothing wrong with you, darling, no matter what he might tell you. You'll always be perfect in my eyes.'

I felt a familiar flash of irritation. 'If I was perfect, Mum, why would I be seeing a psychiatrist?'

'I wasn't attacking you, darling.'

I drew in a slow, deep breath. 'How's your day been?'

'Boring, as usual. I felt like a play on the pokies but I haven't got a cent. Will you be coming up for the weekend? I could sure do with the company.'

'Yep, Ty will be at Adam's most of the time. I'll see you on Saturday, okay?'

'That will be lovely, dear.'

I hung up the phone, aware that my jaw was clenched again.

Chapter Three

The days disappeared. I had to check the newspaper to find out what the day and date was. My only sense of continuity was found in Ty's routine and sitting in front of the television. I watched one program after another till they blurred into meaninglessness. I floated. A familiar, yet strangely comforting feeling of being stranded out in the ether, adrift and alone.

I floated in to our next appointment. This time Phil led me over to the couch and sat in an armchair about three feet opposite. I didn't like it at all. I preferred the desk between us. I fidgeted and squirmed, pushing myself into the sides of the sofa, needing some edges, some protection.

Phil said nothing. He just sat there quietly watching; waiting.

'I don't like this couch,' I finally managed.

'Safer with the desk between us?'

'Yep.' I looked up at him, seeing his warm, caring expression. But I could only look for an instant before needing to lower my eyes again.

More silence. I was getting increasingly uncomfortable. Wasn't he going to say or do anything? What was he waiting for? What was I supposed to do? I stared out of the window, finding his presence almost insufferable. I knew he was looking at me. The attention was making me squirm.

'I don't like this,' I said again.

He just nodded.

God, this is awful! What is he waiting for?

I started fidgeting with my nails. Then I crossed my legs but that felt ridiculous so I quickly uncrossed them again. I looked out the window once more, studying the trees in detail.

This is crazy. Why isn't he doing something?

I was going to have to break the silence somehow; it was unbearable. 'I think I'd prefer to sit back at your desk,' I suggested.

He smiled. 'What are you feeling right now?'

'Totally exposed,' I answered uncomfortably.

'That's what most women who've been sexually abused feel. Wide open.'

God, there he was getting personal again. I squirmed even more.

'Well, anyway, I've had a rotten week.' Anything to change the subject.

'Why's that?'

'I lost all the days. It feels like I haven't been here for months.'

Phil nodded, as if he'd expected something like that. 'Have you been in that spooky space of yours?'

'Yep. Still there.'

'I can see that. You look like you're having a hard time focussing.'

'I am. It's hard to talk too, the words get lost, you know?'

'You don't have to talk if you don't want to.'

That gentleness again. I would have felt calmer if he was gruff or demanding something from me. Having him sit quietly in front of me was altogether way too intimidating. Why wouldn't he talk? What was he expecting me to do or say? I continued to wriggle with discomfort.

'I don't think this will work,' I told him, hoping I wouldn't hurt his feelings. 'It's not you,' I continued slowly, trying to grasp the thick and cumbersome words, 'I just think, you know, I'm probably not cut out for this stuff.' I didn't want to look into his eyes. The softness there was sending waves of unfamiliar feelings through me.

'You're doing really well. Believe me. Just relax and take your time. There's no hurry. Tell me a little more about your week?'

I sighed, but felt relieved to finally have something to get on with. 'Crazy. At first I felt brilliant, then I started speeding up. And I had so many doubts about this place. I got scared. I didn't know what I was supposed to feel. Then I just shot out into space.'

Phil listened intently, and nodded once in a while as I relayed my confusion. I was so aware of his body, his solidness, that I could hardly think straight. 'Is this normal?' I asked him. 'What am I supposed to be feeling?'

Phil shook his head. 'Whatever you're feeling is what you're supposed to be feeling. Remember, there's no right or wrong in this process.'

I felt an irritation rip through my body. 'That's crap!' I snapped. 'Obviously I'm not meant to be this chaotic. You can't tell me that this is normal?'

'I think maybe you've had someone tell you your whole life what you're meant to feel.'

I thought immediately of my mother. The irritation increased. 'I'm only asking you,' I said slowly, 'how should I feel towards you?'

Phil said nothing.

Bastard. I hated bloody silence. I kept my eyes on the floor, staring at his shoes. *He isn't helping at all! Why isn't he talking?*

'If you're waiting for me to solve this,' I began again, 'we'll be here forever.'

'There's no hurry.'

Jesus, I was *dying* with awkwardness and there was nowhere

to go. It was fine for him, sitting there like some smug bugger while I was in chaos. Bet he loves this shit! Women falling all over the place and making total bloody fools of themselves. I watched the clock. Christ, only ten minutes had passed. And still he said nothing.

'Are we going to spend this entire session in silence?' I asked with annoyance.

He shrugged. 'That's up to you, I guess.'

I was hating him more by the moment. How was this crap supposed to fix anything? Why didn't he tell me what I was supposed to do? 'By the way,' I suddenly threw in, 'my mother didn't control me. She can't control anything.'

'Tell me about her. What's your relationship like?'

'Fine. We ring each other all the time and I often spend weekends at her place. She and I are close. Probably the closest in the family.'

He nodded. 'Have you ever discussed the sexual abuse with her?'

There he goes again. What was his deal with this sexual stuff?

'Yep,' I answered, somewhat irritated. 'I told her about ten years ago.'

'What was her response?'

I shrugged impatiently. 'I don't know. Strange, I guess. I thought she'd be shocked and horrified. But she wasn't. She said something like, "Oh, that wasn't very nice, dear". I couldn't quite make it out.' I remembered the incident well. I had left her house feeling peculiar, as though I'd just had some bizarre communication with an alien species.

'What were you hoping for?'

I shrugged again. 'Don't know. I guess I thought she'd feel terrible, and maybe angry with Roger and the other men. I knew how I would feel if Ty ever told me something like that; I'd kill the bastard that touched him and ask questions later.'

'And she didn't react like that?'

'Not at all. It was all very odd. I decided I must have said it wrong or not explained it very well.'

'So you made it your fault?'

'Well, obviously,' I snapped, 'if I'd told her about it properly she would have understood. But she didn't. So I must have missed something.'

'Do you often feel that way with your mother?'

I thought of the million times that I had tried to communicate something important to Mum and the strange, blank expression in her eyes. It made me shudder.

'Sometimes I think she and I must come from different planets. It's like I can't get through to her, can't reach in and affect her in any way.'

'And yet you say you're close to her? How is that?'

'I've no idea,' I answered honestly, 'but we are close. I know that.'

'Maybe that's a fantasy. Something you wish was true?'

'No. It's not a fantasy. It's real.' I was recalling the times I'd laughed with Mum. It was like we were two of a kind. I knew we were close.

'How does she feel about you being in therapy?'

Why was he so interested in my mother? 'Fine.'

'Have you told her why you're here?'

'Yep. Sort of. Mainly about the mood swings.'

'What does she think of that?'

I shrugged. 'Mum says that there's nothing wrong with me. That I've always been moody.' I remembered telling her one weekend that I was scared. I was starting to feel that there was actually something wrong with my mind. She had laughed it off. 'Don't be silly, dear. You're perfectly fine.'

'Actually,' I continued with Phil, 'it annoyed the hell out of me. It was like it didn't matter what I felt, she had it all worked out.'

'Has it always been like that?'

I sighed. 'Yep. I'd try to explain something to her about what was going on for me but it never made any difference, Mum would tell me what I was "really" feeling and what I needed to do, as if she knew me better than I knew myself. Drove me crazy sometimes, like I wanted to scream. But I think it's just because she and I see things differently. She certainly tries hard in a lot of other ways.'

'What do you think she feels about the abuse you and your sister went through?'

Christ, there he goes again. 'Why do you keep harping back to this? She doesn't feel anything. I've tried to find out but she goes blank on me. That's all there is to it.'

'Maybe you should try again.'

'Yeah right. And what would that achieve?'

Phil shrugged. 'I think you need to make some sort of peace with it, and so far that doesn't look like it's been very successful. That will be one of the reasons for your mood swings and dissociation. And possibly why you still haven't left your mother.'

Bloody cheek! 'I left her when I was fifteen years old!'

Phil was shaking his head. 'You may have moved house but you certainly haven't left your mother yet. You told me yourself, you still spend weekends with her.'

'So what? Don't most normal people spend time with their mothers?'

Phil looked dubious and didn't answer.

'I hate it when you say nothing,' I told him angrily.

'What do you want? Me to agree with you? Well, I'm sorry, that's not going to happen if I think otherwise.'

Prick!

'So you're saying that I should bring up the sexual abuse again?'

'I'm not telling you what you should do. It's time you started figuring that out for yourself. But I am saying that the relationship with your mother sounds unhealthy, and part of that is to do with the sexual abuse. Whether you confront her or not is entirely up to you.'

I was looking at his feet again. The thought of dredging up all that slime made my bones feel tired.

'We'll see,' I said. 'I think I'd rather find a way of getting more comfortable with her. I'm sick of being angry all the time. And I know she's always done her best. Some days we're great with each other, we have a ball.'

Especially when we're gambling.

Phil just nodded, letting me talk on.

'She and I have a lot in common. She's an extrovert though, much more confident than I am. I always felt like a wet lettuce leaf next to her when I was younger. And she'd do things that would have me dying with embarrassment.'

'Like what?'

'Oh, the way she dresses, for a start. If it sparkles or shines, she'll wear it. And she was so flirtatious. Men flocked around her. I felt so inadequate next to her. Even when I was in my teens, and bringing boyfriends home, she would sit and talk to them for hours, charming them to the hilt.'

'How did you feel about that?'

'Uncomfortable. When I was sixteen I broke up with a boyfriend because he had a foul temper whenever he touched alcohol. Mum started going out with him a couple of months later.'

'How old was he?'

'About twenty-seven, I think.'

'And your mother?'

'She would have been forty.'

'I can see that would have been uncomfortable for you.'

I nodded. 'It was a bit odd, I guess. Mum said she did it because she wanted to get back at him for being so cruel to me.'

Phil arched his eyebrows. 'How was that supposed to work?'

I shook my head. 'I've no idea. She stayed with him for a couple of years, despite his violent temper. In the end though, she did another midnight flit.'

I sighed, feeling a bit guilty about what I was disclosing. 'She's not all bad though,' I hurriedly added. 'She's very generous, always buying me treats and wanting to know about everything I'm doing. It's important to her that we're close.' I noticed the time and jumped up from the couch. 'Anyway, the session's over.'

Phil smiled gently. 'We'll talk some more next time, huh?'

I nodded, once again, eager to get away.

I stayed away from my mother's house that weekend. I had too much to think about. I was feeling so many powerful feelings towards Phil. At first it was nice, like bathing in a warm pond. But then I got confused. *Isn't he just a doctor? Doesn't feeling this nice mean that I'm getting too close? Are patients supposed to get close? Perhaps he'll get angry and say that this is unnatural and I'll have to sort myself out elsewhere?*

Days passed and the feelings intensified. My body felt as though it would explode. My mind whirled with a mass of conflicting thoughts. On the third night after my session with Phil it all became too much. Ty had gone to bed and I was curled in my armchair overwhelmed by emotions and immobilised with indecision. I needed to let it all out, but I didn't know how. I could feel it inside my skin, building and building till it felt as though all my nerve endings were screaming. An idea came to me. I went to my kitchen drawer and found a pin. I grew excited. Climbing back into my armchair I placed the pin on the table beside me and just looked at it. I had never done anything like this before. I felt adrenalin rushing through me and was hit by a surge of sexual excitement. Could I do this? I imagined scratching the pin down my forearms and hands. It was an intoxicating thought.

Minutes passed. I thought of Phil again, seeing his smile and his strong, solid body, feeling the sickening surge of emotions. I knew I would never get close to him; he was too good, too normal. It was only a matter of time before he would get sick of me, or I would ruin it. And all I would be left with was wishes and hopes. I picked up the pin and scraped it down my forearms. But I hadn't been firm enough; I barely felt it. I tried again, this time pushing the pin deeper into my flesh. The pain was heaven. I was soon drawing blood and swooning in relief. I was letting it out at last. It was a glorious sensation. I continued for an hour or so, till I had ten or eleven welts on my wrists and hands. At last I felt calm. I returned the pin to the drawer and walked through the house, turning off the lights and checking the locks. After climbing into bed I fell into a deep sleep.

I used the pin the following night, only this time I made sure that the cuts were made in a place where they wouldn't be noticed. I was excited at my newfound outlet but scared too. This couldn't be right? How far would I take it? Would I be looking for a knife next? The thought was strangely thrilling. I was in control. It would be totally up to me how far I went. I wouldn't tell Phil. There was no need for him to know. I'd just use the pin for as long as it worked. It would be my secret.

'Debra. Come through.'

I followed Phil into his office. The couch looked unwelcoming.

'Can we sit at your desk?' I pleaded.

He smiled. 'Needing a bit of distance?'

I nodded. I liked the desk between us. It felt safer. We sat there quietly, saying nothing. I kept my hands on my lap, hoping he wouldn't notice the welts. 'Things are worse since I've been seeing you,' I started.

'That's often the case. Do you want to talk about it?'

I shook my head. 'Just too many feelings. And confusion. I don't feel better at all.'

'Unfortunately your therapy will bring things up that have been pushed down for years. It's all part of the healing process. But I'm here with you, you don't have to go through this alone.'

I thought of the previous night and the pleasure of cutting. I *was* on my own. He wasn't there to help with that. I said nothing.

'What's been going on for you?' he asked gently.

I stared at my hands down in my lap. How would he understand that? I wanted to cry but took a deep breath and pushed it down. 'It's too hard. I don't think I can do this.'

'You're a lot stronger than you give yourself credit for.'

'I don't feel very strong.'

I was looking at his jumper. I wished I could just climb into his body; so solid and strong and safe. I'd never felt so lonely in my life.

'What are you thinking?'

Could I tell him? Would he think I was crazy? I took a deep breath. 'I know this sounds odd,' I started, 'but I've got this weird thing where I wish I could just climb into your body. It's so strong and I can't make any sense of it at all.'

I looked briefly at his face for a response. Once again his eyes were looking gently at me. He said nothing and waited for me to continue. I was feeling so little. All I wanted was to be in his lap and have him wrap those lovely big arms around me. But there was no way I could tell him. He'd think I was totally nuts. I felt myself sinking into despair. What was the point?

'It doesn't matter,' I told him, straightening up in my chair. 'No doubt it will pass.'

'I think it does matter. I think that whatever you're feeling right now is very valid. It sounds like you want to get closer to me. Would that be right?'

I felt myself blush from the roots of my hair. How could he be so direct? Now what was I meant to say? I shifted in my seat, unable to look at his face. 'Is that bad?' I asked, dreading the answer.

He smiled softly. 'Of course it's not bad. It's perfectly natural.'

'I don't know how to do it, though. It feels odd. Not right.'

Phil was nodding. 'I guess up until now your way of getting close has been by using your body. Have you been experiencing any sexual feelings lately?'

Oh God, I thought I would die on the spot. How did he know all this shit?

'Some, I guess.' I muttered under my breath.

'I would expect that. Did anyone get close to you who wasn't using you as a sexual object?'

I thought back to all the men. And Mum, who didn't like touching us at all. But then I remembered my dad. He hadn't abused me. 'My dad must have hugged me,' I answered quickly. 'I don't think there was anything sexual with him.'

'And you were taken away from your father at what age?'

'Six.'

'That must have been hard for you; losing your dad, and a brother and sister.'

'I thought he'd find me,' I answered quietly.

'Tell me about that?'

'I would lie in bed at nights in Ireland, wondering when Dad

39

would come and take me home. I was sure he'd find me. I imagined him charging through the front door, gathering all of us up in his arms and taking us back to England.'

'And he never came, did he?' he asked gently.

'Nope.'

'You not only lost half your family but you then had years of constant moves and sexual abuse. That's quite a tragedy for a little girl, isn't it?'

I nodded, feeling removed from it all. 'I guess shit happens.'

'It didn't have to happen like that though, did it?'

I looked up at him in surprise. 'How else could it have happened?'

'Well. You could have had a mother who cared, who looked after her daughters. You could have had a father who took the time to find you and make some sort of contact. And it's a great shame that the only men who came into your life used you like a thing, a sexual object.'

It sounded awful. But still it didn't touch me. Once again I shrugged. 'Well, that's how it was. I guess you get used to it.'

'You survived it, surprisingly well, considering. Some people with your background develop alcohol or drug abuse problems. Others are in and out of mental institutions. Self-harm is another consequence. You're very strong, you know. Somehow you got through it. You should feel proud of yourself.'

Self-harm? Was that like cutting? I decided then and there to never use the pin again. I didn't want to start a bizarre coping mechanism now.

'I don't feel at all proud of myself,' I answered. 'Quite the opposite. I feel like I'm a total failure and completely fucked-up. I'd do anything to be a normal person with a normal life.'

'I wouldn't overestimate "normal" if I were you. Life is hard. Most people struggle with it in one way or another.'

That surprised me. I thought he'd promise me that everything would be wonderful once we'd worked things out. 'Are you saying that even when I'm all fixed up, life will still be difficult?'

Phil laughed. 'Absolutely. Take a look around you, it's hardly perfect, is it?'

'Then what's the point?' I asked, totally perplexed.

'The trick is to find an area in your life where you have some control. But we're getting ahead of ourselves. Right now we need to stabilise you, that would be a good start, wouldn't you say?'

'That would be heaven,' I answered, trying to imagine what it would feel like to have two days the same and a break from the relentless confusion.

'It will happen, believe me.'

'How can you be so sure?'

'This works. I wouldn't do it if I didn't believe in it. For now you're just going to have to trust me.'

'Trust you? Now there's a dirty word.'

He laughed. 'With your background I imagine it looks impossible. A lot of damage has been done to your psyche. We'll need to work on that. But we'll get there.'

I shook my head. 'Beats me how.'

'We're doing it already. Trust me.'

We both smiled this time. Trust. The notion eluded me.

I left the session feeling good. Maybe we *were* on track.

Chapter Four

The week went reasonably smoothly. Despite feelings that threatened to overwhelm me I was able to leave the pin in the drawer.
I found it helped to climb into bed whenever things loomed too
large. I was lying there one night thinking of all the attempts I
had made at fixing myself up. There had been so many. My mind
went back to my first encounter with Personal Growth. I was
living in New Zealand at the time.

It was 1981 and I was twenty-three. I couldn't stand the touch of
my husband. I had lost all interest in sex and it was causing
problems in our relationship. I wished he could just forget about
sex. I thought everything else was great. But lying in bed at night,
his arm would reach for me and my whole body would seize up.
I'd wake in the morning with my jaw aching from grinding my
teeth all night.

Eventually we sought help. There was a commune in Auckland
that was dedicated to the pursuit of intimacy and spiritual growth.
At that time about two hundred people lived there. They had all
sold their worldly goods and committed themselves and their
incomes to the community. It was a fascinating place and looked
nothing like I had imagined when my husband had first told
me about it. I had pictured tents and bearded hippies. But there

were buildings and dormitories, offices, canteens and counselling rooms. Much of the income for the maintenance of such an organisation was derived from therapy groups. We sifted through the literature.

There was quite a choice on offer: private sessions, weekend groups and intensive seven-day live-in marathons. All were designed to break down the barriers between couples and enhance the level of intimacy. The therapists promised to be honest, confronting and supportive. Never being one to do things half-heartedly, I opted for the seven-day marathon. The rules were simple. All participants were to bring their own sleeping bag. No outside contact was permitted. No alcohol or cigarettes were allowed. Meals would be provided.

After talking to one of the therapists, my husband and I decided to do separate groups first. They advised us that this would be easier and allow us to get accustomed to their processes. Once we had completed a group alone we would be better prepared to attend one as a couple.

I wasn't going to be first. The thought alone made me sick with nerves. John got time off from work and we packed his bag nervously. He would be gone for a week. We had no idea what was going to happen. I kissed him goodbye and waited.

During his absence I read more of the literature. It talked about sexual inhibitions and the need to undo the old tapes of conditioning. Each group would have up to fourteen participants and two therapists. Sessions would start at 8 am, break for meals and finish at 10 pm. Although the counsellors would leave the premises at night, everyone else was to sleep in the main room.

I started to get nervous. The days dragged by and my fears increased by the hour. What if he met somebody? Maybe he'd realise that he was crazy being with me? I imagined him telling them all about my strange ways. I started to dread him coming home. I lay in bed on the sixth night, trying to stop the nightmare scenarios.

My husband returned on a total high. It was way beyond words, he said, and had to be lived to be believed. He told me about feedback and tasks and confrontations that had my blood curdling. 'I felt as if I'd relaxed for the first time in my life,' he said. 'It's a fantastic seven days. I've already booked my next one.' I wanted to know about sex. Did he sleep with anyone? No, he assured me, but it wasn't because it wasn't on offer. Sex was a natural part of the whole process, he continued, but none of it would make sense until I'd done a group myself. I was feeling even sicker now.

My turn arrived two weeks later. It was Friday night and I was sitting on the floor in a circle with fourteen 'weirdos', as I saw them. I had already had the runs twice and was sure I wouldn't get through the next hour without throwing up or leaving. The therapists came in and introduced themselves as Renee and Anton. We were then asked to take it in turns and tell the group who we were and why we were there. I didn't feel I could answer either of those questions.

I'm bloody mad, what the hell am I doing here? I eyed the exit. I could hardly swallow and my heart was pounding. *How the hell did my husband find this fun?*

I muttered something inane when it came to my turn. I wanted to go home. I decided I would see the evening session through and then get the hell out.

There were six men and eight women, including myself. We were all between twenty and thirty-five years old. I didn't like the look of any of them. Renee was explaining that it was only natural to feel nervous and that in a couple of days we'd be feeling a whole lot better, especially if we made a commitment to participate fully.

'Now,' she continued, 'let's loosen things up a bit. Everybody stand up. I want you to walk around and pick a partner. Once you've found someone, I'd like you to stand still, look in their eyes and tell them how you feel about them. Take it in turns. Once you feel completed, move on and work your way around the room. The task is finished when you've spoken to everyone.'

You have got to be kidding? Tell them how I feel about them? How the hell do I know?

Now my heart was thumping. My mouth felt like sandpaper and my mind was hastily thinking up a rapid exit. Suddenly there was a lumbering, six-foot bloke standing in front of me and peering into my eyes. 'You look scared,' he started, smiling softly. 'This your first group?'

'Yep,' I answered, thinking that he didn't actually look too awful.

'No one bites.' He was quite nice. Reminded me a little of a huge teddy bear with big brown eyes.

'I'm going to be sick,' I managed, convinced I would be vomiting within minutes.

He actually took hold of my hands. 'I'm Pete and I assure you that you'll be all right. Just take some deep breaths.'

I did as he said, feeling a little awkward with the handholding.

'Now, we better get on with this task. Let's see ...' he gave me that lovely, warm smile again, 'I feel very protective towards you. I think I'd enjoy wrapping you up and making you feel safe.'

Well, he won me on the spot.

I looked into his eyes. It was my turn now. I took another deep breath. 'I feel really relieved that you were the first person to speak to me and I feel better already having spoken with you.' We beamed at each other. Well. Maybe this wasn't going to be too awful.

I had two creeps tell me they had the 'hots' for me and a few of the women shared that they were unsure of me. 'You sound like a snob,' I was told on two occasions. It was my English accent, I assured them. Although to be honest, I was certainly aloof.

The ice was broken. Renee then went over the timetable with us and by then it was 10 pm and she and Anton were bidding us goodnight.

Oh God, here we go.

Everyone was up and about, gathering sleeping bags and finding a spot to sleep. I went into the showers and changed into my pyjamas. I was dreading this. And dying for a smoke! I told myself that all I had to do was get through the night and I'd leave first thing in the morning.

I found myself a corner not too far from the door, laid out my sleeping bag, climbed in quickly and faced the wall. Moments later, I felt a gentle tap on my shoulder. It was Mike, one of the blokes who had the 'hots' for me. 'Hey,' he smiled ever so broadly, 'I'd like to spend the night with you if that's okay?'

What?

'I'm fine by myself, thank you,' I spluttered. It was the best I could come up with.

He laughed. I noticed his pimples and unshaven face. Yuk.

'I think you'd enjoy it, is all.'

I couldn't believe this bloke. He didn't even know me.

'No, thank you. I want to sleep. Really.'

'Please yourself sweetheart.' And he moved on to the next sleeping bag.

Thank God I was left alone. But within about half an hour the noises started. It seemed everyone but me was having sex. I pushed myself into the wall. I'd never heard such a racket!

I finally fell asleep, doubly determined to leave first thing.

Before anyone else awoke, I grabbed a forbidden cigarette from my handbag and ducked outdoors. Having found a tree to hide behind I lit up and sat down, wondering what on earth to do. How was I ever going to last seven days? I thought of calling John. I knew he'd do everything in his power to make me stay. I remembered our problems at home. They weren't going to go away by themselves. Maybe I *was* too inhibited? It wouldn't hurt to give it another twenty-four hours. I butted out my smoke and headed back in.

After breakfast we were back in our circle and Anton and Renee had joined us. 'Well,' started Anton, 'let's have a feedback round. How was your night?'

One by one they 'shared' with the room, naming the person they had spent the night with, how it was, what had come up for them and any other little niggles. I was quite fascinated by it all and relieved that I had nothing to say. I noticed that Mike got quite a lot of negative feedback and I felt pleased about it. The whole thing took over an hour. Then I realised that Renee was looking directly at me. I smiled back. The room was quiet.

'Well, Debra, you're the only one who hasn't said anything. Would you like to share?'

'I just slept,' I answered truthfully.

Renee smiled back warmly. 'Didn't anyone talk to you at all?'

I remembered Mike and told her what had happened.

'So why didn't you fuck him?' she asked me quite calmly.

I gave a nervous laugh. What sort of question was *that*?

'Well, I'm married, for a start.' This got quite a few laughs from around the room.

'Yes, we had your husband with us just a while back. Did you make an agreement not to have sex with anyone else?'

Anton, the other therapist, was smiling broadly. I didn't like him one bit. He was overweight and had a perpetual sheen of sweat on his face. His black t-shirt and saggy track pants looked like they hadn't seen a washing machine for months. What sort of a therapist would dress like that, I wondered? Renee was waiting for an answer. I now doubted how honest John had been with me. Did he have sex? Did he tell them we'd made an agreement?

'Debra,' she prompted, 'there isn't a right or wrong answer. I just want to know how you plan to conduct yourself during the week. Are you saying that you won't be having sex with anyone?'

'That's right,' I answered quietly.

'Aw shucks!' bellowed Mike.

'I think we've got the virgin queen in our midst,' laughed one of the women. I think her name was Charlene. She hadn't liked me from the word go. I was wishing the conversation could change and get the spotlight off me.

'What I'd like to know,' Anton piped in, leaning back against the cushions and placing his hands behind his neck, 'is what happens if you fancy someone during the week? Are you allowed to change your mind, or will hubby get all upset?'

'Is he in a position to get upset?' Renee asked, smiling.

'Ooooh, did the husband break the rules?' I don't know which person in the group asked this, but I could feel myself getting irritated. What had John got up to?

Renee tried again. 'I want you to know that there is no pressure here, Deb. If you don't want to fuck anyone, you don't have to. But I'd like to remind you that you're here to explore doing things differently, and I'm more than happy to support you when you do. Okay?'

I nodded my head. I quite liked her. Even if the language was a bit rich. She was about forty, with short black hair and an open, friendly face. After asking a few more questions about the previous night, Renee stood up and asked us to do the same. 'Task time!' she enthused. My stomach did its usual heave. What now?

'I'd like you all to form a circle, please, and leave a little space between each person. Now, taking it in turns, and I don't mind who starts first, I want you to go inside the circle, and share with each person exactly what you're feeling about being in this group. Only this time, you're not allowed to talk.'

Oh God, I hated this stuff! We slowly formed a circle and I noticed most of the men were looking particularly unimpressed with the task. Pete caught my eye and gave me a wink. I figured he must have done quite a few of these groups before.

Sure enough, Charlene opted to go first. Her red hair, blue eyes and extroverted nature reminded me of my mother. She was pirouetting and dancing around the circle letting us know how delighted she was to be here. I felt even sicker. There was no way in the world that I was going to do that!

Next up was Shane, a quiet, serious-looking man of about thirty. His long blonde hair was tied back in a pony tail and he had the loveliest, gentle brown eyes. I wondered what he was going to do. I certainly couldn't picture him prancing. At first he walked past us all, stopping for a moment, looking into our eyes, and then moving on to the next person. Once he had completed the circle he started again. Only this time, to my horror, he roared! I nearly leapt out of my skin and threw a quick look at Renee. Was this normal? She seemed quite unmoved. Shane's face was wild, his eyes, fierce. As he went from one person to the next, the long, violent roar would erupt from him again. I started to shake. I didn't like this. I wanted to find a corner somewhere and hide. He was getting closer to me. Roaring and bellowing like a man deranged. Then there he was, in front of me. I didn't want to look at him. I waited.

Get it over with, then go away.

Eventually I looked up at him. His eyes were swimming. He looked once again gentle. He was gazing deep into my eyes. Then he smiled and moved on. I nearly fell over in relief. But Mike was standing next to me and copped such an almighty roar that I started to quiver all over again.

This time it was Justine's turn. I hadn't had much to do with her. She was one of the women who had found me 'snobbish'. As she did her first round I noticed what a lovely body she had. She was tall and lithe. Her dark hair fell in soft curls around her face. I thought she must be about twenty-five. The men were eyeing her with interest as she sauntered past them. She walked into the centre of the circle, and to my total amazement, stripped off all of her clothes.

Ye Gads! You're joking?

Justine then proceeded to embrace the circle, one by one. The men were delighted. Charlene looked miffed, like her thunder had been stolen. Then it was my turn. I honestly didn't know where to look. Justine stood in front of me and waited till we had full eye contact. I felt peculiar standing there fully clothed with a naked female three inches away from me. She was assessing me. I took a slow breath and just looked right back at her. A few moments passed. Then she gave a wry smile and wrapped her arms around me. I hugged her back, suddenly relieved not to have been passed over. Maybe she wasn't so bad after all?

Next it was Mike's turn. It seemed roaring was the thing for the men. Only this time I didn't get let off. He stood in front of me and bellowed! Strangely enough I was fine with it. I knew where he was coming from. He was one pissed-off man.

I knew that soon I was going to have to perform. I couldn't for the life of me work out what to do. Nothing I had seen so far came anywhere close to how I was feeling. How do you portray 'scared' without words? Or feeling out of your depth? The circle was waiting. Then suddenly I knew exactly what to do. I stepped forward into the ring. I decided to start at a place where I felt reasonably safe. I stood in front of Pete. The big bear. I folded my arms tight in front of me and hunched my shoulders. Pete beamed, as if to say, that's right, just show the truth. I went from person to person, standing before them and conveying my withdrawal, my desire not to participate. It all went fine till I got to Mike. I was looking into his eyes, seeing his aggression, his annoyance at being rejected by me the previous night. Suddenly I wasn't feeling at all withdrawn. There was a slow anger building up inside of me.

You bloody bastard! Just 'cause you don't get a fuck! Standing there like some angry prick who hasn't got his way.

The anger turned to rage; my hands were tingling. I looked for Renee, unsure. She just nodded. I uncrossed my arms and stared into Mike's intimidating gaze. It wasn't Mike anymore. It was my husband, annoyed at my distance. It was Roger and all those other angry, sick pricks I'd ever come across. I exploded! A roar came out of my centre like it had lived there for centuries. I couldn't stop it. I just roared and roared and roared into his face. I wanted to rip him to bits, to thump and hit and kill him.

Then as quickly as it had started, it disappeared. I was drained. I wanted to cry. I folded my arms again and walked before the remaining groupies. When I took my place back in the circle, I was exhausted.

At lunchtime I found myself a cushion and sat alone. I wasn't nervous anymore. I was numb. Justine pulled up a cushion nearby.

'That was amazing,' she said.

I smiled. 'Not sure where that came from.'

'It came from you, Deb. Must be a lot of anger in there?'

I looked at her. She was so pretty; so sure of herself. I felt cumbersome, awkward beside her.

'Well, hopefully it's gone now,' I answered.

Justine laughed. 'Just like that, huh? I wish.'

'What do you mean?' I thought I had just gotten rid of something that had held me back for years.

'This is my fourth group,' Justine explained. 'I'm still working my way through the anger. It's a slow process. But you're doing great.'

'Am I the only first-timer here?'

'Yep. And five of the groupies live in the community, including me. We're really old hands at this stuff.'

'I bet Pete's one of them too?' That would explain his high comfort level.

'Sure is. Like him, do you?'

I was watching him making a cup of coffee. 'Yeah, he's nice.'

Justine was looking at me intently. 'Think you might change your mind about being celibate?'

'God, no!' I answered quickly.

She laughed. 'He's my partner. I wouldn't mind at all.'

I gulped. 'Your partner? But I haven't seen you together once.'

'We plan it that way. It gets too tricky otherwise. And anyway, I'm doing this group for me, I don't want to be seen as half of a couple.'

I was still stunned. 'And you wouldn't mind if I slept with him?'

'Debra, we're an open couple. We can fuck anyone we fancy. It works for us.'

There was that lovely confidence again. I felt like a dinosaur, trapped in ancient rules and some invisible code of 'nice' behaviour.

Justine was watching my face. She smiled gently. 'Can I give you a hug? You sure look like you could do with one.'

I sighed. 'Yep, that would be nice.'

We curled up into the cushions and lay there for the rest of the lunch hour.

That afternoon we were told that an art therapist from the community would be joining us for a few hours. I felt relieved. I'd had enough of tasks. I was snuggled up into a cushion next to Justine. It was pouring outside. I wished we could just do nothing for the rest of the day. But right on the dot of two, our door opened and in came Maria, loaded with paper and crayons.

She was quite a sight. I wondered if these community people had washing machines or irons. Maria was wearing a tie-dyed kaftan that was so creased it looked like it had lived in the bottom of a wardrobe for years. She had enormous, pendulous breasts that were clearly visible through the thin fabric. Her hair was a frizzled mess of red curls. She reminded me a little of a blown-up Orphan Annie doll. Really blown-up. She plonked herself in the middle of our circle.

'Hi. I'm Maria, your art therapist for the afternoon. I always love coming to these groups. So exciting!' She beamed a smile at all of us. No one said anything. We were all still pretty mellow from our lunch.

'All right then. Let's get started!' She handed out the butcher's paper and crayons.

This would be a nice break. I hadn't drawn in years.

When we were all organised Maria sat back in her place and looked slowly around the room. 'Now, we're going to pretend that you're throwing a dinner party. I want you to draw me a picture of three people who you'd love to invite and three people who you would hate to have there. That's all. Nothing too complicated, is it?' Once again she beamed.

I felt like she was talking to a bunch of three-year-olds.

'Nothing is ever harmless in these groups,' muttered Justine.

I laughed. 'Drawing is pretty safe, I reckon.'

'Ah, to be that innocent.'

I wasn't sure what she meant. Anyway, I had to get on with

this task. Soon we were all engrossed and the room was quiet. A dinner party. Who would I invite? Half an hour into the exercise I developed a sickening headache. I kept drawing, almost finished, when the pain got so bad that I could hardly see. 'Justine? Where can I get some Panadeine? My head's killing me.'

Justine looked at me with sympathy. 'Sorry, Deb, no pills allowed. Told you nothing is harmless.'

This had nothing to do with the exercise. I just had a rotten headache. I finished the drawing and sat there waiting for the others. I was irritable and impatient. For God's sake, how long does a bloody picture take? At last we were all done and Maria collected the crayons.

'Excellent!' she piped. 'Now, let's go around the room and share our experience.'

Oh fuck off.

I wanted some painkillers. Who cared about a bloody stupid drawing?

One-by-one the groupies held up their drawings and discussed the reasons for their choices and how it had made them feel. Maria mostly listened and sometimes asked a couple of questions, but generally things went smoothly. My turn arrived. I held up my drawing and told the group why I had invited each person. But my head was pounding!

'I'm sorry, Maria,' I said halfway through, 'I'm not up to this right now. I've got a rotten headache. Can you just move on to Justine?'

Maria frowned. 'I guess I'd like to hear about the people you would hate to have at your party first.'

Jesus. I glared at her. 'Okay, fine: Charles Manson, Phyllis Diller and Robert Mitchum.'

'Why Robert Mitchum?' she persisted.

'He makes my skin crawl.'

'Have you got any reason as to why you feel that way?'

What the hell did it matter! I suddenly hated this bloody place and wanted to go home.

'Debra. Your headache may have something to do with this. Why not give it a shot, huh?'

'Fine,' I answered abruptly. 'He makes my skin crawl because he looks like a child molester.'

Maria was nodding. The room had gone quiet.

'What about him makes you think of a child molester, Deb?'

God, my head was hurting so bad. I didn't want to talk, or to think. I saw everyone waiting. 'I'm sorry, Maria. But that's it. I don't want to keep going over it. Okay?'

She nodded again, but kept looking at me. I just looked straight back at her, daring her to challenge me. I had nothing else to say. Eventually she moved on to Justine and left me in peace.

My headache wouldn't go away. For the next two days I totally withdrew from the group. I talked to no one. Thankfully they left me alone. I knew that Renee was watching me, but she didn't push. I went through the tasks like a robot. During the breaks, Justine or Pete would sit next to me for a while but nothing was said. At night I was the first in bed, by now unconcerned about the moans and groans around me.

On the fourth day I couldn't stand it anymore. As soon as Renee entered our room I went up to her and asked for an individual session. We were allowed to do this if we got 'stuck'.

'I wondered how long it would take you. Quite a stubborn madam, aren't you?' She gave me a hug and said she'd see me in an hour or so, after feedback round.

'I was fine till that bloody drawing,' I told her. Renee had grabbed a couple of cushions and found us a corner to sit in.

'Tell me what happened,' she asked.

I filled her in and once again my head started hurting.

'I take it you've had some experience with child molesters?' she asked quietly.

I nodded.

'Why don't you tell me a little about it? Take your time.'

'I don't want to. Stuff went on, you know, with men. I didn't know what to do.'

'Where was your mother throughout all this?'

My mother? What did she have to do with it?

'I don't know, work, classes, you know, she was pretty busy.' It seemed irrelevant.

'Did you ever tell her about what was going on?'

'Nope.'

'How come?'

'What would that have achieved?' I asked irritably.

Renee smiled, her eyes ever so gentle. 'I guess it might have been a relief for you to hand over to someone. It can't have been easy to keep all that stuff to yourself.'

I shrugged, but I felt a pain inside me. It hurt.

'Deb?'

I looked up. 'Everything hurts,' I told her.

She took hold of my hand. 'Tell me how it hurts, hon.'

My throat felt strangled. I thought I'd burst. And my head was pounding.

'It's too much,' I whispered.

'It was too much, Deb. Way too much for such a little one.'

She was stroking my hand.

'You've got to let it out, darling. That's why your head is hurting you so badly. Let it out. It's very safe here. I promise.'

'I don't know what to do,' I wailed.

'Yes you do. Let go, hon. Just let it all go.'

And then I did. An awful noise came out of my throat, like a long, drawn out moan. It went on and on. Then I was bawling my eyes out like a child. I felt totally bereft. Renee was quietly encouraging, assuring me that I was safe. After what felt like an age, I curled up on the cushion and fell fast asleep.

For the next few days I roared and wept and raged. It seemed to come from a bottomless pit. As other groupies let their defences down, a closeness developed between us that was like nothing I had ever experienced. I fell in love with Justine and Pete and even Mike. On our last day we swore eternal friendship. I had done it! I had stuck the whole seven days out and discovered things inside myself that would have me thinking for weeks.

I arrived home elated, much like my husband had after his own gruelling seven days. We talked for hours into the night, sharing our experiences and working out when we could attend a group together. I believed I had found the answer. It was simply a matter of letting the feelings out.

In the next five years we participated in various groups, some alone and a few as a couple. We learnt how to 'vent' and 'share' and 'explore our feelings'. It had come as quite a shock to me at first, when on my second group I had walked into the main room during a lunch break and come across Renee having sex with one of the group participants. I eventually got used to it, though. And even had sex myself with the therapist who ran my fourth group. Despite our efforts however, I still remained detached from my husband. I couldn't bear to be touched by him and the distance between us grew wider. My mood swings were increasing.

The decision to separate was one of the hardest things I had ever done in my life. What hurt the most was taking my son away from his father. I felt that I was no better than Mum. I resolved that Ty and his dad would have constant contact. I would do my utmost to keep their relationship functioning.

I left New Zealand with my four-year-old boy. We flew to Australia, to Adelaide, where my mother and little sister Kim resided. My life was to change dramatically. However, what didn't alter was my determination to fix myself. I was to spend the next ten years exploring some weird, some wonderful and some vaguely useful avenues for personal development.

And here I was, ten years later, seeing a psychiatrist. What would Phil make of those seven-day groups? I imagined he'd be a little horrified; all that raging and wailing, not like his style of therapy at all. I wondered too what he would think of the therapists sleeping with the groupies? Sex was everywhere and a huge part of their belief system; so different from my sessions with Phil. But would his approach be futile too? Would I find myself exactly where I started; confused, lost and detached from reality? I thought of his office and the couch. It seemed so innocuous. I just hoped with all my heart that this was going to be the one; I had nowhere else to go.

Chapter Five

'I don't like humans at all. They're so bloody difficult to work out.'

Phil smiled. 'You don't see yourself as a human?'

'Nope. I can't possibly be from this planet. I've felt like an alien all my life. People talk to me about buying new curtains or redesigning their kitchen and I wonder what on earth they are talking about.'

'So what do you do?'

'God, I think I've tried everything. I used to ask them point-blank, could we cut the crap and get down to the *real* stuff? I was sure they were hiding it from me, but I never got anywhere. Most people ended up feeling really annoyed with me, not understanding what it was that I wanted. I tried that for years till I finally gave up. Then I decided that maybe I just needed to rattle their worlds, you know, by asking them how secure did they *really* feel about their marriage, or their job? How meaningful was it?'

'I bet that went down well,' Phil suggested, amused.

'It was a disaster. Most people got quite nervous around me.'

'You could be pretty formidable, I imagine.'

Formidable? I quite liked that idea. I saw myself more like a terrified rabbit, gnawing away at people who wished I'd hop off and go pester somebody else. 'I have been told that I'm too confrontational.'

'Who's called you that?'

'Most of my family. I think they wish I would just leave them alone.'

'What are you trying to accomplish when you have those conversations?'

'God only knows. I get so incredibly frustrated though, like they're all so closed-off and safe in their predictable little worlds and there I am, wide open for all to see, trying to make sense of the fucking basic things, like who I am and what's it all about? How the hell am I meant to get interested in bloody curtains?'

Phil just nodded. 'I can see how that would be frustrating for you.'

'But it's no different than being with you.'

He arched his brows. 'How so?'

'Well, it's like you've got some thick concrete wall around you and there's no way you're going to let me in. That's what it's like with everyone, they talk about safe shit and boring crap and they keep all of their deep, dark secrets inside. I hate it. I feel as though I'm so bloody transparent.'

'It's actually quite remarkable that you're even aware of boundaries. I doubt whether you had much experience of them in your childhood.'

Boundaries? I thought of them more as walls to keep me out. 'Well I wouldn't mind some,' I told him fiercely. 'I'm sick of being so "out there".'

'That's a familiar feeling for you?'

'I've had it all my life. Whenever I meet people I'm immediately aware that they have fences around them. I get this strong desire to pull them down, get to what's behind them.'

'And people have resisted this?'

'God yes! My mother especially. I swear sometimes I think that I'll go crazy if I can't get her to open up. She's like a bloody fortress!'

'What do you think is behind this fortress?'

I had to think about that. What had I been looking for? Why was I so convinced that something was lurking on the other side of the wall? I had no idea. I only knew that I had to do it. I shook my head. 'It's like I'm driven,' I finally managed.

'We'll do some work on that. I'd like to know a little more about your relationship with your mother. Do you spend much time with her?'

'Heaps. We get together on weekends and talk on the phone at least once a day.'

He nodded slowly. 'What do you talk about?'

'Anything and everything. We always have.'

'You told me a little about your childhood, that you moved around quite a lot. Does your mother still do that?'

'Not so impulsively. When we were little it was always on the spur of the moment. My sisters and I would come home from school and find a suitcase packed and Mum ready to take off.'

'How often did this happen?'

'Gosh, all the time.'

'How was that for you?'

I shrugged. 'I guess we got used to it. Sometimes it was great, especially if we were getting away from another of Mum's violent boyfriends. Other times though it was hard, losing friends, changing schools, that sort of stuff.'

'Was this once a year or what? I'm just trying to get a picture.'

'It varied. We might settle somewhere for a while. Mum would always tell us that this would be the last move. But it never was.'

'And this wasn't just houses, or suburbs? You switched countries I believe?'

'Yep. We went from England to Ireland, then left Ireland and went back to England. We stayed there for about two years, that was in Southampton, with Roger, and then we returned to County

Cork again, in Ireland. We stayed there for about ten months before we immigrated to Australia.'

'Did things settle in Australia?'

I laughed. 'Hardly. We did actually stay in Melbourne for about four years, even though we shifted house quite a lot. But Mum had found herself another violent boyfriend and eventually we did another midnight flit, this time to Adelaide. I think I told you about that?'

He nodded.

'I loved that school in Melbourne; it was the best one I'd ever been to. I think the four years helped, it was the longest time that I'd stayed in any school. I got to know all the teachers and actually made some good friends. I even went to the career's night. That's when I made my mind up to be a journalist.' I laughed, looking up at Phil and feeling a little ridiculous. 'A dopey idea, I guess.'

He smiled. 'Doesn't sound dopey to me at all. So what happened with all that?'

I shrugged. 'As I said, we had taken off to Adelaide. We were gone for about three months, by the time we returned to Melbourne, Mum was planning to give the bloke another chance and the school year had ended. I got a job as a typist.'

'That must have been hard for you.'

'I don't know. You get used to it. We were off to Sydney a few months later.'

Phil was shaking his head. 'It sounds like hell.'

'I guess it looks like that from the outside. But it really wasn't that bad.'

'How do you feel when you tell me about it?'

'It's odd, I don't feel anything much at all, sort of removed from it, you know?'

'That's what it sounds like too. As if it happened to somebody else.'

I wondered about that. 'I don't think I would have survived if I'd let myself get emotional about it.'

'On some level, you did, believe me. We just need to get to that place. But there's no hurry. We can take it slowly.'

I noticed the time on the clock. There were only a few minutes left to go. 'Aren't you going to give me some homework, or something?' I asked again.

He laughed. 'No. Would you like some?'

'Well, it would make me feel as though I was getting on with it.'

'With what?' he asked, a little puzzled.

'With getting myself fixed.'

'We'll do that together.'

I didn't understand what he meant. I left his office feeling a little confused. What did that mean, together?

Once again, the week between sessions was a mixture of mood swings, spaciness and manic mental activity. I blew way too much money on the pokies, adding to an already heightened sense of anxiety. I was so uncertain. Was it a good idea bringing the past back to life again? What would that achieve?

Luckily Ty kept me grounded. I welcomed the routine and structure of school times and meals. I think too that Ty was relieved that I had found someone to talk to. He had seen my fluctuating moods and watched on as I started new jobs, filled with enthusiasm, only to leave them three to four months later. I knew he felt helpless and couldn't understand what was going on. My mother-mode was precious to me. I believed it was the only thing that kept me from spinning out altogether. As Ty had grown older though, and needed me less, I had more time on my own. I knew that this was contributing to the mood swings. Who was I if I wasn't a mother? The thought of Ty leaving home was too scary to dwell on.

Phil was waiting. I wriggled uncomfortably on the couch, wishing yet again that we could sit back at his desk. I still didn't know what I was meant to *do*. Did he want me to tell him about the past? Was I supposed to just blurt it all out? But he'd heard most of it already. I inspected my nails, wishing he would break the silence. But as I was beginning to learn, his patience was far greater than my own. Minutes went by, each one feeling like an hour. I tried taking in the objects around the room: a picture on the wall, a neat and orderly bookcase, items on shelves; but I couldn't see details or colours. They were just 'things' and too far out of my range of relevance. Not able to stand it for a second longer, I finally found my voice.

'This is awful,' I groaned. 'I don't know what you're waiting for.'

He smiled and patiently explained to me again, 'I'm not waiting for anything, this is your time. It's up to you what we do.'

'That's easy for you to say, you're not sitting here.'

'I have been in your position, if that's any help. I was in therapy during my training; they recommended it back then.'

'Really? How did you find it?'

He shrugged. 'A bit awkward at first, much like you're feeling now. But it got easier.'

'Have you been a psychiatrist for long?' I preferred this; asking questions was my forte.

'Fourteen years.'

'God, so you've seen it all, I guess. What on earth made you decide to be a psychiatrist?'

He smiled. 'It wasn't my first choice. When I was younger I read a lot of science fiction, I thought I'd like to be an astronaut.

Once I got into university I took a Bachelor of Science, then I entered medical school. I became a doctor and spent two years specialising in neurosurgery. It was only then that I decided to focus on psychiatry.'

'That was one heck of a lot of study.' I was impressed.

'Years,' he answered, smiling warmly. 'It took me a while to make up my mind.'

I envied him the years of continuity. What must that be like, to have a goal and stick to it? 'Do you like being a psychiatrist?'

'It has its ups and downs, but generally speaking, yes, it's very satisfying helping someone to change their life. By the time most people decide to see a psychiatrist, they're feeling pretty desperate.'

'You're my last shot,' I told him honestly. 'If this doesn't work, then I'm done.'

'I understand,' he said, smiling softly, 'I do realise how difficult it is for you to be here.'

'I've just about given up. I feel like I'm hanging on by a thread.'

'A thread is good. We'll just have to build on that, won't we?'

I sighed. Would he always be this patient? This understanding? He hadn't seen how impossible I could be. What if *she* turned up?

'Tell me,' I asked, 'why are my moods so erratic? What's wrong with me?'

He shook his head. 'It could be a number of things, I won't be able to say until I've got to know you a little better. But we will find an answer.'

'Well, can you at least explain what the spaciness is all about?'

'I'll certainly try. As you're probably aware, most people "blank out" quite regularly. You hear stories about someone driving some-where and when they arrive at their destination, they're rather surprised, their mind has been elsewhere. In a way, that's what happens to you, only you go out a lot further, if you know what I mean. And you have a lot less control over when it occurs.'

'I've never been able to stop it, once I've spaced out. It can last for ages, it's like floating out into a vacuum, miles away from everybody.'

'It must be very unsettling for you?'

'I was used to it at first, wasn't even aware half the time that I was out there. But just lately it's got a whole lot worse. It's frightening me. I'm afraid that something really bad is going to happen, like maybe I'll flip out and lose it altogether.'

'That hasn't happened so far, has it? I think what you're going through now is pretty normal, now that you've made the decision to confront the past. Unfortunately it has to get worse before it can get better.'

'So it can be fixed?'

'Oh yes.'

I sighed, needing to believe him. 'I think I want that more than anything in the world.'

His eyes filled with tenderness. 'Trust me, it will happen.'

I spent the following weekend with my mother. She wanted to know everything about Phil and I was keen to have a listener. I talked for hours, telling her every little thing; his words of encouragement, his lovely smile. I couldn't speak highly enough of him.

'Well, dear, it certainly sounds interesting.'

I could hear the unspoken words. 'Maybe you should try it, Mum? It's a neat feeling having somebody listen to you.'

'I don't think so, darling. I couldn't stand having someone pry like that.'

'It's hardly prying,' I answered, bristling, 'he's simply interested. And he seems like a really nice man. It might give you some answers, you've certainly tried everything else.'

She smiled. 'I'll stick to my books, dear.'

I wasn't prepared to let it go. 'I don't understand, Mum. You've gone to all sorts of odd people in your life, some of them downright weird. Now I'm telling you about Phil, and how safe it is with him, and you wouldn't even give it a second thought?'

'No, dear, I've already explained that. I wouldn't like the idea of someone putting me under a microscope.'

I gritted my teeth and decided to shut up.

'What's it like at your mother's house now?' Phil asked.

I sighed. 'Pretty much like it's always been, I guess. She still has heaps of weird people visiting and quite a few creeps. I tend to go down to the garden and stay there till they leave.'

'What do you mean by "creeps"?'

'She attracts them all. There are at least two alcoholic men; there have been three paedophiles over the last couple of years and loads of others who just visit for her advice. They're not all bad, though; there are a couple of women who I quite like.'

'She has paedophiles visiting?' he asked, somewhat surprised. 'How do you know they're paedophiles?'

'They tell her. It only takes a short while before they pour out their story to her. They love her, always have done.'

He was shaking his head. 'And what does she say to these paedophiles?'

'The usual. That God forgives them and it's not her place to judge.'

'That's quite bizarre.'

I could see he was mystified.

'So how do you feel about that?' he enquired.

I shrugged. 'I'm used to it, I guess, although I do get pretty antsy about the molesters. They make my skin crawl.'

'Why do you think your mother attracts them to her?'

'I have no idea.'

'So,' he continued, still trying to get a grasp of it all, 'she attracts child molesters, invites them into her home and gives them advice. And then what happens?'

'They usually become her friends. One of them just got out of jail for molesting a fifteen-year-old; he got eighteen months. Another younger man has just gone to jail for molesting his two daughters, I think he's in for four years.'

Phil was trying to take it all in. 'And you know these men?'

I nodded. 'Quite well.'

'And how is that for you?'

'Well, it's not like I have deep and meaningful conversations with them. They know I don't like them. I make that quite obvious by leaving the room whenever they visit. But I can't throw them out, they're Mum's friends.'

'Have you ever questioned your mother about this?'

I rolled my eyes. 'Constantly. It's like watching her being surrounded by the dregs of society. But I know she loves it. They're so captivated by her. Sometimes she even lets them live in her spare room. I usually stay away when that happens.'

He was still shaking his head. 'I'm just trying to take this all in. Your mother knows how you feel about the paedophiles, you've told her about the sexual abuse, and yet she fully justifies having them as her friends?'

'I guess that's her right, isn't it? It's not for me to tell her who she can and can't like.'

'No,' he said slowly. 'But you'd think she'd be a bit more sensitive to your feelings, given what happened to you as a child.'

'We're talking about my mum. She's not like normal people. And I wonder too if maybe it's trying to teach me something, you know, like acceptance? I'm not the most tolerant person in the world.'

'I think that might be asking a bit much of yourself?'

'I don't think so, I mean, what's the point of being angry about it? Mum sees everything so differently.'

'I'm beginning to see that. What I don't understand is why you spend so much time with her, given the visitors? Isn't that difficult for you?'

I sighed. 'Yes and no. They're not always there. We only run into trouble if one of them turns up when I'm in the house. I think she's starting to realise that. And anyway,' I stated, suddenly bristling, 'I don't think this is so much about Mum as it is about men. They're the creeps, remember?'

'True,' Phil said slowly. 'Tell me a little about them.'

I sighed. 'I don't have a terribly high opinion of men.'

'I'm not surprised.'

'I'm always hoping that one is going to surprise me, though.'

'In what way?'

I shrugged. 'I don't know, I guess I'm hoping that they'll be different. I always start off believing them.'

'But why would you do that?'

I frowned. 'Why wouldn't I?'

'Well, doesn't it take time for trust to develop?'

I thought on that for a moment. 'I don't know, I guess I just hope that *he'll* be the one who doesn't let me down, but it never takes long before the inevitable happens.'

'Like what?'

I shrugged. 'It's always about sex for them. Give them that and they all roll over on their backs. It's quite pathetic really.'

'What are you hoping would happen?'

'Oh, I don't know. I think it would be amazing to meet a man who could say no to me, you know? Now that would be something.'

Phil arched his eyebrows. 'And you'd like that, would you?'

'Well of course I would.'

'I doubt whether you'd ever let a man like that come near you.'

I frowned. 'Yes, I would.'

He shook his head dismissively.

'Yes, I *would*,' I repeated.

'So, where is he?'

'Oh, you're very funny.'

'I'm not being funny at all. Where is this man with such great control?'

I racked my brains, there had to be at least *one* who I could think of.

Phil looked smugly satisfied.

'Oh sod off.'

'I thought as much.'

'I just need time to think, that's all.' But my mind was blank. I decided to change the subject quickly. 'I feel sorry for Mum most of the time.'

'Why's that?'

'She's getting on now, only a few years away from being seventy, and still she's restless as hell and no closer to finding whatever it is she's been looking for.'

'What do you think that might be?'

'I don't know. I just wish I could help her to find it.'

'I imagine you've tried?'

'God, yes. She'll come up with a new idea, or I will, and for a brief while there's a flurry of excitement. But it never lasts.'

'Maybe she's happy with the way things are.'

'If she is, then she's not showing it. She gets depressed quite a lot, and doesn't have the enthusiasm she once did. I always feel guilty, as if there's something I should be doing for her.'

'Is that one of the reasons you spend so much time with her?'

I nodded. 'That, and the fact that I'm really the only daughter left who she's close to. It feels like it's my job to stay with her.'

'Hmm. Why do you feel that it's your responsibility to take care of her? It sounds like you're the mother.'

'I feel like that most of the time. Always have, I guess.'

'But you're not. She's an adult and able to take care of herself.'

I shook my head. 'I don't think so.'

He smiled.

'You disagree?' I asked.

'Your mother has managed for all of these years; she sounds like quite a survivor.'

'She is.'

Phil said nothing. And I was left to ponder.

Soon there was nothing in my world except Phil and my mum. I was still spending weekends at my mother's house. We discussed virtually every detail of my therapy, but I left out the bits about her. I wasn't sure how to broach that.

My moods were chaotic and I was finding it increasingly difficult to sort out my relationship with Phil. I had started to have dreams of him that left me cringing with shame when I awoke. They were always sexual. The desire was intense and I became riddled with guilt as persistent sexual fantasies occupied hours of my time. Whatever would he think of me? After weeks of a recurring dream where we were rolling around naked in his foyer, I decided to bite the bullet and confess.

'It can't be that bad?' he prompted. 'Believe me, I've heard everything.'

I was squirming in my seat. Was there no nice way of putting this?

'You'll feel a lot better afterwards. Just get it out.'

Oh God, when would the day come when I had something nice to tell him? There was so much slime. I took a deep breath and launched in quickly. 'Okay, I have this dream ... well, we're in your foyer. Naked. And you're on top of me. But you're having second thoughts, so I tell you that I won't tell anyone. And that I'll make sure there's a happy ending.' I feel myself blushing in shame.

'It sounds like you're telling me that it would be safe for me to take advantage of you?'

'What do you mean?' I asked, immediately defensive.

'Well you're telling me that if I were to make a sexual advance on you, you won't tell anyone. You'll make it safe for me.'

'It's a bloody dream!' I snapped.

'Yes,' he smiled, 'but it's your dream. You created it. Did we have sex, by the way?'

I groaned, the picture still vivid. 'Yes, we did.'

'You realise that there will never be a sexual relationship between us?'

Oh God, how embarrassing was that? 'Yes I do realise that. You've only told me about a hundred times. And I don't want that, anyway.'

'That's not what your dreams are saying.'

I gazed into space. Bloody dreams! I should have kept it to myself. I knew he didn't want sex from me. How could he? Someone as normal and clean as him wouldn't want to touch me with a barge pole. I felt disgusted with myself. Suddenly I didn't want to be in the same room as him. It was like I could see me through his eyes; a pathetic, soiled weirdo.

'What are you thinking?' he asked softly.

I kept my eyes on the floor. 'Nothing much. I guess I'd like to change the subject.'

Phil stayed quiet and we sat in silence for a few minutes. I just wanted to leave but the clock still had twenty minutes on it.

'Having sexual feelings and dreams like this are very normal, given the circumstances. I guess they're telling us what's going on in your subconscious. And that's good. We know what to work on.'

I didn't want to talk about it anymore. I shrugged. 'What does it matter?'

'You matter,' he answered firmly. 'Very much so.'

'Does it make you sick having to listen to all this crap?'

He shook his head slowly. 'You had to live with all that crap. It must have been horrible for you. But it was never your crap; you were innocent. Sick adults who were unable to control themselves dumped it on you. That's their rubbish, not yours.'

His words were like nothing I had heard before. I was innocent? Really? Sick adults?

'I have always thought that it was all my fault,' I told him quietly.

'How could it have been? You were a little girl.'

I shook my head. 'But sometimes I liked it. It felt good. I didn't tell them to stop and I could have.' I felt miserable with the disgust of it all.

'I imagine you felt quite powerful at times, too?'

His question stopped me dead. I looked up at him in surprise. 'Powerful?'

He nodded. 'Having that effect on grown men, knowing what you could do to them?'

I went quiet. I was remembering when I was ten or eleven and Frank had turned up, a revolting, watery-eyed drunk of about fifty; I knew exactly what he wanted and I gave it to him.

Phil was watching me. 'What are you thinking?'

I relayed my thoughts. 'I used to get this feeling of strength inside me, so strong, but I didn't know what it was. I just lay there, opening my legs to make it easier for him, and hearing him getting more excited by the minute.'

He nodded. 'In my experience that's quite a common feeling. It's just not a very popular view these days. But it exists, and

I think it's important to acknowledge that; even though some people would scream for my blood if they heard me suggesting that children could feel powerful during sexual abuse.'

My mind was racing. 'That's the same feeling I get just before sex. My body surges with power. I couldn't work out why it stopped dead once sex started though.'

'It's another unfortunate outcome of sexual abuse. You were exposed to sexually aroused adult men, often asked by them to keep it all a secret; that's a lot of power for a little girl.'

I grimaced. 'It's all so grubby.'

'It was the only form of contact you knew. You weren't bad just because your body responded. You can't even be blamed for seeking it out. What else did you know?'

I so wanted to believe his words. 'So it wasn't all my fault?'

Phil leaned forward and looked directly into my eyes. 'It was never your fault. You were innocent.'

I tried to take the words in, but they wouldn't ring true. I was a lot of things, but I don't think 'innocent' was one of them. It was nice of Phil to say it. I guess he had to tell his patients that, but he didn't really know me yet, it wouldn't be long before he'd change his tune. 'There's so much to sort out, isn't there?' I asked, wanting to let the subject go.

He smiled warmly. 'We'll take it a bit at a time. It took a lot of years to cause this damage.'

'I talk to you all the time, you know? Especially at night when I'm in bed. We have conversations for hours.'

'Really? What do we talk about?'

'Gosh, everything.'

He smiled. 'I wish I could be there. Tell me something,' he asked, 'when we're talking like that, where am I?'

I tracked back to the previous evening; we'd been discussing my mother. 'You're on your chair usually, about the same distance

74

from me that you are now. And you're far more amenable too,' I added, smiling.

'Is that right?'

'Yep. Not so hard case.'

'Well, you're hardly a piece of cake yourself, you know.'

I laughed, not many men had talked to me like this before; his honesty was refreshing.

'Eventually you're going to have to bring me inside you, you know.'

I looked at him in surprise. 'Inside me? What do you mean?'

'When you have these conversations with me, you'll need to internalise me.'

The concept was completely alien to me. 'Gosh, that's pretty personal, isn't it?'

He nodded. 'That's what most sexual abuse survivors say. But ultimately that's where you'll need to place me.'

What a strange notion. Inside me? I was going to need to give that a lot of thought.

It was on that note that the session ended. I left feeling very uncertain. Was that right? Should he be saying things like that? It sounded so intimate that I could feel a familiar doubt worming through my being. Could he be trusted?

Chapter Six

Within twenty-four hours my system was in chaos again. The confusion was sickening and I had no one to discuss it with. What if Phil really was a creep and was waiting for me to trust him? What was all that stuff about placing him inside me? If that wasn't sexual, what was?

The erotic dreams returned. I would spend the day trying to push the pictures aside: Phil in a bathrobe with his penis sticking out; another time dreaming that I had turned up for my session and Phil had opened the door, his fly undone and his penis erect and dripping. Should I tell him? Couldn't I just ignore them and hope they'd go away? As each day passed, my confusion and sense of shame intensified. I should have been able to predict what was going to happen, but I still believed that I had a handle on it all.

She was growing stronger. Her fantasies were disturbing. She pictured herself undoing his zip and giving him the best blowjob he'd had in his life. She longed to tear his clothes off and spend the entire session in one long, drawn-out fuck. How fantastic would that be? What would the power feel like in that exquisite moment when he finally weakened? She knew it would happen. It was only a matter of time before he'd expose the chink in his armour.

On the day of Phil's appointment, it was she who climbed out of bed. Energy was coursing through her. She flicked through the wardrobe; irritated by the abundance of dreary, lacklustre clothing. Was there anything that actually *fitted*? After trying on what seemed like a dozen or more sack-like garments, she finally settled on a clingy white top and a pair of reasonably close-fitting jeans.

This'll show him. She stood in front of the full-length mirror and surveyed the results. *And maybe a little make-up won't go astray either. It's about time this fellow Phil realised exactly who he is dealing with.*

Her stomach lurched at the thought of him.

Hmmm, alive again at last.

She sat on the couch with her legs crossed and looked directly at him. 'I'm not a mouse, you know. Even though I may have come across that way.'

Phil arched his eyebrows. 'I hadn't found you mousy, but go on.'

'All that self-pity, that's not me at all,' she explained, flicking back her hair. 'I'm not afraid of anything.'

'Really?' he asked, smiling, 'tell me more.'

'Gosh. Where do I begin? I feel like we haven't really met yet. I'm Debra, by the way. Nice to meet you.'

He smiled warmly. 'Likewise. So who have I been talking to all this time?'

'Let's call her Miss Mouse.'

Phil didn't bat an eyelid. 'Okay, and who are you?'

'I'm the real person. I'm strong and tough and don't blubber about anything. In fact,' she added confidently, 'I'm not even sure why we're coming to see you at all.'

'We? Tell me, do you all have different names?'

'Of course not!' she replied, hotly. 'We're not crazy, this isn't one of those multiple personality things. I know there's only one body here. It's just that sometimes when things get too messy, I get a shot. I have more fun than the rest of them put together.' She smiled broadly, knowing he'd be finding her far more enticing than Miss Mouse.

'I'd like to hear more.'

She was having an excellent time. 'Sure,' she continued, 'let's see. I love blowing money; I think gambling's in my blood. Mind you, I do get a little carried away at times. Miss Mouse always turns up eventually and manages to spoil everything.'

'How does she do that?'

She rolled her eyes. 'You've met her, she's so bloody *sensible*. It might have taken me hours sometimes to set up a fun night, you know, phone calls, clothes, that sort of thing. And I'll be just about to start having some serious fun and ping; she turns up and puts an end to it all. She's the *bane* of my existence.'

'Maybe that's kept you safe?'

'Safe? Who the hell wants to be safe? I want to let down my hair and live a little. I can't *stand* this dreary, sensible, well-behaved life she's set up. No wonder I have to break out.'

Phil smiled warmly. 'You get a bit frustrated, do you?'

'To say the *least*. She has us living the nun's life. It's just as well that I'm around or we'd all *die* of boredom. I don't know how you can stand it, having to listen to her for hours on end, moaning and groaning about her miserable existence.'

Phil just listened, allowing the conversation to take its course.

'She's just pathetic, I hate her. Most of us do, in fact. If she had her way we would sit in a room all day, see nobody and do nothing. That's her motto, you know, "nothing, no one and nowhere".'

'And what's yours?'

'Mine?' she asked, tilting her head back. 'Fuck 'em all! That's how I see it.'

He smiled. 'And you do that, do you?'

'Well, whenever I can. As I said, we're presently living the nun's existence. It's all the Catholicism, you know, she loved that stuff. But not me, I'm here to have fun. I've done so many exciting things in my life, you know. It hasn't all been doom and gloom.'

'I'd like to hear about it.'

'Gosh, there's so many. I've flown in a helicopter, been down a mine in Coober Pedy, given a talk on existentialism, sung in front of hundreds of people. I'm not afraid of anything, you know?' It felt so good to finally tell him some of this stuff; he must have thought she was such a wimp before.

'I guess you must have needed a lot of courage when you were younger.'

She flicked his question aside with disinterest. 'The problem is *her*, you know, Miss Sensible. She drags us into the most *boring* of jobs, desperately seeking a *normal* life, for God's sake; as if that's what we're here for? I just won't have a bar of it.'

'So what do you do?'

'I get us the hell out of there! I want to *live*, you know? Life is too short for her sort of crap. Who *cares* about being normal? Who *wants* to be just like everybody else? Not me, for one. I've watched those so-called normal drones, doing the right thing, buying a house, watching the children grow and then waiting for death. Fuck it, they can have it, it's a bunch of crap.'

'You seem a little angry about this?'

She shook her head. 'Not angry, just passionate. I won't have anyone tell me how I should live. I do as I please.'

'I see, and that works for you, does it?'

'Absolutely, if you could just get *her* out of my way.'

'And why can't you do that?'

She glared at him. 'Because she thinks that she's the main one, you know, the *real* Debra.'

'Maybe she is?'

'Of course she isn't, nobody could be *that* dull.'

Phil smiled. 'So you're just out to party, are you? I guess there wasn't much of that around when you were younger?'

'Ah, who cares about then? This is now, that's all that matters. Oh yes, before I forget, I want to let you know that I'm certainly not afraid of you, nor am I embarrassed. After all, there's nothing wrong with feeling sexual, is there? It's not a crime.'

Phil was nodding slowly. 'No. It's not a crime. Are you aware,' he asked, looking directly into her eyes, 'that you've been playing with your hair since the session started?'

She hadn't actually noticed. 'So? Is that *bad*, or something?' she teased.

He smiled. 'No. It's not bad. But I'm aware that you're giving me very strong sexual signals.'

It was her turn to smile. 'Don't worry. I know your rules. Tell me,' she asked seductively, 'is there anything on that list of yours that you can actually say *yes* to?'

He arched his eyebrows. 'Are you flirting with me?' he asked playfully.

'Am I? Gosh, heaven forbid.'

'It's a very enjoyable experience but I'm afraid I'm not going to change my mind. I can resist you, you know.'

She crossed her legs. 'So bully for you.'

'Is there anything else you'd like to talk about?'

She shrugged. 'It all seems pretty darned serious to me. When do we get to have some fun?'

'Fun?' he asked, somewhat amused, 'and what might that entail?'

'I don't know. You tell me. You're the expert.'

'I'm getting the impression that you're testing me.'

'No, no test. I know how good you are. And I don't think your sort of sex is the type I'd be interested in anyway. I bet it's all tissues and niceties. I just wish we could do something other than discuss the dreary past. It gets so bloody boring.'

'I think I have a rather eager young teenager in front of me, would that be right?'

She twisted her hair again. 'Me? A teenager? You wish.'

He laughed. 'Why would I wish that?'

'What man wouldn't?'

'I guess I'd like to talk to you in a way that isn't sexual. But maybe you'd rather be treated like a thing. More familiar.'

'That's a prick of a thing to say,' she snapped.

'Well you're the one throwing your body at me.'

'I'm not *throwing* myself at you. In your dreams, mate!'

'I think it's in *your* dreams, isn't it? Don't you have us cavorting naked in the foyer?'

Where did he get off? 'You're a total prick you know.'

'Is that right?' he asked, his eyes lit with amusement. 'You're going to put me in the same place as all your other men, are you?'

'Yeah right. All my other men. I have them waiting in the sidelines with their tongues hanging out.'

He laughed. 'I bet you do. And I imagine they're pretty eager when you call them in. But I'm not one of them, you know, no matter how bad you might want me to be.'

She groaned. 'God, do you ever fancy yourself.'

She gazed out of his window. This was getting her nowhere.

'I'm really enjoying this session,' he continued, smiling broadly.

'I bet you are,' she snapped.

He laughed again. 'Feeling a little gypped, are you?'

She shook her head in wonder. 'Where do you ever get off on this stuff?'

'It seems to me that you're feeling a little frustrated. Not getting your way?'

'Look, mate!' she grumbled. 'The last thing in the world I want is anything from you.'

'Is that right? That's a lot of energy from somebody who doesn't want anything.'

She recrossed her legs. She wasn't going to say another word. Fuck him.

The clock ticked by. As usual he wasn't going to do anything.

'Don't you ever take control?' she asked with a rising irritation.

'What would you like me to do?'

'Anything! Other than just sitting there.'

'These are your sessions. You're in total control here.'

'Oh sure I am. You get to tell me when I can see you. You limit how long we spend together. You decide where I sit. How much control is there in that?'

'Yes, that's true. But I'm always here. You can stop coming at any time. You might decide that I'm talking a bunch of crap. You can end this relationship whenever you want and I can't do anything about it. That's quite a lot of control for you, isn't it?'

She hadn't thought of it that way. 'I guess so. I hadn't seen it like that.'

'Unfortunately our time is up,' he said smiling, rising from his chair. 'But thank you for such an enjoyable session. It was very tempting, but I think I can resist.'

She rolled her eyes and walked straight past him. Bloody prick.

She was angry for the rest of the afternoon. After eating her dinner she flicked through her little yellow book and found the number of an old flame. She was going to get drunk as a skunk and have a wild night of fun and games. Rob was surprised to hear from her.

'A call after all this time? How long has it been, Deb? Three, four years?'

'I imagined you'd like some time with your wife,' she answered sarcastically.

'So why call now?'

'Who knows? Maybe I just feel like letting my hair down a little. I've been so good lately it's enough to make me ill.'

Rob laughed. 'That sounds like my girl. I won't finish here till at least ten though. You think you can stay awake till then?'

Four hours? Was he worth it? 'Sure. And make sure you bring a bottle of wine.'

'I've got a hard-on already. Don't start without me.'

She hung up the phone feeling restless. What would she do for four hours? She put the radio on but it just irritated her. How dare he make her wait? She couldn't get Phil out of her mind. If she could just fuck her brains out and tell him every little detail. That would show him.

An hour ticked by and I suddenly wasn't feeling so wild anymore. What was I doing ringing Rob? I had ended that relationship because of how dirty and deceitful it had made me feel. Sneaking behind his wife's back and knowing that in some naughty-little-boy way, Rob was getting his kicks from it. I certainly hadn't called him for the sex; that had always been a disaster. He struggled with ejaculation while I tried to hide my extreme spaciness. It was a relationship that should never have happened. I paced around the house trying to make my mind up. There was a football game on television that I had planned to watch. It seemed at once far more appealing than a night with Rob. I decided to call and cancel. He was a little disappointed but I promised I'd ring him back soon. We both knew I was lying.

The football game was riveting. My beloved Crows won by five points. I went to bed feeling satisfied and immensely relieved that

I hadn't followed through with Rob. What on earth had I been doing? Why did I think it would prove something to Phil? I was mystified.

Phil thought it was quite funny. 'So you missed out, huh? Boyfriend not running to your beck and call?'

'Fuck off,' I told him, half jokingly. 'He would have. Only I didn't feel like waiting for hours. The mood wore off.'

'How many men have you got on the sidelines?'

'Oh millions,' I quipped. 'Sometimes it's hard to keep track of them all.'

'Sarcasm, huh? You resort to that quite a lot, I notice. But I mean it, do you have something like a black book with all their phone numbers?'

'It's yellow actually.'

'I see. And they come running when you call, do they?'

I glared at him. 'You make it sound awful. But it's not like that.'

He shrugged. 'Sounds like it to me. A bit like having your own brothel on the side.'

'How charming.'

'Sort of like your childhood, isn't it? Lots of men floating around, wanting you for your body?'

'I do *talk* to them, too, you know? It isn't just sex.'

He looked dubious. 'And this Rob you called, he's married, you say?'

'Yep.'

'Who is he?'

I frowned. 'What do you mean?'

'What's his full name, where did you meet him?'

'Well I'm hardly going to tell you that.'

'Why not? Anything you say in here is confidential.'

I shook my head. 'This is a small city, you may well know him.'

'I somehow doubt that, but why would that matter?'

I looked at Phil as though he was thick. 'He's *married*.'

'So?'

'*So*, I don't think it would be fair to him to tell you his full name.'

He was unimpressed. 'So you're protecting him?'

'I suppose I am.'

'Are they all married?'

I rolled my eyes. 'All? The hordes, you mean?'

He shrugged. 'You're the one with the little yellow book.'

I didn't want to discuss it anymore. The whirlwind had passed and I was enjoying the relative peace. 'I don't feel like arguing with you. Can't we talk about something else?'

'Of course we can. Your choice entirely.'

I stared out of the window. It was a grey, wintry day. Splatters of rain were running down the glass. 'When I was thirty-two, I went back to England and met my dad. And Mark and Cheryl.'

He looked surprised. 'That was very brave of you. How did it go?'

'Strange. But okay I guess.' It was hard to say really; such a big event. It had been a spur of the moment decision. Ty had wanted to spend some time with his dad in New Zealand and it suddenly seemed like a perfect opportunity. Slowly I recounted the details to Phil. It still felt surreal.

I had landed in Frankfurt, a city glistening like a fairyland with the first snows of winter. I was immediately entranced. It was bitingly cold and my body didn't know where it was, having left a searing forty-degree heatwave only twenty-four hours previously. I strolled through the town in my jeans and white cotton shirt feeling more excited by the minute. I was soon way out there, euphoric and electrified by everything I saw. Once I had booked into my hostel I went straight back outside into the wintry wonderland and walked for hours and hours. Once again I was captivated by the idea that I could be anyone I wanted; do anything I wanted.

Armed with my Euro-rail ticket I spent the next two months, spaced out and manic, backpacking around Europe. I had a ball, loving everybody I met and convinced that I was finally being who I was meant to be, detached from everything and free as the wind. I visited Paris, Milan and Florence, adoring the freedom of waking up and choosing which country I might journey to that day. In the far recesses of my mind I knew too that I was trying to get up my nerve. My dad was just across the waters. What do you say after twenty-six years? Would they even want to hear from me? My mind kept going back to the day my mother had taken us away. I wouldn't blame any of them for not wanting to see me. But what if Dad was dying to know how I was? How his three daughters had got on? I had so many questions too. Like why hadn't he found us? Did he know we had moved to Ireland; and then Australia? Did he care? I let the questions swirl in the background of my mind.

I met an American in my Venice hostel and we stayed together for five or six days, spending most of our time in bed, drinking very cheap Italian wine. I was barely eating one meal a day and had lost over seven kilos. At one time I was standing with him in the middle of St. Mark's Piazza and everything had spun around me in a kaleidoscope of colours. I had had to sit down and try to ground myself, but I knew I would be in danger if I continued to live so precariously. On my seventh day in Venice I said goodbye to the American and booked a flight to London.

After settling into the bed and breakfast I headed down to the foyer and rang directory assistance. To my amazement it only took a couple of minutes before I was staring at my father's telephone number. He was still in Essex, still in the seaside town where I had been born, about an hour from London. My hands were shaking as I dialled the number.

'Drake speaking.'

I gulped. 'Is that Ernest Drake?'

'Yes. Who is this?'

What a strange accent. 'It's Debra. Your daughter.'

Only a moment's silence.

'Hello, love. Where are you?'

Was that it? No shock? No elation? I felt odd, like maybe I had rung the wrong number. 'I'm in London. I've travelled over from Australia.'

'Are you going to come down and see us?'

Us? So Mark and Cheryl were still in Essex too. I couldn't believe it. Somehow I managed to continue talking. My father gave me the train times and we arranged to meet at the station the following day. He would come with Mark and we'd all go to Cheryl's place and get re-acquainted. I hung up the telephone feeling strangely distant. None of it felt real. After years of fanta-sising it had come to this? And what was that odd accent? None of the rest of my family spoke like that.

The train trip was sickening. My stomach heaved and I wanted to change my mind and head back to Europe. What if I didn't recognise them? I imagined walking around the station and harassing strangers with the bizarre question: are you my dad? The thought made me shudder. Time was flying. The train was due to arrive in five minutes. Oh God, had I made a mistake?

I got off of the train quickly and found a bench to sit on. So far no one had approached me and my eyes were scanning the crowd trying desperately to pick out a familiar face. I wanted to throw up. My hands were shaking so much that I couldn't hold my cigarette. And then I saw him. He was standing at the entrance with my brother, Mark. I could have picked them from a hundred paces. How bizarre. They spotted me at the same time and we walked towards each other. I took a deep breath, thinking here ends twenty-six years of questions.

We stood there awkwardly. There were no hugs or exclamations, no tears of joy. Mark was shifting from foot to foot. Dad looked as uncomfortable as hell. 'How was your trip?' he asked clumsily.

'Good. Quick.'

'Yep, it's a fast train they've got now. Though it's always breaking down.'

I didn't know what to say. Mark finally grabbed my bag and suggested we head to the car. 'Chez is waiting for us,' he explained.

Chez? Is that what they call her? My big sister, I wondered what she looked like. We made small talk about Europe and hostels as we headed towards Cheryl and her husband's home. It still didn't feel real. I was way out there in the ether, watching it all from a distance.

You're with your dad; you're with your dad.

It wouldn't sink in.

We knocked on their front door. A man of about forty answered and his mouth dropped open. 'Chez, quick, come and have a look at this.' I was wondering what he was talking about till I saw Cheryl heading down the corridor. My God! She looked exactly like me. We both stared at each other, not knowing what to say.

'Quite a similarity, isn't it?' Dad said quietly.

It was eerie. Once again Mark got us all moving and we were herded into the kitchen where Cheryl had tea and cakes prepared on the table. I wasn't able to eat a thing. Inane small talk continued as we all stole quick glances at each other. Mark looked just like my sister Jo; they could have been twins. And my dad? It was like seeing the other half of myself that had always been missing. We were all talking but I don't remember a word of what was said.

That night my father and I were sitting in his lounge room. He had downed a scotch and seemed to relax a little. I decided that this was the time to ask some questions. But where to start? As usual I just plunged in at the deep end. 'Dad? How come you didn't look for us?'

'Ah darling,' he started slowly, 'if only you knew how hard I tried. Every weekend for six months I piled Mark and Chez into our car and we checked out every caravan park within a hundred mile radius. At one stage we had missed you by two days. We got so close. Then it was like the trail just dried up.'

Two days? My dad had been two days away from finding me? 'We went to Ireland,' I explained.

'I found that out about twelve months later. Social Welfare had tracked you down. They told me you were all fine.'

I looked up at him in amazement. 'Fine? However did they work that out?'

I was remembering the small room we had all lived in, the nights of being forced to listen to their foreplay and sex games. The scars on Jo and my wrists from scalding water; had they seen them? How was that fine? Who the fuck would see that and say fine? I felt a rage flood through me.

Dad sighed. 'I thought they were telling the truth, love. Not a night passed when I didn't pray to God to look after my three little girls.'

Well God wasn't fucking listening.

'You were okay weren't you, love?'

I looked at this old man who was my father. His eyes were

pleading with me for reassurance. What could I say? That I had cried night after night for months waiting for him. That I had never given up on him? That I had pictured him walking through our front door and rescuing my sisters and I from the madness of our mother's house? I suddenly knew how futile it all was. Just a little girl's dream. I had made a mistake and thought it was real.

I managed a smile for my father. 'Sure, Dad, we were fine.'

Chez was quite a different story. It was the following morning; her husband was at work, her children at school, and Dad had dropped me off at her place so that we could 'get to know each other'.

We were sitting at the kitchen table and I still couldn't get used to her appearance. Despite the fact that she was six years older than me, it was like looking in a mirror. 'So,' Chez blurted out suddenly, interrupting our chatter about Europe, 'what's the bitch like?'

I was at once silenced. That was my mother she was talking about. 'It's hard to say,' I started, not knowing where to begin. 'I guess she's been with me all of my life, I've grown used to her.'

Chez was waiting. I knew she wanted more, but there had been so much venom in her voice that I was still uncertain.

'You know what I dream of?' she said bitterly. 'I'm walking down the street and the bitch comes up to me and says: "I'm sorry, I want to explain everything," and I look her straight in the eye, spit in her face and walk straight past her.'

I was stunned by her hatred, and wanted to defend my mother somehow. But Chez just kept going.

'You know the day that you all left? That was my birthday. Mark and I came home to an empty house. We figured there was going to be a surprise party. We waited for hours, until Dad finally got home.'

Jesus. I hadn't known about that. For once I was seeing that awful day through Cheryl's and Mark's eyes. Their mother had abandoned them. My mother. How the hell had her mind been working? On a birthday? Cheryl continued to fill me in on the years that passed. How for months she and Mark had raced each other to the mailbox on first sight of the postman, sure that Mum would write, especially if it was near Christmas, or a birthday. How she kept hoping, and waiting, convinced that Mum and her three sisters would roll up any day now. And how that hope eventually turned into hatred. I sat and listened to it all. It was bizarre. I had done the same thing with Dad.

'What was it like for you three?' she finally asked.

I didn't know what to say. In Cheryl's fantasy it was her three younger sisters who got the better end of the bargain. I felt like I had entered a crazy farce.

'I think the whole lot of us suffered in some way, Chez,' I finally managed.

She looked at me and knew that I wanted to close the subject. We returned to small talk.

I stayed with those people for three more days. They were nice. Normal. I couldn't help but wonder how different my life would have turned out if I had been one of the children left behind.

When the time came for me to return to Australia there were more awkward hugs, but at least this time I got to say goodbye. I knew there would be no more contact and I think they were aware of that. The train ride back to London was slow.

Phil was shaking his head. 'Thank you so much for sharing that with me. It's all terribly sad, isn't it?'

'I felt stupid, really, imagining some sort of glorious homecoming. But in the end they were just strangers.'

'Why did you let your father off the hook so easily?'

'I don't know. He so wanted us to have been all right.'

'So once again you took responsibility?'

I nodded. 'What could he have done, after all that time?'

'Well, maybe he could have taken some of the burden off you.'

'Ah, I don't think so. In a funny sort of way he's just like Mum. They both kept giving us to God to look after.'

Phil smiled sadly. 'Maybe He did?'

'Oh, don't you start,' I snapped. 'Bloody God wasn't listening. He was stone deaf. He always has been.'

That evening I was curled up in my usual chair, watching television, and trying to ignore a slow paralysis that was creeping into my body. I pulled my knees up, wrapping my arms around them, trying to squish into as tight a ball as I could. There was something inside me that felt so *starved* that I could hardly breathe. I could feel the pressure building; everything in me was screaming for attention; desperate for somebody to come. I tried to make sense of it, tried to hear the words, but there was only a feeling; an awful, empty, terrifying feeling. My eyes were clenched tight, pushing, pushing for something to happen. I felt sure that I was going to die.

For God's sake, what the hell is happening to me?

I wanted to get the pin out again; it was too much, too intense. I somehow managed to get myself to bed. I lay there in the foetal position for hours, freezing cold and alone.

Help me. For God's sake, someone help me.

'It's *awful*,' I told Phil, still feeling the emptiness inside.

'Describe it to me.'

'It's like I'm starving for something, only I don't know what it is. My body feels as though it will explode.'

'Go on.'

'I can't hear words or anything. Just a desperate need, it's like my life depends on it. But I don't know what it is.'

'I imagine that's because you were very, very young when this happened. What do you think you were needing?'

'I don't know,' I wailed. 'But I wanted it so bad!'

His eyes were filled with tenderness. 'Take a guess.'

I shook my head. 'I really don't know. I just felt so alone.'

He nodded slowly. 'Whatever damage was done to you occurred in the first few years of your life, that's why you're not able to find the words for it.'

I looked up at him in surprise. 'What would that be, though? I don't think I was molested when I was in my dad's house.'

'It isn't that, it's more about neglect.'

'Neglect? In what way?'

'We're still uncovering things, but from what you've told me, I doubt whether your most basic needs were attended to properly. That's what that empty feeling is all about.'

'Like food, you mean?' I asked, still unsure about his meaning.

'And love.'

'Love?' I spat out. 'I hate that word.'

'I wonder why.'

I shook my head. 'It's just another bloody word that people throw about. What is it, for God's sake? What does it look like?'

He smiled softly. 'It's not like a thing that I can show you. It's more like a feeling.'

'I don't believe in it.'

'Why don't you let yourself receive a little?' he asked gently.

I looked into his eyes, but the utter tenderness there was too unsettling. Quickly I returned my gaze to the floor. Something was hurting inside; a slow, constant ache. I pushed it aside. 'I don't know what you mean.'

'I understand that, I really do. You've suffered a lot from the hands of those who were supposed to love you.'

'But what am I meant to do now?'

'You're already doing it now, even though you may not feel like that.'

I kept my eyes to the floor, so aware of his closeness, his gentleness. I could feel the little one inside, wanting him more than anything she had ever wanted before. If she could just climb onto his lap and merge into him, connect to him in some way, she knew she would find heaven.

Ask him for a hug, she pleaded. But I kept my eyes glued to the floor.

He won't hug you. For God's sake, you're too big for that.

No, I'm not, he will hug me, just ask.

I pushed her aside, struggling to maintain control. 'Tell me,' I asked Phil, 'what is this stuff about wanting to connect with you? What does it actually *mean*?'

Phil paused for a moment, his eyes looking sad. 'It's what is supposed to happen between a child and the parent. That connection you're talking about occurs very early on in life; it's when the bonding takes place.'

'And that never happened with me and Mum?'

'No. That's why you experience that sense of emptiness. I'm not surprised that you've found it difficult to deal with, it must be very frightening.'

I nodded, deciding to tell him at least some of the truth. 'It's overwhelming at times. I want to cut myself.'

'That's very common. There are a number of people out there who use it as a coping mechanism. I guess it feels like letting it out somehow.'

'Yep, but I don't think it gets rid of it.'

'No. It takes a lot more than that. The damage needs to be repaired, that's what we're working on together here.'

'But how?' I asked again.

He smiled. 'It's achieved through the relationship that you're forming with me now. I know that sounds very mysterious, but it does work.'

'I just have to trust you, huh?' I joked.

'Exactly.'

Chapter Seven

The sexual dreams returned with a vengeance. One night I dreamt that Phil had invited me to his home for lunch. We spent hours in the kitchen, preparing the meal, joking and laughing. I suddenly felt tired and Phil suggested that I lie down for a nap; he would wake me when the meal was ready. I climbed onto a large double bed and fell asleep. But I woke with a start to find him on top of me, trying to kiss me. I was terrified and struggled to get away. He wouldn't stop. Somehow I managed to escape and raced into the kitchen to get a knife. Phil walked slowly towards me. I knew exactly what he was going to do. He was going to take the knife away from me and cut me into tiny pieces. I wondered desperately whether my mother was going to rescue me. Did she know where I was? Would she get to me in time? I awoke from the dream with my heart thumping and drenched in sweat. I finally calmed myself down.

Oh fuck; I'm going to have to tell Phil.

'That's pretty telling, isn't it?' he asked.

'In what way?'

'Well, that's what happened as a result of the sexual abuse. You were, psychologically, cut into little pieces.'

Gosh, I would never have seen it that way. Was that why I was so changeable?

'And I guess the mother stuff is pretty self-explanatory. You were hoping she would rescue you, and she didn't.'

I just nodded.

'One other thing that this dream is telling us,' Phil continued, 'is that you're still a long way from trusting me. You believe that eventually I will ruin everything and do what all those other men did.'

I shook my head. 'I don't think that at all.'

'Not consciously, perhaps, but certainly a part of you will be waiting for me to abuse you, to destroy this relationship. How could it be any other way?'

I frowned. 'I think you're wrong. I don't see you like those creeps at all.'

'So you've cut off my dick, have you?'

I was taken aback and surprised by the language. 'No,' I said slowly, 'I don't think I've done that. I just have you in another compartment, that's all.'

'Safe and castrated?'

I was squirming in discomfort. 'No. You're different, that's all.'

'How do you know that?' he asked, frowning.

'Well, I can tell, you know? I don't sense that "thing" that most men have towards me. You don't have it.'

'What "thing" is that?'

I scowled at him. 'You know what I mean.'

'Honestly, I don't.'

'It's like you don't give me any openings, any way of getting in, you know?'

'And that's unusual for you, is it?'

'It's very uncomfortable. I'm not at all sure of how to deal with you.'

'I can see that,' he answered, smiling for the first time that session.

'And you're not going to make this any easier, are you?'

'How many men actually sexually abused you?'

I sighed; here we go again. 'Roger, Ray, Terry and Frank. That makes four.'

'And these were your mother's boyfriends?'

'Roger was the only real boyfriend, the others were more like men friends. She had males around constantly.'

'How old were you when it started?'

'I'm not sure. But it finished when I was eleven. By then I had learnt how to make it easier for the men; it felt normal.'

He nodded slowly. 'And your sister was abused as well?'

'My big sister, Jo, was. In fact, I think there were even more men where she was concerned.'

'And your youngest sister escaped somehow.'

'Yep. Maybe because Jo and I were quite a bit older than Kim, and she was very talkative. That might have scared them off. They could have thought that she'd tell Mum.'

'Did you or Jo ever discuss this with your mother?'

I grimaced. 'You could never have done that. She was too frightening.'

'In what way?'

'We weren't allowed to get angry, or raise our voices. Mum would get livid. We sort of tiptoed around her, trying not to get her angry or upset. Telling her that Roger was molesting us would have caused all hell to break loose.'

'Do you think she knew?'

I shrugged. 'I don't know. Obviously something weird was going on the night Roger called me into bed with them. But, who knows?' My mind was starting to drift.

'Can you tell me a little more about that night?'

I squinted my eyes, trying to bring Phil into focus; he was starting to look fuzzy. 'I'm sorry,' I stammered, 'I've lost what you said. Would you mind repeating it?'

He smiled gently. 'That's all right. Is this getting uncomfortable for you?'

'Not at all. I'm just, you know, losing focus.'

'Spacing out?'

I nodded, suddenly feeling myself miles and miles away, floating in space and detached from whatever was going on.

'This is how you must have coped, back then,' he said quietly.

But he was gone. And I was cut adrift.

I can't remember the session ending.

The sexual fantasies became relentless. Only now it was the little one who was filling my mind with ghastly pictures. She was finally in Phil's lap. And he was telling her to take her clothes off. His penis was huge and he showed her how to rub it. She only wanted to please him, relieved at last to be doing her job. He put his hand between her legs and she lay back against him in a state of bliss.

I was disgusted with myself. What would Phil think if he knew? I felt as though I was covered in filth and everybody around me could see it. There was no way in the world that I could let Phil know what was going on in my mind. I would die of shame.

She would not let up though. The only safe place to be was on Phil's lap and she drove me to distraction with her pleas.

Ask him for a hug, she begged again. She pictured his thick, warm jumper and snuggling in close.

I can't, I tell her. *It isn't like that here. We're just meant to talk to him. And how would you feel if he said no? How awful would that be?*

Then just ask him, she begged. *How else will we know what he'll say?*

For days I was driven crazy with indecision. Should I ask? Or was I meant to grow up and get over it? I couldn't sleep. I lay in bed at night desperately looking for a solution. I didn't know what was expected. Why hadn't Phil told me how this stuff works? Should I ask him for a hug or was that being stupid and childish? Was this therapy about growing out of such ridiculous desires or was it normal to want the hug? What would he say? The night prior to my next session with Phil I finally came up with an alternative: I would ask him to sit next to me on the couch. That should go halfway to a solution, without making me look totally absurd. It would also, hopefully, put an end to the relentless yearning for his lap. For the first time in weeks, I slept like a log.

'I think I'm going to throw up,' I told him, my stomach heaving.

'Would you like a bucket?'

'Ugh! I don't think so, thank you.'

Phil laughed. 'It won't be the first time someone's vomited in front of me.'

'I think I'll skip that experience all the same, thanks.'

'Why do you think you're feeling sick?'

I knew exactly why. There was a small voice inside me giving me hell. *Ask him to sit next to you*, she persisted. *Don't you dare finish this session and not do it.*

Phil was waiting for an answer. My hands were clammy and I was finding it hard to swallow. What if he said no? What if he got angry? 'I guess I'm feeling sick because there's something I wanted to ask you,' I finally gushed out.

'Go ahead,' he prompted.

'Oh God,' I groaned, staring at the ceiling, 'I wish it was that easy.'

'What are you afraid of?'

I looked at him in dismay. 'Everything!'

He smiled. 'Come on, it can't be that bad. I won't ever hurt you, you know.'

He was convincing and oh so gentle. I continued to gaze at the ceiling. I knew that if I left the session without saying it, I would be given hell. I took a long, deep breath. 'Okay, here goes. I was thinking, well, more like wondering, if . . .'

I couldn't do it.

'If what?' Phil asked firmly.

'Oh Jesus, if . . . you would . . . sit next to me.' I blurted it out and stared fixedly at my shoes.

'Of course I can. Let's swap places first, huh? You come and sit in my chair and I'll sit on the couch.'

That sounded like a fun idea. We switched places. 'Gosh, it's heaps better sitting here.'

He smiled. 'Why's that?'

'Your chair has got edges.' It was an odd feeling, seeing Phil sitting on the couch. 'Maybe I should ask you questions now?' I joked.

'Fire away.'

My mind went blank. 'Maybe not. I'll just enjoy sitting in your chair. In a way, it's almost like being in your lap.' The little one was already feeling better.

Once again, he smiled warmly.

I looked nervously at the empty space next to him. Suddenly the couch looked tiny! If I sat next to him we would almost be touching.

'What are you thinking?' he asked.

I sighed. 'I don't know if I can do it.'

'You don't have to, you know, you can always wait till you feel more comfortable.'

I shook my head, remembering the past few days and the

relentless, conflicting desires. 'I've got to do it,' I answered, 'or there'll be no peace.'

'When you're ready, just take your time.'

Oh God, why had I ever brought this up? I was about to plunge into the sea of doubts again.

Fuck it, get over there. In a second I leapt out of Phil's chair and plonked myself next to him on the couch. I looked straight ahead, holding my breath, terrified. He was so *close*. In that instant I spaced out into the ether. 'I'm miles away from you,' I told him, still staring straight ahead.

'Is that right? What are you feeling?'

'Scared.'

'That's okay, remember to breathe though.'

'Could you please not make any sudden moves?' I asked him, afraid that I would leap out of my skin if his hand moved even an inch.

'Sure. I'll just sit still.'

I let myself take a few deep breaths and allowed my eyes to sneak a quick glance at his legs, only an inch away from mine. He had his hands on his lap, where I could see them. Phil stayed quiet. I was starting to calm down. He wasn't going to grab me or lunge at me. I was doing it; I was sitting right next to him! 'Nothing's going to happen, is it?' I finally asked.

'No, we're just sitting together.'

He's not touching me, the little one said. *Look at his hands, so close, why isn't he doing anything?* I told her to be still, I had done what she'd wanted.

'And I had nothing to be afraid of?'

'That's right, but I imagine it was a very scary thing for you to do.'

I nodded, still not able to turn my head and look at him. 'I feel a lot better now.'

'That's good, you've done very well. Are you still spaced out?'

'Not as much. You know, I've wanted to get closer to you for a long time. I was just too scared to ask.'

'What were you afraid of?'

I shook my head. 'That you'd get angry or say no.'

'And maybe that I'd take advantage of you?'

'Yep, I guess that too.'

Doesn't he want me? The little one was dismayed.

'Then this was a really brave thing for you to do.'

'Now I'd like to go back to how we normally are, if that's okay?'

'Sure,' he said, getting up and returning to his chair.

I heaved a sigh of relief, aware that the background voice had at last been silenced.

He smiled. 'Better now?'

'Much. Thank you for doing that.'

'My pleasure.'

'I have so many odd thoughts about you,' I confided, feeling a little braver. 'Some of them are really awful.'

'Why don't you tell me about them.'

I grimaced, but felt weary from keeping so much to myself. 'They're very sexual. I'm usually in your lap.'

'And what am I doing?'

I hung my head. 'What those other men did.'

It was his turn to grimace. 'That's not a very nice picture.'

'I know,' I wailed, feeling terrible. 'It's relentless though.'

'How about your dreams, have they continued?'

I nodded.

'Want to tell me about them?'

'Not today, maybe in our next session. They're so embarrassing!'

'This is all to be expected, you know. At some time or another you will try to sabotage this relationship, try to sexualise it.'

I shook my head fiercely. 'No I won't. That's the last thing I need.'

He smiled softly. 'It's inevitable; you will do everything in your power to seduce me. You've already tried a number of times.'

I wriggled in discomfort, wanting to deny it fiercely but knowing that he was speaking the truth. 'Am I just a rotten person?'

He shook his head. 'Of course you're not. It's just the way this works. There hasn't been much in your life that was good. You'll want to destroy this, because it will feel too unfamiliar.'

I sighed. 'But that's awful!'

'It's just the way it is; it's not your fault.'

'I know, but everything that's coming up is so sordid! And I feel as though I don't even have the basics on how to handle it. My mind is like an alphabet; only it goes from A to F then M, missing some of the vital steps. I don't know how to make sense of this business with you. Do you know what I mean?'

'I do. And in a way, that's exactly what happened to you. You missed out on quite a few of the formative processes of growing up. Our job is to fill in those blanks for you.'

I frowned. Was that like teaching me how to be a human? 'So are you sort of civilising me?' I asked, not quite sure I liked that idea.

He smiled. 'In a way, yes.'

'Hmmm.'

'Don't like the sound of that?'

'I guess it conflicts with my elevated picture of myself. I know this sounds ghastly, but I've always felt somewhat superior to others. Now here you are teaching me the basics of being human. That's a little deflating.' I had a sudden image of a wild child being rescued from the jungle. 'I'm not completely clueless, you know,' I continued, trying to muster some dignity, 'only in this confusing stuff. If it wasn't for that, I think I'd be fine.'

He looked a little puzzled. 'What "confusing stuff" are you referring to?'

'You know!' I answered, feeling increasingly frustrated. 'This personal stuff.'

'I'm sorry, but I'm still not quite with you.'

'*This*!' I said, pointing to him and me.

'A relationship, you mean?' he asked, suddenly laughing out loud.

I scowled, but another part of me was charmed. God, it was so neat to hear him laugh. 'Don't be such a sod.'

'I'm sorry,' he said, still thoroughly enjoying himself, 'it was just the way you said it. But yes, forming relationships is pretty fundamental to being human.'

'Well I think they suck.'

'It gets better, believe me.'

'Hmmm. Well at least one of us is enjoying the process.'

'Come on,' he said, smiling warmly, 'it's not *all* bad, is it?'

I looked up, liking him more by the moment, despite myself. 'No, I guess not. My ego is just struggling a wee bit.'

'More accustomed to being in control?'

'Exactly. And floating above everybody. This is like a crash course in humility.'

'Humility is okay. Good for the soul.'

'Well, I'll just have to take your word for that.'

'Wow. There's a giant leap forward.'

I laughed. 'God, you're certainly firing on all cylinders today.'

'Good to let some humour in once in a while. It can get a bit too serious otherwise.'

I nodded. 'You can say that again.'

I left the session feeling warmed and relieved. Perhaps now, I would get some peace.

The thoughts calmed down. I could think of Phil without being set upon by wildly conflicting desires. I felt another glimmer of hope. However, I was finding it increasingly difficult to be in my mother's company. It took only the smallest thing to upset me. I was continually angry with her and didn't know why. Every word that came out of her mouth rubbed me the wrong way. I challenged her constantly. Even our trips to the pokies brought little reprieve; we sat at different machines, miles apart and barely acknowledging each other. I knew she was feeling hurt but I was tired of making her feel better all the time. After a few more sessions with Phil I decided that it was time to confront her. I had nothing to lose; our relationship had totally deteriorated.

It was a Saturday afternoon in Aldinga and we had just finished playing Scrabble. I had come up for the weekend so knew that I had all the time I needed to sort things out with her. I waited till she had made a cup of tea before tentatively broaching the subject. 'Mum, I need to talk to you about things that have been coming up with Phil.'

She raised her eyebrows. 'I thought you had told me everything, dear.'

I shook my head. 'Not everything. I guess that's one of the reasons why I've been so angry lately. There are things I need to get off my chest.'

'Oh not again, dear. Haven't we covered all that old stuff?'

'Obviously not well enough, or I wouldn't be feeling like this.'

Mum looked annoyed and I knew she was hoping I would back down. But I just kept direct eye contact with her. She sighed. 'Go ahead, dear. What's the problem?'

I took a deep breath. 'It's about Roger and the sexual abuse. I figure that maybe I haven't explained it well enough. You don't seem surprised or even angry with Roger. Don't you think it was awful, what he did? And Frank and Terry? They all molested Jo and me, Mum. Numerous times. Don't you feel anything about that?' I wanted desperately to reach her, but her eyes remained blank.

'Yes dear, it's all very unpleasant. But it's not like they had sex with you, is it?'

I was stunned. What sort of a question was that? My mind started whirling. Was I crazy or something? Was it me that was making a big fuss over nothing? But what about what Phil had said? I tried again.

'No Mum, they didn't have sex with us. At least, I don't think they did. They just pawed us and used us whenever they felt like it.'

She looked like someone had passed a plate of rotten fish under her nose. 'Well, yes, that couldn't have been very nice.'

'Not very nice? Mum,' I pleaded, trying to get through to her, 'that was *four* men, all of them either your friends or boyfriend. Didn't it occur to you to keep an eye on things? In most cases, it was you who had suggested they pay us a visit while you were at work. Didn't you *see* that that put us in danger?'

She shook her head. 'It was different back in my day. There hadn't been all this publicity about sexual abuse. It didn't even enter my mind.'

Was that right? Was it a generational thing? Maybe mothers weren't so aware of the risks back then? It didn't make sense though. I brushed it off as a ridiculous excuse. 'That's crap, Mum. Parents have always protected their children. It's not a new thing. I could make allowances for one creep getting into our house, but *four*?'

'Well, I don't know how it happened, dear,' she answered tiredly. 'I certainly did my best with you girls. I had to work to keep a roof over our heads. That wasn't always easy, you know. I couldn't be aware of every little thing that was going on.'

I was still shaking my head. Was this conversation insane or was it just me?

'There's something wrong with your response Mum. It doesn't make sense. Don't you feel *anything*?'

Her face turned red with anger. I knew what was coming next. I had heard it a thousand times before.

'Look, dear,' she said, in a clipped, irritated tone. 'I feel what I feel, and I'm sorry if that's not good enough for you. I loved you girls more than anything and it appears to me that not one of you has any gratitude. Frankly I sometimes wonder why I bothered.'

It was like a broken record; I'd been listening to it since I was five years old.

She got up to make a cup of tea and I sat there, doubting myself again. Why couldn't I just leave her alone? She wasn't a bad person; she just didn't have a clue. I felt so different towards my son; I wanted to keep him safe more than anything else in the world. Why hadn't Mum felt like that for my sisters, or me? It just didn't make sense. I got up from my chair and went outside for a walk.

It was a cold, blustery day and the sea looked grey and uninviting. I wrapped my jacket around me tightly and headed for the tip of the peninsula. I thought of all the cities in the world that I had walked in: Paris, Auckland, Sydney, Milan; the list seemed endless. But where was my home? Was there somewhere that I belonged? I stepped up my pace as the wind whipped through my coat. I wished once again that my spaceship would come and get me. We're so, so sorry, they would say. You should never have been left here. I would race into the craft, swooning with relief.

They would ask how it was, still mortified at their mistake. I would roll my eyes. This planet sucks, I'd tell them. People are awful to each other. And none of them say a word that makes sense. My fellow souls would nod and tell me it's all over. We're taking you home.

Home, I'd think, hugging the word like a long-lost friend. I'm going home.

I walked back into my mother's house. She looked up at me with a smile. 'Fancy a game of anagrams?'

I nodded, keen to put it all behind me. 'Why not?'

We sat at the dining room table and set up the board. Like me, Mum had a love of the English language. I beat her in virtually every game we played, however, which annoyed the hell out of me for some reason. She wasn't stupid, and she read as much as I did, how come she couldn't find the words? On this particular day, we were halfway through the game and I could feel my irritation rising again. There was no way Mum was going to win. I couldn't understand it. She was struggling to find a word with her ten letters and I could see a beauty. Usually I would point it out to her, or if I were too bad tempered I would ignore it and wait till she found her own, smaller word. I was watching on, trying to find the source of my anger. Mum loved playing this game, and despite her frequent losses, she was always eager to start another one. Was it so important for me to win? I felt that in one form or another, I had been beating her for years. No matter what she said or did, I would find a way to challenge her. I felt a pain in my heart again. Could I let her win this time, would that be so hard for me? I had to take a deep breath so as not to cry. That's my mum, I thought, noticing how grey her hair had become and how old she looked. She had done her best, and no one could say her life had been easy. All those violent men, the crappy jobs, the constant shortage of money, and here she was now, not far off seventy. Couldn't I for once forego a victory? I let myself lose that day, and enjoyed watching her light up like a child.

'You're mothering her again,' Phil stated.

'I know. I just felt so sad for her. And I've been relentless with her. I feel guilty as hell.'

Phil said nothing.

'I'm not stupid, you know, I do know that in a few days, or a week, she'll do or say something that will have me leaping off the deep end again. It's no different from what happened with a photograph, just a few weeks ago.'

'What's that about?' he asked.

I sighed. 'Well, years ago my husband had taken a photo of me, I had lost a lot of weight and was quite enjoying my new slim body. It was done quite tastefully. I was lying on a double bed, naked except for a pair of knickers. Anyway, I'd had it tucked away with dozens of other old photographs. Mum and I were going through them about three weeks ago. When I got to the nude shot she was quite taken by it.' I shuddered a little, remembering my discomfort.

'So what happened?'

'I'd found what I had been looking for. It was an old picture of Jo, Ty, Mum, Kim and myself. We looked like a really close family, all smiling with our arms wrapped around each other. I showed it to Mum and she made quite a fuss of it. Anyway, the next morning she rang me and asked could she have the negative, she wanted to blow it up poster size and put it on display in her lounge room.'

Phil was nodding, and listening intently.

'Well, I said sure, but I thought she had one like it somewhere in her own albums. We had crossed wires though. It took me some time to realise that she was talking about the nude photograph of me.'

Phil looked horrified. 'She wanted a poster-size picture of you naked to hang up on her wall?'

I nodded. 'I know. I was astonished too. I asked her if she was joking. What about all the creepy men she has in her house, how would she feel about them gawking at my naked body?'

'What did she say?' he asked, still in disbelief.

'She said she'd be proud. She liked showing me off.'

Phil was speechless. 'How did you feel about that?' he finally managed.

'I was shocked, I guess. Couldn't quite believe it. I said no. No way. But she couldn't understand why. I tried to imagine myself wanting to do something like that with a photograph of Ty. It made me feel ill.'

He was shaking his head. 'It's no different than your childhood, is it? In some odd way she made you girls available to her men. Almost gave them permission, as it were.'

I nodded. 'What's that about?'

He continued to look baffled. 'I've no idea. Obviously there's something wrong there. She gets something out of men lusting after her daughters.'

'She used to parade us in front of them.'

'And from the sounds of it, she's still doing it.'

I asked him a question that I had been avoiding for some time. 'You think she knew all about the sexual abuse, don't you?'

He nodded. 'In your case especially, with the incident in bed with her and Roger, I'd find it pretty hard to believe otherwise.'

I shuddered. 'That night was so awful.'

'Do you want to tell me about it?'

Could I find the words? I took a deep breath. 'I had just gone

111

to bed. Mum and Roger were in their bedroom, watching television. I heard Roger call out my name. I leapt out of bed quickly; it didn't pay to keep him waiting.' God, I hated him.

'What happened next?'

'I went into their room. It was dark except for the light coming from the television. Roger had asked Mum to move over, he'd made a space for me next to him. He told me to climb in.'

'So he was in the middle of the bed?'

'Yep. Mum on one side, me on the other.' The memory of what happened next flicked across my mind. I shook my head. 'It's just too awful,' I told Phil, looking up at him and hoping he'd let it go.

He just waited.

I had kept it a secret for so long. What would Phil think of me? And how could I even say the words? My body squirmed with indecision. I looked down at my feet.

Tell him, for God's sake. I took a deep breath.

'Roger put his hand down my pyjamas and started, you know, touching me. I was terrified. Mum was only about a foot away. I could almost hear my heart thumping. I was thinking, for God's sake, she'll *see*, any minute now and she'll see. But it was like she wasn't even there. Well, a few minutes later, he took my hand and . . . put it, you know, between his legs.'

'Did he have an erection?' Phil asked softly.

I nodded, still dying of shame.

'What did he do with your hand?'

Did I have to say this? Wasn't it all pretty obvious? I swallowed hard. 'He got me to, you know, rub him up and down.' Oh God, I felt so *bad*. Take me away from this, somebody, let me fall through the floor and disappear.

'What was your mother doing?'

I shook my head. 'Nothing. She didn't say a word.' Why, Mum?

Could you see it? Didn't you feel the bed moving, and hear Roger's breath, fast and excited? Where were you, Mum?

'Did he ejaculate?'

'I don't know. I don't know what happened next. It just goes blank.' I hung my head, feeling covered with slime. I sat quietly for a few moments, trying to take it all in. How could Mum have let that continue? 'I don't understand her,' I told Phil, looking at him for answers.

'She would have known what was happening, don't you think?'

I so wanted to believe otherwise, but how could she have not noticed? 'I've told myself for years that she must have been unaware.'

He smiled gently. 'You've been covering up for her in one form or another for most of your life. I guess you had to, she was all you had.'

I nodded, not able to comprehend for a moment how that woman's mind worked. 'I always feel so sorry for her, as if I'm making her life hard by bringing everything up again.'

Phil kept quiet.

'Should I just let it go, where she's concerned,' I continued, filled with confusion. 'Am I being mean? It's not as though she did it intentionally.'

'So explain the photo to me.'

I slumped back into the couch. I didn't understand that at all.

I left the session feeling dirty again. Would I ever get rid of this filth? I stopped at the supermarket on my way home, still feeling grubby and deflated. As I walked up and down the aisles, I looked at the women passing by. They all seemed so *clean*. Did they sense my dirtiness? Was it obvious to everyone who met me?

Later that day, I was in my doctor's surgery, needing painkillers for an ache that had started up in my jaw, when an idea came out of nowhere. 'There's another thing,' I told my doctor, deciding to chance it, 'I'm having a lot of trouble sleeping. Normally I'm fine and maybe it's just this cough, but I wonder could you prescribe something?'

'Sure,' she answered readily. 'Have you ever used sleeping pills before?' I shook my head. And before I knew it I was heading into the chemist with a strange thrill going through me. It was the same sensation when I had cut myself. I left with the sleeping pills in my handbag and decided to visit some other nearby surgeries and collect as many bottles as possible. It was a cinch. I arrived home euphoric. Excited. Once again I was in control.

When Ty had gone to bed, I took all the bottles out and placed them on the table in front of me. Would that be enough to kill me? I wondered where I could do it without Ty finding me. Maybe I'd need to go interstate, or wait till his next trip away to New Zealand. I opened one of the bottles and shook out some of the tablets. They looked so tiny and innocuous. I held them in my hands and thought back over my life. It was going nowhere still. Wouldn't the next forty years be exactly like the last forty? I knew I wasn't up to that. Slowly I sank into the familiar darkness within. Nothing was ever going to change. I was a nobody, with no one, and going nowhere. These pills would at least put an end to that. I placed them carefully back into their bottles as though they were tiny, little friends of mine. I was freezing cold and so bloody tired. I climbed into bed, shivering.

Phil was furious. 'Was that the same doctor who referred you to me?' he asked in disbelief.

I nodded, trying to ignore the pain in my jaw.

'I can't believe how irresponsible she was. It makes me angry when they prescribe so readily, especially since she knew you suffered from depression.'

'It's hardly her job to monitor me,' I explained. 'And anyway, there were other doctors too. It was easy getting quite a horde together.'

Phil was shaking his head. 'So what do you plan to do with them?'

'I don't know,' I answered truthfully, feeling hopelessly confused. 'I just like to line them all up and look at them. Gives me a small sense of control, you know?' I rubbed the side of my face, trying to ease the sharp jabs that felt like somebody was piercing my jaw with a hot poker.

'What's up?'

'I don't know, this pain came out of nowhere. I've got some painkillers, but they're really strong, so I'm trying just to take them at night.'

'Have you had it before?'

I shook my head.

'Hmmm, what do you think it might be about?'

'I'm not sure, it only started a few weeks ago, but it's getting worse. And I hate going to doctors. I leap out of my skin the minute they come near me.'

'You don't like them putting objects inside you?'

'I can't stand it. I have to fight down the urge to shove their hand away, especially if they're trying to put something in my mouth, or ears.'

'Did that happen to you as a child?'

I frowned. 'What do you mean?'

'Those men, did they put things in your mouth?'

I could hardly think for the pain in my jaw, so I simply nodded.

'And what else?'

'Roger, when he was giving me a bath once, he had a metal object, I'm not sure what it was.'

'What did he do with it?' Phil asked gently.

'He put it ... you know, inside me.'

'In your vagina?'

God, I hated that word. I just nodded again.

'Do you have problems when you're giving oral sex?'

'Yep.'

'You gag?'

I nodded.

'Then that might go some way to explaining what's going on for you right now, do you think?'

I held my jaw. 'I guess so. It hurts *so* much though.'

Phil's eyes were full of sympathy. 'I can see that.'

'I'm so fed up with everything. I think that's why I got those pills, you know?'

'I know, but it's also partly to do with what went on recently with your mother, don't you think?'

'But I tried to talk to her. It's useless. I just keep getting it wrong. And I'm sick of trying. I don't know what else I could have done.'

'I think you do.'

I shook my head, feeling totally defeated. 'Honestly, I don't. I talk to Mum and nothing makes sense again. I don't know what more I can do?'

'*What more could you do?*' Phil suddenly roared. 'You could tell her to *fuck off* for a start!'

I nearly fell out of my seat. I'd never seen him angry.

'What would that achieve?' I asked, still in awe over his response.

'For God's sake, it's about *you*, not her. When will you *get* that? It's not about getting a response; it's unlikely you ever will. It's about you standing up for yourself, saying no to all that fucking crap and pretence. You're still protecting her, still trying to keep everything nice!'

I was speechless. I'd never heard anyone so passionate about something concerning me. I felt a warm glow permeate my being. What a neat person he was. 'Tell her to fuck off, you say? Well, that would certainly be novel.'

'Do *something*, for God's sake; you're not gathering sleeping pills for nothing.'

I couldn't do it though. Instead I sank further into despair.

Chapter Eight

Our sessions continued. I slumped in and said very little. One day merged into the next. The only thing that got me out of bed was my appointment with Phil and my routine for Ty. Nothing else existed. I knew I was in trouble but didn't know how to pull up from the dive.

My contact with Mum increased. I had once again put the past behind me and was determined to get our relationship back on track. She wasn't a bad person; everyone else loved her. Why was it so difficult for me? I would just shut up about the past and be grateful for the good things about her. I was sure I could get there. But the spaciness was getting worse and some days I was so disorientated that I lost track of time again. One Monday morning I knew I had to get out and get some groceries for the house. I was standing in the aisle trying to choose a pack of toilet paper. I went to reach the one I usually bought when my eye was caught by the brand next to it, thirty cents cheaper.

Ah, I'll get that one instead. But then I noticed that it only had seven-hundred-and-fifty sheets, whereas my initial choice had a thousand.

Hang on, though, that one's two-ply. I'd never even known such a distinction existed! I was totally baffled. Before I knew it I was scanning the rows of rolls and gathering masses of information. There were scented ones, patterns, recyclables, economy packs,

118

luxury rolls, twelve packs, double packs, one-ply, two-ply; it seemed to go on and on and I was standing there absolutely paralysed.

For God's sake, just grab a bloody roll and get out of here.

But I couldn't. It seemed such an important decision and more than anything I wanted to make a meaningful choice; to get it right. Why did they have to put so many there? How did normal people know which one to choose? My body had gone rigid and my throat was constricted. Something inside me wanted to scream. Then ping! I was miles and miles away in the ether and talking to myself in a slow gentle voice.

Hey, Deb, it's all right, it doesn't matter, it really doesn't matter.

And just as suddenly, it didn't. I grabbed a roll and paid for it, so far away from the cashier that I could barely bring her into focus.

Everything was getting crazy. My moods were swinging wildly and I didn't know how I would be from day to day. Phil hung in there with me, constantly assuring me that this would pass. I held on to him like a lifeline, terrified that I would cross the threshold into that huge, vast space and not be able to get back. I eventually blanked out, and handed the controls over to whoever wanted them.

She curled up into the couch and didn't know what to say.

'How's it all going, Deb?'

She shook her head. 'I had to drive here,' she told him, 'all ... by ... my ... self.'

'That must have been tough,' he said, ever so gently. 'You're not very big, are you?'

'Nope. And I was *scared* too. It took me ages to get here.'

'I bet it did,' he smiled.

'You know what I don't like?' she confided eagerly.

'No, you tell me.'

'I don't like it when you tell me that it's time to leave here.'

He smiled softly. 'I know, but what else can I do? If I let you stay here, the next patient might find it a bit uncomfortable. You know, with you sitting in the corner.'

That made her laugh. 'Maybe she wouldn't mind. I'd be quiet as a mouse.'

'I don't think that would work somehow.'

'No,' she said sadly, 'probably not.' She looked around his office, now such a familiar room for her. 'I wish I never had to leave here.'

'Safe, is it?'

'Yep. I don't like going out there. Not one bit. I get too … confused by everything, you know?'

He nodded, his eyes kind. 'You can come and visit me whenever you like, you know?'

She looked at his lap, so tempting. 'Why do you sit all the way over there?'

'Would you like me to sit closer?' he suggested.

She nodded. 'That would be real nice.'

He pulled his chair nearer to her and she gasped with surprise. 'You're in my space now,' she told him, her eyes wide with wonder.

'You invited me,' he said softly.

It felt so good to have him that close by; so strong and solid. 'I like you a *whole* lot, you know. Sometimes I think of you and everything gets all warm.'

'Thank you.'

'That's not all,' she continued happily, delighted to be talking to him, 'I think I love you.'

He nodded slowly. 'That's okay. Lot's of people fall in love with their therapist.'

'No,' she said firmly, 'not like *that*. Like *real* love, you know. All warm and safe.'

'Well I'll make sure that I look after that love very carefully. I promise not to mess it up for you. You deserve that, you know. You're a very lovable little girl.'

She reckoned he must be the neatest, nicest person in the whole world.

'I'm freezing cold,' she told him, suddenly aware that her teeth were chattering.

'Would you like to lie down?' he asked softly.

She nodded, and curled up on to the couch.

'What are you feeling?'

Something had changed. She didn't like it.

'It's all right,' he said gently, 'you can tell me.'

'I get scared, you know,' she confided shakily, looking around the room. 'Real scared, and my jaw hurts so bad.'

Phil pulled his chair a little closer. 'What are you scared of, Deb?'

She shook her head. 'It gets dark and I'm frightened. Frightened that ... someone's going to come in.' She shuddered.

'Who's going to come in?'

'I don't know,' she whispered, only aware of the danger, 'but he's ... big.'

'You're right there in that moment now, aren't you?'

She nodded, feeling tiny and very alone.

'What is he doing to you?'

She didn't want to tell. Her body was frozen to the bone.

'Where is he?' Phil asked again.

'He's on my bed and ...' She felt her mouth clamp shut.

'It's okay, you can tell me.'

'I'm so ... cold.'

'Would you like a blanket?'

She shook her head, not wanting him to leave.

'What's the man doing on your bed?'

It's too awful. 'He's got his hand ... down my ... jarmies.'

'What are you doing?'

'I'm ... looking away from him, staring at the wall. But I can hear his breath; it's fast and ... horrible. I don't like it one bit.'

'What happens next?'

'He ... gets in my bed. He's got ... his thing out and he's ...' She doesn't want to go on, she is too embarrassed.

'What's he doing with his penis?'

She lowered her head in shame. 'He's pulling at it. The bed is shaking and I don't know what to do.'

'Is he still touching you?'

'Yes.'

'Does he ejaculate?'

She frowned. 'I don't want to say anymore.'

'You'll feel better if you can, Deb. You've needed to get this out for some time.'

'I don't like it though. It feels yuk.'

'I know,' he said softly, 'it is yuk. But you've been carrying it on your own for too long.'

'I'm covered ... in slime.'

'Where did he ejaculate?' he persisted.

'I don't like this. It's not one ... bit ... nice.'

'You can tell me, though. It's okay.'

She chewed the inside of her lip, the words sticking in her throat like pieces of wood. 'On ... my ... tummy,' she finally whispered.

'Where is your mother?'

'She's *gone*. And Jo and Kim are out too.'

'So you're home all by yourself.'

She nodded.

'There was no one there to help you?'

She shook her head, wanting to cry.

'I would have helped you if I had been there,' he said softly.

Her throat was so constricted that she could barely breathe. 'Would you ... have made him go away?'

Phil nodded gently.

'Nobody was there,' she told him again.

'I know. And someone should have been.'

She gazed into his eyes, wanting him to take her home with him. How neat would that be? 'I don't want to leave here,' she told him quietly.

He smiled softly. 'That's okay, you just lay there for a while, there's no need to rush out just yet.' She felt herself getting drowsy and the pain in her jaw diminishing.

Why aren't you my daddy? You would have made all those men go away.

It was okay to doze, she had Phil close by now, big and strong and safe. Something warm wrapped itself around her heart and the icy chill began to fade. For the first time in her life she was secure, able to let a grown up do all the thinking. Phil sat quietly beside her. It was as if his strength was pouring into her little body. She wished she could fall into a deep sleep, knowing for once that she could do so safely. Quiet moments ticked by, with her curled on the couch, warm and sleepy, and Phil only inches away, strong and solid.

Please God, let this moment just go on and on and on.

They stayed there for the remainder of the session. She got up to go and had the odd sensation that she had forgotten something. She looked back at the couch.

'I feel like I've left something behind.'

'That will be your innocence,' Phil answered quietly. 'But don't worry; it will be safe with me.'

She took a deep breath. What a lovely thought.

'You drive carefully,' he told her, 'I doubt you're anywhere near old enough to hold a driver's licence.'

She left his office in a glorious state of happiness. She loved him. She had told him and it had been fine. She didn't want the day to end.

Something changed that day. I felt different but couldn't explain how. I just knew in my heart that Phil had reached inside and repaired a part of me that had been broken for years. I started to feel some hope. Maybe this therapy was really going to work. What a fantastic thought!

The world became a sparkling, magical place. I stopped and gazed in awe as a flock of rainbow lorikeets flew overhead, dazzling in their blues, reds and greens. I saw sunsets for the first time and people's smiles. I loved everyone and everything. My heart soared.

At night I lay in bed and replayed my session with Phil over and over again. It was like hugging a warm, precious gift. I could hardly wait to see him again. I wanted to tell him everything about my week, how the planet had changed, how I had changed. I counted the hours.

'You look a little down,' Phil observed.

She's always bloody down, aren't you bored with her yet?

'I guess I am,' I answered, trying to shut out the background racket. 'I feel like I haven't seen you for weeks.'

'You've lost some time?'

I nodded. 'I know I've been here, it's just that I don't feel like *I've* been here, you know?'

You haven't, Miss Mouse, we've been having a ball.

'So, you are aware that other parts have been turning up?'

'Sort of. It's like I'm way in the background, not able to speak.'

Too right, we managed to shut you up for a few days.

'But you know what's been going on?'

I nodded, trying desperately to hold my place. 'They hate me, you know.'

'Why do you think that is?'

'They think I spoil all of their fun. And I guess I do. They leave me with so much mess to clean up. I get exhausted.'

Tell him we think he's gorgeous!

'You've been doing that all of your life?'

'Yep, in one form or another. I feel as though I'm a million years old.'

You are. That's why we want to dump you.

Ask him for a hug.

He smiled gently. 'Why do you think the little one has been turning up to see me?'

He's talking about me. Tell him that I want a hug real bad.

'I don't know,' I answered, finding it increasingly difficult to concentrate. 'Why do you think that's happening?'

'You have no idea?'

'No. It's like I'll be on my way here one day, with something really important that I want to discuss with you, then, ping, I'm gone.'

He nodded. 'Maybe those other parts want to be heard.'

Yes. Give us a chance to speak.

'But I don't like it. It's like I lose control.'

'Yes, in a way I guess you do. But they're carrying quite a load, and perhaps its time that some of it got handed over. There wasn't

125

much opportunity for that when you were younger, was there?'

Please ask him for a hug.

I shook my head, struggling to keep control. 'But I can't let them take over. They wreak havoc. And you know what they've been saying?'

'What?'

'That I'm the one who should go. I'm the one who's making their life impossible.' I paused, and looked up at him nervously. 'Do you think that too?'

Of course he does, Miss Mouse, he'd much rather talk to me.

'You all have conversations, do you?' he asked, smiling warmly.

I nodded. 'It's absolute bedlam inside just lately. Everyone wants to speak; all of them want to talk to you.'

'That's good. You must be starting to feel a little safe here.'

'Good? It's insane! There's absolutely *no* agreement between us. Getting dressed in the morning is a total farce, it's like we all have our preferred clothes. Am I crazy?'

Not crazy, just boring. Tell him that I give a great blowjob.

'Not crazy, just very confused. Your therapy is bringing everything up, things that have been pushed down for decades. It's not surprising that this is happening.'

'But who am I? Which one of the parts is the real one?'

I am, no, I am.

'I don't think it works like that. You're the sum of all those parts. Our job is to glue them all together somehow.'

For once, there was silence. I paused to think that over and shook my head. 'I don't think that will work at all.'

He smiled. 'Let's just give it some time, see who turns up next, huh?'

I grimaced. 'Don't say that, you'll start a riot inside.' I could hear the rabble already. But I pushed them to the background, determined to keep my place.

The journey home was a nightmare. I could hear them all, pestering me for my attention. *I'm going in next; I'm going to tell him how much I like him.*

No, it's my turn, I want to tell him what he's missing out on.

He's already heard that, and I don't think he's interested.

Oh fuck off, you're just a child, how would you know? I'll have him begging for it soon.

I reached into the glove compartment for my Enya cassette.

Not that one.

I like this one, it's fun to sing to.

It's crap.

Put Enya on, that'll calm everything down.

Not fucking Enya!

I slammed the compartment shut. Sod them all; we'll drive home in silence.

His new secretary looked up and smiled at me. 'I've been trying to reach you, Miss Drake. The doctor isn't in today.'

All the blood drained from my face. 'Not in? But … we had an appointment.'

'Yes, but it's been cancelled. He should be in next week though.' She went back to her papers. I just stood there, stunned. I was falling into a deep, black hole. He'd just disappeared! Where had he gone? Why hadn't he told me?

I left the office and sat in my car, shaking. Bastard! After all that crap about trusting him and he can just disappear when he feels like it. He didn't even speak to me, just got some bloody woman to pass a message on like it was nothing! Rage was searing through me. I suddenly saw it all. Saw exactly how it was for him. I was just a time slot. He could wake up on any morning and say, 'Fuck it, I don't feel like those weirdos today.'

I started the car up and somehow managed to drive home. I still couldn't believe it! What a total, bloody idiot I had been. I thought I had actually mattered. He *knew* that change frightened me. But it hadn't made any difference. I was nothing. Just the eleven-thirty. I wasn't even a *person* to him. Bastard!

I couldn't calm myself down. I headed into my kitchen and took a writing pad out of the drawer. I wrote about ten drafts trying to explain to him why I was stopping therapy. But it only made me angrier. Why did I owe him any sort of explanation? I picked up the phone and dialled his number. The secretary answered swiftly, 'Doctor's Rooms.'

'Yes, hello. It's Debra Drake here. Would you pass a message on to Phil please that I wish to cancel all future appointments?' My voice was still shaking with rage. Did I need to add anything? 'Oh yes, and tell him thank you. That's all.' I hung up feeling slightly better. It was good to be rid of him.

I felt better for all of three hours and then I sank into despair. Now what? He had been my last hope. I had nothing left to try. But it was his fault. He shouldn't have disappeared like that. I climbed into bed and curled into a tight ball, my bones frozen to the core. There would be no point in getting up. Everything was gone. I lay there miserably for hours, wishing time would just leave me alone and the world would stop. But I knew Ty was due home. I dragged myself out of bed, slipped into mother-mode and headed into the kitchen to prepare dinner.

At 9 am the following morning, my telephone rang. I reached for the receiver hoping with all my heart that it wasn't my mother.

'Debra? It's Phil here. Is there a problem?'

I was speechless. I hadn't for a moment thought he would call. In all these months he had never contacted me. The voices started.

Tell him to go fuck himself.

No, no, go and see him, I've missed him.

I started to shake. 'No, not a problem. I'm just, I've just decided to finish therapy, that's all.'

'That's your right, of course, but I wonder has something come up that you need to talk to me about?'

I thought of that terrifying moment with his secretary. 'I've just been thinking that I've probably made a mistake, got things wrong, you know? It would be better if I stopped our sessions, I think.'

'Okay, well why not come in and see me and if you still want to end therapy after that, you can. How does that sound?'

Tell him no, tell him to fuck off. He's just a prick like all the rest of them.

'I'll be in tomorrow,' I told him quietly.

I was so angry that I couldn't look at him.

'Do you want to discuss it?' he asked.

It would feel like giving in. The minute I showed him my anger he had won. But I knew I couldn't sit there in silence. I glanced hatefully at him. Prick!

'I feel like I'm conceding defeat just by being here,' I spat out.

'What's been going on, Deb?'

That's right; the bastard didn't even know what he'd done. He hadn't cared. The words were right there but I didn't want to give in. The constriction in my throat was killing me.

'You're obviously very angry with me,' he prompted.

Once again I looked up at him. I *hated* him! He was so fucking calm.

I took a long, slow breath, trying to release some of the tightness in my throat. 'Yes, I'm angry with you. Pretty stupid, huh? Given the circumstances, that is. But don't worry, I'll deal with it.'

Phil was nodding slowly. 'I don't think it's stupid. I think it's probably very important for you to share it with me.'

'I bet you do,' I snapped, 'I get to share everything while you sit there in your safe little world. Meanwhile I'm trapped in some bloody fantasy that it actually matters. Well not anymore, this will be my last session.' I was shaking again.

'As I said, that's your right. But I'm still not sure what's brought this on.'

Bloody bastard. I thought my throat would seize if I held it in much longer. 'Okay,' I started at last, 'I'll tell you. You fucking set me up! You told me to trust you! Then one day you just disappear. You didn't warn me or anything! You got some fucking strange woman who couldn't have cared less to tell me you weren't there.' I felt like I was going to cry and pushed it down as hard as I could. There was no way in the world that prick was going to see me in tears.

To my utter amazement, Phil was smiling. I couldn't believe it! 'You're a rotten prick!' I spat at him. 'This isn't a fucking relationship! This is just me being a pathetic, weak weirdo and you just sit there soaking it all up.'

His smile broadened. What was going on? I tried again, feeling the anger pouring from my every atom. 'And I'll tell you something else. I hate the fucking way we're always talking about *me*. When do *you* get to show something, or is that bloody unheard of? How come it's always me that has to do the work? Oh that's right, you're the fucking psychiatrist. I keep forgetting that.' My body was electrified from tip to toe.

He was positively beaming!

I finally gave up. I'd never seen such a response. 'What's so *bloody* funny?'

'Not funny,' he said, 'just an absolute delight. This is the first time I've seen you angry. I'm honoured.'

I couldn't believe it. I had been waiting for him to rip into me or demand that I leave. I'd been so nasty to him. And he was honoured? Something in me melted. I felt the tightness in my throat finally loosen up, the anger dissipating. 'I was so scared when you weren't there yesterday.'

'You thought I'd abandoned you?'

'Yes,' I cried, 'it was *awful*. I didn't know what to do or where to go.'

'Is that a familiar feeling for you?'

'All the time,' I answered, remembering my terror at sudden changes. 'It's like falling down a dark hole, with nothing to grab onto.'

'You've lost a lot in your life, haven't you? Your family, your home and country and really just about everything that was ever important to you.'

I could finally look into his eyes. 'I thought I'd lost you too.'

'You'll never lose me,' he assured me, 'and that's a promise. I'm committed to you till the very end. No matter how long it takes.'

I felt a lump in my throat. 'But you disappear!' I accused him, still shocked by his sudden absence.

'Sometimes that's going to happen. My wife and my baby were sick. I had to stay home. Life does that sometimes. You're going to have to make some allowances for that.'

His wife and baby? Jealousy ripped through me. 'How many children do you have?' I asked, trying not to look too interested.

'Three. Three girls.'

Ouch. That hurt. 'Just like my sisters and me?'

He nodded, smiling softly. 'That's right.'

God, I was *so* jealous. Imagine him actually taking a day off from work to look after them? How neat must that be? Then I thought of his wife and immediately hated her.

'What are you thinking about?'

I shook my head. 'Nothing much.' I'd exposed enough vileness for one day. Hopefully they had a rotten relationship anyway, I consoled myself.

'I'm not good with change, am I?' I asked him, changing the subject.

He laughed. 'No, I'd have to agree with that. But that's to be expected. Your mother dragged you from pillar to post for years. Any sudden changes are likely to bring up memories and any feelings you may have suppressed. It was very brave of you to come here and express some of those feelings. You should be proud of yourself.'

Proud? He had such a different way of seeing things. My mother would have ignored me for days if I had lost my temper like that with her.

'I'm sorry for being so vile.'

'That wasn't vile. Not even close. It was honest.'

God, was there no end to his patience? 'I get scared by how I feel about you.'

'Because you need me?'

That pulled me up short. 'Need you? I don't need anyone. No, it's not that.'

'Really?' he asked, looking amused. 'So why are you coming here?'

'To get fixed,' I answered. What did that have to do with need?

'I see. And why do you think you reacted like you did when I wasn't here yesterday?'

I grimaced at the thought. It couldn't be? 'Because I need you? That's a repulsive notion.'

He laughed. 'Come on now, it's not that bad, is it?'

'It's awful. Pathetic!'

'The whole point of this therapy is to put you in a position of dependence. It's something you missed out on as a child. How could you have, when there was no one there for you to rely on?'

'But I didn't come here to become dependent. That's an awful thought.'

'It won't be forever. Once you become strong enough you'll eventually move away from me. That's what would have taken place if you'd had a proper childhood. We need to go back and repair the damage.'

'Is that why I keep feeling so little lately?'

'Exactly. In some weird way when something goes wrong in our formative years, the child remains with us. That's why you get tripped up so much. It's *her* reactions that keep surfacing.'

'Will she eventually go away?'

'Not so much go away as integrate. But there's been a lot of damage done to you. This will take a while.'

I sighed. 'So it's normal for me to feel so needy?' I shuddered; it was such a gruesome thought.

He smiled. 'It's exactly what we want. But believe me, it won't last forever. Eventually you'll move away from me and become independent.

'I promise you, it will happen.'

Leave Phil? Never. It was a thought too awful to imagine.

That evening, after Ty had gone to bed, I put on some quiet music and let my mind replay the session over and over again. Something inside me had changed and I was trying to pin it down. I kept seeing Phil smiling while I had ranted and raved. It was such an unfamiliar response. Mum would not tolerate her daughters' anger. If we so much as raised our voices she would be incensed at the outburst and demand an immediate apology. I became afraid of my anger, inventing numerous ways to subvert or deny it, or turning it instead into a whining, pleading request. Yet Phil had simply smiled, enjoying the outburst. He'd even told me that it was healthy! I was entranced.

'I'm beginning to get a handle on how this therapy stuff works.'

Phil smiled. 'How's that?'

'Well, I've been thinking about my anger and how much I've hated it. I wonder is that because somewhere inside me I had Mum's reaction to it? And what you're trying to do is to give me a new response that will replace hers. So that in future when I feel angry, I immediately see you, smiling at me and thanking me for being honest. And because of that, I have a whole new way of seeing my anger. Is that how it goes?'

'Very perceptive. That's exactly how the process is meant to work.'

'Hmmm. Then why hasn't that happened to me before? I've met other people who've managed to stay calm when I've lost my temper.'

'It isn't as simple as that, unfortunately, otherwise we'd all find this change business pretty easy. There may have been instances when other people have not become angry in response to your anger. But in other ways the relationship was dysfunctional. For some reason we tend to seek out relationships that are familiar to us, no matter how unhealthy they may be. And that only helps to reinforce our picture of the world and ourselves. In a way, we're collecting more proof. What you and I are doing here is recreating the setting of your childhood, and in the process, I try to repair the damage by offering alternative, healthier responses. That's why the therapy relationship is unique.'

I let that sink in. 'Not all my relationships have been bad, though.'

Phil arched his eyebrows.

'I mean it,' I said, suddenly feeling defensive. 'Not all the men I've been with have been creeps.'

Still Phil said nothing.

'My life has had some good things in it.'

'I find that highly unlikely.'

I could feel an irritation rising. 'Well, you're wrong. I've had some amazing times in my life.'

'So what are you doing here?'

I glared at him. 'Very funny.'

'I wasn't trying to be amusing. I'm being quite serious. From what you've told me so far, you've been out of control for most of your life. What's so amazing about that?'

'I know that!' I answered, suddenly wanting to stamp my foot. 'But it wasn't *all* bad.'

Phil shrugged, looking totally unconvinced.

I rolled my eyes. 'Well, obviously I'm not getting my point across here.'

'What exactly *is* your point?' he asked, frowning.

I tried another tack. 'I can't look back at forty years or more and say that it was all a waste.'

'Well, wasn't it?'

'*No*. My *son* is in those forty years. He's probably the only good thing that came out of it.'

'I think that's what I've been trying to point out to you. But for some reason that I'm not quite clear on yet, you want to convince me that you're life has been quite good up to now.'

I was getting confused. 'Not all of it. But I can't say that it was all bad.'

'You *won't* say.'

I glared at him. 'Why are you being so bloody hard-case?'

'*Me*?' he asked, smiling in disbelief.

'Yes you. All that I'm trying to say here is that I can't, won't look at everything in my past and call it "bad". There must have been a reason for it.'

'And what would that be?'

'Well, it all led me here, didn't it? To you?'

He sighed. 'So let me get this right. You want us to look back at your life, men sticking their fingers and dicks into you, your mother treating you like a thing, and you living without a scrap of control in your life; and you want us to say there was a good *reason* for it?'

His words stung. I wanted to prove him wrong somehow but he hadn't said anything that wasn't the truth. I slumped back into the couch. 'So other than Ty,' I said quietly, 'my life has been a waste?'

'Isn't that what we're trying to change here?' he asked gently.

I shook my head slowly. 'But that's awful.'

'It is, and very sad. But we're working on turning all that around.'

'I've been putting a good spin on my life for years. Telling myself that one day I'd finally see why it all happened the way it did.'

He nodded. 'What other choice did you have? It's only as you learn that there can be another way of living, that you're able to view the past differently.'

I sat there quietly, looking at all the years and the effort. My spirits were sinking rapidly. 'I used to tell myself that there was a purpose to it all.'

Phil took a slow, deep breath. 'I think you can turn it around and *use* it somehow, but you've got to be a little wary here. Your mother has always justified what happened to you, or offered some pretty bizarre explanations for it.'

'That's what I'm doing too, isn't it?'

'You're re-visiting everything, that's bound to create a lot of confusion for a while. Don't be so hard on yourself.'

'It just makes me feel pretty stupid.'

'That's what I mean about being hard on yourself. I don't see it as stupid at all. You did what you could, given the limited tools you had.'

Another thought occurred to me. 'How come I think I'm either incredibly smart or completely stupid?'

'There's a lot of black and white in your thinking. Much like a child would view the world.'

I grimaced. 'That's wonderful to hear. It just keeps getting better, doesn't it?'

Phil laughed. 'Hey, we're working on it. It won't be like this forever.'

I could only hope that he knew what he was talking about.

After Ty and I had eaten that night I decided to skip television and treat myself to some music. I flicked through the ancient records and found one of my favourite albums from the seventies. After dimming the lights and throwing a few cushions on the floor, I lay back and let the sounds transport me.

'Hey Mum.'

I sat up suddenly, surprised to see Ty sitting on the couch. 'I thought you were going out.'

He shook his head. 'Change of plans.'

'You want to watch television?'

'Nope. Leave the music on. Who is it?'

'Neil Young, his Harvest album. Bit before your time.'

Ty smiled. 'Not bad.'

'Takes me *way* back.'

'Did you and Dad listen to this stuff together?'

I shook my head. 'No, this was a couple of years before we met. I was living the high life in Sydney.'

'Dad wasn't really into all that hippie stuff, was he?'

'Not at all. He was working his way up the corporate ladder.'

Ty lay back on the couch, making himself more comfortable. 'What were you doing?'

I grimaced. 'Gee, everything I guess. I was pretty much stoned all the time; thought I'd found the answer to the universe. I went on most of the marches, especially the ones for women's rights. They were neat.' God, it all felt so long ago.

'Why'd you stop smoking dope?'

'A friend offered me some LSD. She told me it was the quickest route to God.' I laughed, amazed at my own naivete.

Ty smiled. 'I take it you didn't find Him?'

'Nope. Think I visited his mate instead. I had nearly twenty-four hours of terror, seeing monsters and fire wherever I looked. After that, I couldn't even get stoned again. I was too scared.'

'Maybe just as well then.'

I looked up at him and smiled. He was so perceptive. 'What about you?' I asked.

He rolled his eyes, 'Yeah right Mum, like I'm about to tell all.'

'I'm not asking for everything, but I know you've tried dope.'

He shrugged. 'It's okay, I guess, but I get bored with everyone just sitting around. I prefer to go out and have a few beers.'

I got up to turn the record over. This was so neat, a night with my son; I didn't want it to end. 'Has Dad told you much about when we met?' I asked him.

'A little. He says you were barefoot most of the time.'

I settled back onto my cushions. 'That was when I was between jobs.'

'What brought you together then, it doesn't look like you had much in common?'

'I think we were total opposites actually. That's what the main attraction was. He had a five-year diary, would you believe?'

Ty laughed. 'I can somehow picture that.'

I wondered if he knew how much he resembled his father. They looked almost identical, same fairness and slim build. And they were both very practical and goal-orientated. 'I thought he was the most amazing person I'd ever met. I fell madly in love with him.'

'And he was married at the time?'

I grimaced. 'Afraid so.'

Ty went quiet for a while and I wondered what he was thinking. I had been the same age as he was now, when I first met his father. Seventeen; it looked so young.

'Dad said he'd never met anyone like you before.'

I smiled. 'That sounds about right. I was all over the place, happy to have two dollars in my purse, enough for a train fare and a packet of smokes. It all seemed so much easier back then.'

'In what way?'

I sighed. 'I guess it was more about enjoying the here and now. There was great music, concerts to attend, sitting with friends and dreaming of how we'd change the world. It looked for a while like everything was going to be different. Free love and all that.'

'I think the seventies would have been a lot more fun than the nineties were.'

'I think you're right. You lot seem to have so much on your plate these days. It's far more serious.'

Ty nodded. 'All about careers and not becoming one of the unemployed.'

'Can't say your music does much for me either.'

He laughed. 'Some of it's all right.'

I was so enjoying having my son sit with me. He'd been so busy lately, caught up in his final year of high school. When he wasn't studying he was out with friends, surfing or going to parties. It had felt like a while since we'd had much time to talk. Was he okay? Were there things going on his world that were worrying him? Did he feel he could still come to me?

'Hey Ty, I'm not getting all deep and meaningful on you, but there's something I'd like to say to you.'

Ty wasn't convinced. 'Here we go.'

I smiled; he always squirmed whenever he felt I was about to go mushy on him. 'I just want to say that I know it hasn't been a breeze having me as a mother and . . .'

'You've been great, Mum,' he interrupted, wanting to reassure me.

'I could have raised the bar a little,' I said, feeling a lump in my throat. 'I was so obsessed with keeping you safe.'

Ty shook his head. 'You did a good job, Mum. I've got lots of neat memories of my childhood.'

'Really?' I asked, trying to hold the tears back.

'Yep. I remember being little and sitting on the lounge-room floor playing with my toys while you were close by. And playing rugby with you in the park. You've always been there for me.'

God, I loved him. 'You've been a piece of cake to raise, you know.'

'You've been a piece of cake to have as a mother.'

I laughed. 'I don't think that's quite true, kiddo.' The record had stopped and I looked up at Ty.

'Put on that other one of yours,' he suggested, 'the Cat Stevens record. I like that one.'

We spent the next two hours talking about the past and discussing Ty's plans for the future. It was a magical evening.

As usual I was at my appointment fifteen minutes ahead of time. I flicked through the magazines but could find nothing to hold my interest. I walked around the waiting room, visited the toilet, and brushed my hair to kill time. I went back to my seat. He should have come to get me five minutes ago. I knew my watch was right; I was obsessive about being on time for everything. What was keeping him? There was a clock in his office. Couldn't he see that he was running late? Five more minutes passed. I could feel my anger increasing. What was he doing? We only had forty-five minutes together and he was chewing into them as if it didn't matter. I bet he was sitting in there laughing his head off with somebody and thinking, fuck Debra, she can wait. I was in a rage. He was fifteen minutes late! I wanted to charge into his office and tell them both to fuck off! In fact, I wanted to leave and let the prick come out to get me and discover that I'd disappeared. That would show him.

'Debra? Come in.'

I followed behind him seething with anger. He sat in his chair and bid me to take my place on the couch. I couldn't even look at him. I stared out of the window trying to calm myself down. Bloody bastard, there was only half an hour left of our session. Well, fuck him, I didn't care. As usual he was saying nothing, waiting for me to take the lead. But the thought of giving in made me even angrier, that would be like saying, sure, go ahead, you be late whenever you feel like it.

The clock ticked on. It was ridiculous! Why bother being here?

'I had an idea, while I was sitting in the waiting room,' I started curtly. 'If this is going to happen regularly, you know, you being fifteen minutes late, why don't we simply change my appointment time? Then I wouldn't have to wait at all, would I?'

Phil smiled. 'I guess it happens once in a while.'

Well fuck you too.

'You don't like to be kept waiting?'

I looked at him like he was a two-year-old. 'No,' I said, deliberately slowly, 'I don't like to wait. Is that novel, or something?'

He laughed. 'Not at all.'

'I felt like putting a brick through your window.'

'Really?' he answered, arching his eyebrows. 'That's a little dramatic, isn't it?'

'Well we have such a bloody short time as it is.'

'Do you usually fly off the handle when somebody is late?'

I nodded. 'It makes me furious, like they're telling me that I don't matter.'

'That certainly wasn't the case here. If one patient runs late it affects the entire schedule. Maybe you take it a little too personally?'

Brick throwing *was* a trifle over-reactive. 'But what about my session? I lose almost half of it?'

'Not at all. You'll still get your full time.'

'Oh,' I said, suddenly feeling ridiculous, 'I didn't realise it worked like that.'

He smiled. 'That's okay, you weren't to know. But maybe it would be a good idea to make room for some things like this. Life has a way of tossing the unexpected at you.'

'I hate that. It always throws me.'

'I know, but change is everywhere. There's no way you're going to be able to control that. It would be far easier to make allowances for it, don't you think?'

I nodded sheepishly. 'I'll work on that.'

It'll only take another century. Just add it to the pile.

'My mother is late for everything, always has been. She says she needs to be free to change her mind.' I sighed. I must have had a dozen discussions with her about her lateness, but as usual I had to give in. Mum just couldn't understand my annoyance.

He nodded. 'I imagine you have strong abandonment issues. Speaking of which, we won't have a session for a couple of weeks. I'm moving premises and I'll need time to get the new place fixed up.'

'Moving?' I asked, feeling that familiar worm of fear. 'Where to?'

'I'm setting up my own practice. I'll give you the new address when you leave, but it's only about twenty minutes south of here.'

That wasn't too bad, I could deal with that. But two weeks? 'Why do you need so long?' I asked him.

He laughed, 'I thought two weeks was pretty good, given the amount of work I have to do.'

I nodded, trying to be gracious. 'I guess that I already have such a hard time with just a week between visits. It makes me a little nervous, that's all.'

'Okay, well maybe we need to look at increasing your sessions?'

I looked up at him, stunned. 'Can we do that?'

'Of course we can. What would you like?'

I was still in total surprise; for some reason I had believed that I was only allowed to see him once a week. 'So I can see you twice if I want to?'

He smiled. 'You can see me every day if you like.'

'Is that right?' I asked in disbelief.

'Why so surprised?'

'I don't know. I didn't realise there was a choice.' I scanned my week and tried to work out a new schedule. 'Could I see you Tuesdays and Thursdays?' I asked.

'Yep, just give me some time to work it out. We'll slot you in for Tuesday, two weeks time, and get a more regular schedule after that.'

I was delighted. Twice a week? Neat!

Unfortunately my delight was short-lived. Within twenty-four hours I started to panic. What if he didn't come back in two weeks? He could change his mind and decide to throw in psychiatry altogether. Ty was going to be in New Zealand visiting his father for the next three weeks. That meant I would be alone in the house with no routine and no Phil. I knew I would be in trouble.

I saw Ty off at the airport and headed home. I drew the blinds, locked all the doors, took the phone off the hook and climbed into bed. Fourteen empty days loomed large before me. How would I get through it? Didn't he realise how important he'd become to me? Doubts and insecurities plagued me. After hours of turmoil I struck upon a brilliant solution. I decided that *I'd* go away too.

I leapt out of bed, went to the phone and booked a return seat to Melbourne. I would take the train. I had always loved trains. There was one due to leave at eight o'clock that evening. After packing a small bag and ringing Mum to let her know, I sat down to work out what sort of holiday I wanted. There were people I knew in Melbourne, but I didn't feel like company. Maybe I could find a cheap hotel room right in the middle of the city? That could be fun. I could even stay longer than two weeks and skip my next appointment with Phil. That would show him how independent I had become. It seemed like the perfect solution and I was thrilled with myself for being so imaginative.

A few hours later I was sitting in the railway station, rippling with excitement. This was more like it! Free again. How I loved this feeling, transient and detached, not needing to be anywhere or see anyone. Soon I would be walking in a new city again, a stranger to everyone. My spirits were lifting by the moment. I was *born* to live like this. I imagined Phil sitting with me, watching everything through my eyes. I silently talked to him, telling him about the adventures we would have and the new things we would see.

Melbourne was magical. I visited the casino, wandered through the markets and drank cappuccinos by the river. I caught trains to distant suburbs, relishing the unknown and the freedom to be wherever my impulses took me. Despite the smallness and rather dingy atmosphere of my hotel room, I enjoyed lying on the single bed and flicking through the daily newspapers. Where would I go today? What new thing could I try? I was spaced out into the heavens, but that was fine too. Maybe that was where I belonged?

My money was tight. I could only afford to eat once a day, so I would find a pie-cart or hot-dog stand and savour each little bite. I visited the museum and the art gallery and walked for miles around the city, all the time feeling Phil close by. Days passed quickly but I had lost track of where I was in the week. At least twice a day I would need to check the newspaper to find out if it was Monday or Friday. I had a card in my bag with Phil's appointment time written on the back. But he had gone somewhere, disappeared. I turned his card over, reading his name on the front, and his new address and phone number.

Will he be there?

Wouldn't it be nice to call him and let him know that I was in a new city and having a wonderful time? I doubted that he was there, though. I couldn't find a picture to place him in. He had gone. I put the card back in my bag and headed out for another mystery tour of Melbourne.

I ran out of money and was starving hungry. Maybe I should head back to Adelaide? I checked the newspaper in the hotel foyer. It was Sunday. I had been away for nearly a fortnight. I could have sworn I had only been here for about five days. Where had the other ones gone? I went back to my hotel room and lay on the bed, determined to track each day. I managed to find most of them, lost in the blur of spaciness and mania. Feeling somewhat relieved I decided it was time to go home.

I entered my quiet, empty house and called Mum. She invited me to stay with her till my next appointment with Phil. I didn't hesitate in accepting.

Chapter Nine

My first appointment at the new premises was booked in for 5 pm. For some reason I felt a great deal of trepidation about our session but was unable to track down the source. I sat in the waiting room with a growing sense of unease. Other than Phil, I was the only person in the house, and shortly it would be dark.

'I've never had a late session before.'

He shrugged. 'Not much different, is it?'

'Oh, I don't know. It'll be dark soon.' I didn't know where I was going with that but I knew I had to say something.

'Afraid of the dark?' he joked.

I shook my head. 'There are so many empty rooms in this house. Doesn't that seem odd for you?'

'No, not really, but it's obviously doing something to you. What's your concern?'

A vision flicked across my mind. I pictured double beds. Maybe he took his other patients there. And there was nobody else around to see.

'Care to share?' he prompted.

I wasn't sure what to say. But my nervousness was increasing by the minute. 'It's the other rooms.'

'What about them?'

'Are they empty?'

He looked slightly puzzled. 'Well, some of them have a few bits of furniture, but I'm renovating the house, so most of them are pretty stark. Why? I'm not sure where you're going with this?'

The light outside was fading fast.

'What do you think I have in the other rooms?'

'I know this sounds ridiculous, but a picture keeps flashing in front of me. And I wonder if, you know, you've got ... beds in there?'

'Beds?' he asked, surprised. 'What would I have beds for?'

I took a deep breath. 'I don't know, maybe, I'm not sure. I was thinking ...' I couldn't finish. I felt way too uncomfortable.

'I assure you,' he said firmly, 'that there is not one bed in the entire house.'

I nodded, eager to let the subject drop. 'Okay, that's fine, I know I'm just being stupid. I'll let it go.'

'No,' he said slowly, rising from his chair. 'I've got a feeling you won't. Come with me.'

I was surprised. Phil was heading out of the office and into the corridor. 'Come on,' he urged, 'follow me.'

One by one he took me through every room, opening the doors, even the cupboards and letting me look inside. I felt ridiculous, like a little girl whose daddy was showing her that there were no monsters under the bed. It was also somehow beautifully reassuring. By the time I got back to his office I was beaming from ear to ear.

'Feel better?' he asked, smiling broadly.

'That was so neat of you.'

'My pleasure. But obviously we still have some work to do on the trust issue.'

I grimaced. 'I'm sorry. Just when I think I've settled, something else seems to crop up.'

'That's to be expected. Are you sure it's a fear though, and not a fantasy?'

'What do you mean?' I asked, feeling a blush creep up my neck.

'You know what I mean. Maybe you like the idea of a double bed in the house?'

I cringed with embarrassment. How could he say that?

'Not at all,' I managed, trying to muster up some dignity. 'It wasn't with *me* anyway. I imagined you using the rooms with your other patients.'

'Really? And why ever would I do that?'

I shrugged. 'Well obviously you have dozens of weird women who want to throw themselves at you. It would seem perfectly natural for you to make use of that.'

His eyebrows couldn't have arched much higher. 'Is that right? So not only would I be prepared to risk my career, but I'd also feel fine about abusing the trust of my patients?'

It sounded awful when he put it like that. I tried to sink lower into the couch.

'How do you think I might feel about myself if I resorted to that?' he continued.

I was shaking my head. 'I ... don't know.'

'I'd be disgusted with myself.'

I felt dreadful. 'I'm sorry. Really sorry.'

'Believe me there are a lot of psychiatrists out there who are prepared to abuse the situation. Some of them have no problem with the idea of forming outside relationships with their patients. But I've always found that idea a little too risky. Wouldn't you agree?'

I could only nod. I was dying with mortification.

'Hey, I'm not berating you here,' he offered, in a gentler tone, 'I just want you to know where I stand with this. I think it's important for our relationship.'

More nods. How ever could I get myself out of this mess? 'I'm sorry,' I repeated. I couldn't think of what else to say.

'Don't apologise, you've done nothing wrong. I'm glad in a way that this came up. Lets us clarify things.'

I just wanted to get out of there before I let something else out of the bag. But only twenty minutes had passed. It felt like hours.

'What are your plans for the weekend?' he asked, blessedly changing the subject.

'I pick Ty up from the airport on Saturday. And then I'm going to watch the football on television.'

'Is that right? I didn't realise you were a footy fan. What's your team?'

'The Crows, of course,' I answered, lightening up. 'Is there any other?'

He smiled, 'I'm a Port man, myself.'

Wow. I'd had no idea that he followed the football. It was my only real interest. 'You support Port? They're doing well this season.'

'So far, so good. I don't like to get my hopes up too early.'

'I'm not altogether clear on all the rules yet. In fact, some of it quite mystifies me.'

'Well, let's change that, huh? Fire away and I'll answer as many of your questions as I can.'

I was utterly delighted. It was such a nice change to be talking about something fun. For the rest of our session Phil explained some of the more intricate moves in Aussie Rules, even drawing pictures to clarify a few of the players' positions. He was quite the expert and obviously loved the game. I left the session feeling a million times better. It took a couple of hours to dawn on me that I had forgotten to tell Phil about Melbourne. Ah well, maybe he didn't need to know.

The following Saturday I was curled up in my chair watching the afternoon game. It felt like Phil was right there with me. I soon had a dozen questions that I wanted to ask him. Like had he ever been to a game? What was it like? Had his team ever won the grand final? I could feel the little one inside, imagining what it would be like to be his daughter. 'I bet he takes them to the football,' she daydreamed, 'and lets the youngest sit on his shoulders.' I ached inside. It seemed the saddest thing in the world.

I leapt straight in at our next session. 'Do you ever go and watch a match live?'

He nodded, 'I'm a member.'

'Really?'

'Haven't you ever been to a game?'

I shook my head. 'Nope.'

'Did you ever go when you were little?'

Once again I shook my head. I could feel the sadness inside again.

'That's a real shame, isn't it?'

I nodded, thinking again about his children. 'I think my dad liked soccer, but I don't remember going to a game with him. It would have been neat, I guess.' I sighed deeply. 'Ah well, there you go. It's not as if I can change anything.'

'I'm not so sure about that. Maybe I can do something here?'

I looked up at him in surprise. 'Like what?'

'Leave it with me.'

I felt a flicker of excitement, but couldn't imagine what he could do. 'I need to confess something,' I suddenly blurted, recalling my trip to Melbourne.

'Shoot.'

I took a deep breath. 'I sort of went walkabout when you disappeared for that two weeks.'

'Where to?'

'Melbourne.'

'Really? How did that come about?'

I grimaced. 'I think it was my reaction to you going away. I decided that I'd go away too.'

He smiled softly. 'A bit of a pattern is it?'

'It's like I get angry or something, I don't know, it's my way of saying, hey, I don't need you either.'

'I understand. But I didn't disappear, you know. I was still here.'

'One day maybe I'll believe that. I guess I imagine the same thing will happen with you that happened with Dad. One day you'll be there and the next day, ping, you'll be gone.'

'I'm not going anywhere, I assure you.'

'But what if you get sick of being a psychiatrist? You might wake up one day and decide you've had enough.'

'I don't see that happening for a few years yet. I like my work, remember?'

'I wish I could make that feel real.'

'It's about trust. When you were younger you were constantly hit with sudden changes, your mother changed her mind from one day to the next. It's not surprising that you think I'm going to do the same thing to you. Were you okay, in Melbourne?' he asked, changing the subject.

I smiled, 'Yes, a bit spacey, and pretty high. Blew a bit more money at the casino than I had planned, but luckily I kept away from people, so I didn't get into too much trouble. And I took you everywhere with me, that helped a lot.'

'Did we have a good time?' he asked, his eyes smiling warmly.

'We sure did. But next time I think we'll need a bit more cash.'

He laughed. 'Sounds good to me.'

I felt better after telling him.

On the drive home I thought about Melbourne again. I had

been doing that for years; taking off suddenly if someone close to me had plans to go away. Sometimes it was only for a weekend. No wonder my work history had been so erratic. I just couldn't settle into anything. But Phil's reaction had surprised me. He didn't tell me that I shouldn't have taken off, or comment about my gambling, not even to suggest that I quit, or at least try. Why was that? Maybe he was hoping that I'd figure it out myself. It was a totally new experience for me; having someone in my life who wasn't convinced he knew what was 'better' for me. But could that be because he didn't really care?

The next couple of days were strangely calm. I didn't make any contact with Mum, stayed away from the pokies and kept busy at home. It was a nice feeling to know that I had an appointment booked with Phil. The world felt as though it had finally gained a bit of structure.

Chapter Ten

'This is getting to be a habit,' I joked, settling down onto the couch.

'A good one, I hope?'

I smiled. 'Most of the time, if I can stop my head from thoughts of doom and gloom. Hey, guess what?'

'What?'

'I just had two lovely, calm days with no mood swings, no spaciness and barely a trace of confusion.'

'That is promising. What do you put that down to?'

I shook my head. 'No idea. I'm just letting myself enjoy it. And I'm making a real effort to stop blowing money; I can't stand the tension of always being broke.'

Phil just nodded, seeming a little distracted.

'Why do I blow money?' I finally asked him. 'What's that all about?'

'What do you think?'

'I'm not sure. I do it if I'm in a great mood or a rotten one. My adrenaline level picks right up and I don't stop until every cent is gone. I always feel dreadful afterwards, and make all sorts of promises that it will be the last time. But it doesn't work.'

Phil just looked back at me.

'Aren't you going to say anything?'

He shrugged. 'Like what?'

'Well, you must have a view on it?'

'Not really.'

I was getting exasperated. 'You don't have a view on it? Not one, single opinion?'

'Why would my opinion matter?'

I sighed, 'I'm supposed to figure this out for myself, is that right?'

He merely smiled again.

'Well, that should be really productive.'

'I think the good thing here is that you're experiencing some periods of stability.'

'I guess so,' I agreed reluctantly.

To my surprise, Phil suddenly got up from his chair and walked over to the desk. 'I've got something for you,' he said slowly, reaching into his briefcase and taking out a small card.

'What is it?' I asked, wondering for an awful moment if one of my cheques had bounced.

He returned to his seat, handing it over to me. 'It's my membership card to Football Park. I'd like you to use it, go see your beloved Crows team.'

I didn't know what to say; I was too stunned. I turned the card over in my hands, seeing his name written upon it. He had given it to *me*. I felt a lump in my throat. I looked up at him, not trusting myself to speak.

'I think you deserve to see a football game, if only once, don't you?'

I could feel my eyes starting to water and looked down quickly at my shoes, not knowing how to respond. I wrapped my fingers around the card, holding it like a precious jewel. 'I don't know what to say,' I finally managed.

'Just say yes.'

My throat was so constricted I was afraid I'd stop breathing. He was being so *nice*. It felt strange and unfamiliar to me. I took a deep breath and pulled myself together. 'Of course I'll go. I wouldn't miss it for the world. But I can't believe you're doing this for me.'

'Maybe some fantasies can come true, huh?'

I was still finding it hard to find words. 'So I'll be like a member?'

'Yep. And you get to sit in the member's stand. So you won't have to queue and you'll have the best view of everything.'

'Can I pick what match I want to go to?'

'Of course you can. In fact,' he continued with a flourish, 'I've brought the season's schedule along. So we can look through it together and pick the best match.'

I wanted to cry. I wanted to wrap my arms around him. Instead I stayed sitting on the couch, awash with emotions.

We chose a game that was three weeks away. It was expected to be an almighty clash. 'Now make sure,' he advised, 'that you take a cushion to sit on and a blanket or rug. It can get pretty cold there.'

I nodded, still not trusting myself to speak.

'Who are you going to take with you?'

'My son. He'll be happy to go, even though he doesn't follow football. We'll take his car too, so I won't have to drive or worry about traffic.'

'Good choice.'

I turned the card over in my hands again. It felt so special to have something that belonged to him, with his name on it. I was so overcome that I blanked out, and the little one butted in.

'You know what I wish,' she said, gazing up at him, her eyes full of hope. 'I wish you were going to take me.'

Phil smiled softly. 'I know you do, Deb. And you know what?' he said, pausing for a moment and leaning forward. 'In an ideal world I'd adopt you and take you home with me and we'd go to heaps of football games together.'

Oh God, that hurt! It was all too much for her. Why wasn't he her dad? Why couldn't he adopt her? Why did she have to be so alone? It just wasn't fair. A pain started in her heart and wouldn't let up.

'Well, I don't like the real world one bit then,' she pouted.

'I know, it can be pretty tough. But I don't hand that card out to just anybody, you know?'

She looked up at him, adoring him with every atom in her being. 'This is the best thing that anyone's ever given me. I won't lose it or anything, I promise.'

'I trust you.'

She wouldn't let the fantasy go. She wanted so much for him to take her to the game. She needed him to keep her safe from the crowd, to explain everything that was going on and to keep her all wrapped up and warm. Why couldn't she be his special little girl for just one match? Couldn't he make an exception this one time? It wouldn't hurt anybody, would it? She'd be so good and well behaved and promise not to ask him for another single thing.

It kept playing itself through my head till I thought I'd go crazy, but for once I didn't push the little one aside. Nor did I tell her that her wants and needs were selfish or stupid. I could feel her pain too strongly. I knew though, that it was never going to happen. Phil's rule was clear; there was no outside interaction. She was overwhelmed with the unfairness of it all and I knew it threatened to ruin the match altogether if I wasn't careful.

Days passed. Sometimes I let her cry it out. Phil continued to encourage me, knowing what I was going through. Finally, about a week before the match, the little one and I were able to make an agreement. We would go to the match and enjoy every minute of it. It was true, in an ideal world Phil would have been her daddy and they would have gone to the game together. But this was the real world. And what we did have was his membership card and his desire to make this little girl's dream come true. That was special. That was more than we'd ever had. We finally made peace.

The match was the most thrilling, exciting thing that I have ever attended. Despite his lack of interest in football, Ty let himself get swept up into the atmosphere. Forty thousand Crows supporters roared and waved their banners as our team trounced its way to victory. It was exhilarating!

I arrived home from the match and climbed into bed, exhausted but immensely satisfied. As usual, I imagined telling Phil every wonderful little detail. It was only after ten minutes or so into our conversation that I realised I wasn't addressing him in a chair three feet away from me. I was talking to the warmth inside. My God, I had internalised him!

I sat up in shock. Is this what he had meant when he told me I would need to bring him inside me? Had I finally managed it? I hugged the warmth within like a new found gift. Was this Phil? I felt like leaping out of bed and dancing around the bedroom.

Now fully awake I started to explore a little further. I wondered about this thing that I called the 'warmth'. What was that? Did everyone feel a warm inner glow when they were close to someone? Was it normal? And did it have a name? A tingle suddenly rippled through my body and I lay there hardly believing what had just flicked across my mind.

Surely not. I was still too scared to let the idea in. But it wouldn't go away.

This is love, a voice within explained to me. *This warm inner glow is what love feels like.*

I couldn't accept it. I *hated* that word, even more than 'trust'.

No matter how hard I tried to close the subject down, it wouldn't go away. The warmth was flooding through my entire being. So I was forced to ask myself what I felt for Phil. Had this warmth *come* from Phil? Is that what he had been giving me throughout all these tumultuous months? I was stunned by the very notion. I tossed and turned for hours. I would need to discuss this with Phil.

'I want to hear absolutely everything about the match,' he started enthusiastically.

I beamed, handing his card back to him. 'It was magnificent! Brilliant! And we won!' I enthused, and commenced to fill him in with all the wonderful details.

'I'm so glad that you let yourself have it; it looked touch-and-go there for a while.'

I nodded, 'Sure did. And look, thank you again for doing that for me, it meant so much.'

'I know it did. I think it's been a turning point for us in some way.'

'In more ways than I would have dreamt. I need to talk over something that happened last night.'

'Sure.'

'It's about this feeling I have inside, whenever I think of you. Up until now I've called it a "warmth", but I wondered last night if maybe it was more than that.' Oh God, I suddenly didn't know if I could even say the dreaded word. I started to feel uncomfortable and riddled with doubts. What if I was wrong? I'd look ridiculous.

'Go ahead,' Phil urged.

'I don't know,' I said, back-pedalling quickly, 'maybe it's not that important.'

'I think it must be, seeing you brought it up.'

I looked out of the window. I would simply die if I had got it all wrong. It had seemed so convincing last night. But maybe I was just bathing in the glow of the game. I could feel myself retreating by the minute. I wished that I was out there in the garden, under the tree or better still, home in bed tucked safely away.

'You know that you always feel better if you take the risk here,' Phil reminded me.

I looked at him and sighed. 'Easier said than bloody done.'

'Come on, out with it.'

I took a deep breath and launched in. 'It's about that word I hate.'

'Hang on,' he said, 'let me check that long list of yours.'

I laughed. 'Shut up, I'm serious. It's the first one on the list.'

'Which one would that be?'

Oh sod him; the bugger was going to make me say it. I grimaced. 'Okay then: love.'

Once again, he laughed. 'You look like you're spitting something very distasteful out of your mouth.'

'I am.'

'So, what about it?'

'Well, I wanted to know, if, you know, if that's what ...' Oh shit, I couldn't say it; I wanted to throw up.

Phil said nothing and waited for me to continue. *Why* was this so bloody hard? Once again, I took a deep breath. 'Is that what you've been giving me?'

Phil just nodded slowly.

I felt a lump in my throat. 'Okay.' I continued, determined to work this out. 'Is it meant to happen that the love from you ... goes inside me?'

'That's right,' he said softly.

Gosh. 'So what I've been feeling inside, has come from you?'

He nodded, smiling.

'That's incredible!' Then something even more astounding occurred to me. 'Tell me,' I asked, almost too scared to hear the answer, 'can you feel what I feel for you?'

'Yes, I can,' he answered simply.

I sat there in total awe.

Moments went by as I tried to absorb these incredible new insights. He could feel how much I loved him? How fantastic was that? I didn't have to do anything or say anything to prove it; he could already *feel* it. 'I didn't realise that the feelings went through,' I explained, hoping that he understood.

'They do, that's a good way of seeing it.'

I was shaking my head, still stunned. Then another idea leapt into my head. 'My mother couldn't have loved me?' I asked, suddenly understanding. 'It didn't come through to me, that's why I never felt it?'

'That's right. Of course, in her own way she loved you.'

I cut him off, needing to stay on track. 'But she didn't ever feel anything *from* me either,' I told him, 'and I loved her so bad it almost hurt!' From out of nowhere I burst into tears. I thought of all the years that I had tried to show my mother how much I loved her. But she had never believed me. There was always some condition I had to meet, like if you loved me you would know what I wanted, or if you loved me you wouldn't act like that. I ran myself ragged trying to find the *right* formula. But I had loved her from the word go. And for some sad reason she had never been able to feel it. Phil sat quietly while I let the truth dawn upon me. I had loved my mother the same way that I loved Phil now. It had been a wonderful, warm and unconditional love. There hadn't been something wrong with it, as she had taught me to believe.

I looked up at Phil, feeling overwhelmed by the sadness of it all. 'I *loved* her,' I told him again.

'I know you did,' he said gently.

The tears still fell freely, 'She never, ever knew it, or even felt it.'

He shook his head.

'It wasn't about me not getting it right?'

'No. I doubt you would ever have succeeded in convincing her.'

I was lost for words. It was just all too, too sad.

Chapter Eleven

Despite, or maybe because of the inroads we were making in therapy, the sexual dilemma was still ever present in one form or another. Either I was a little girl who wanted to make Phil 'happy' by attending to his needs or a rampant teenager whose only desire was to fuck him and ditch him. The latter was the more challenging opponent. As soon as I got close to Phil she would appear and throw a spanner in the works. I felt completely disconnected from her, as though she was some ghastly being who inhabited my mind but certainly wasn't 'me'.

And there lay the problem; my constant denial of her almost guaranteed her emergence.

Like the day she spotted a job in the paper for escorts. The advertisement was at once appealing and terribly exciting. She rang the number and made an appointment for later that day. As brothels go, I'm sure it was a lovely place. There were soft apricot drapes and matching bedcovers, beautiful chandeliers, thick plush cream carpet and really friendly staff. She was quite entranced.

I belong here! This is what I should have done years ago. No wonder I've been so lost.

The woman who ran the brothel was somewhat unsure. I doubt she'd come across such unbridled enthusiasm before. She asked the eager teenager if she had ever done this type of work before, and if she knew what it entailed.

'Absolutely!' she answered, delighted. 'I think I'll love it!'

'Good, good. We like to keep our girls happy here, but there are some rules. No drugs or drinking while you work and I don't look kindly on a "no show". If there's a reason you can't work one night, then I expect a call.'

'Certainly, but I doubt if that will happen, I'm *very* reliable.'

'That's good to hear. So, how many nights are you available for?'

'Gosh, are you open every night?'

'Yes, although some evenings are quieter than others.'

'Well, I'll fit in with whatever you need. I'm very flexible.'

'Good, good. And you say ... you've never done this sort of work before?' the owner asked again, still looking a little perplexed.

'No, but I know I'll be good at it. I know how to keep a man happy,' she smiled broadly, eager to please.

'Well, you will need to be firm, too, at times. We can get some customers who try their luck, you understand?'

'Absolutely. Don't they *all*?'

'Yes, yes ... of course. Well, when would you like to start? We'll have a trial night, see how you go, okay?'

'Excellent!'

Well, she danced all the way home. At last she'd found something that made sense, something that felt almost like her second nature. She imagined servicing the men, feeling born to it. And getting paid for it! She was incredibly excited. The only glitch was Ty. There was no way in the world that he could ever know about it. She'd have to let Miss Mouse deal with that.

She rang Mum as soon as she got home to tell her all about it. Mum was pleased for her and equally fascinated. She promised to call her as soon as she'd finished her first night and fill her in on all the details.

She told Phil with equal delight.

'A brothel? Is that right?' he asked, eyebrows arched.

'Why not?' she responded, flicking her hair back and crossing her legs. 'It's good money, great hours and I can still come to your sessions.'

Phil was nodding slowly. 'You feel this would be a good experience for you?'

'Absolutely. It's about time I explored this sort of work. In a way I've trained for it all my life.'

'Yes, but I thought we were looking for something healthier. You'd been talking about going back to university. What happened to that idea?'

'Ugh! Like how *boring* would that be? This job has got a lot more going for it. Although I will have to go shopping, I haven't got a single piece of lingerie at home.'

'I imagine not,' Phil answered dryly.

'I'll just give it a try, see how it works out. I truly couldn't spend one more day of my life sitting in an office job. That's not who I am, its no wonder that they always fall through. But this, gosh, I'm *so* excited about it!'

To his credit Phil just heard her out. She left the session still delighted with her new found career, and fantasising about the night that Phil might turn up as a willing customer.

Well, thank God for mood swings. I awoke the next morning feeling horrified. A brothel? Me? You had to be kidding? And she'd told *Phil*? Oh God, how was I going to explain that? Just the thought of those revolting, pathetic, and probably drunk men pawing away at me, made me want to throw up. I rang the owner and explained very nicely that I had made a mistake; I wouldn't be starting on Saturday after all. She didn't sound in the least bit surprised.

Jesus, I need to get a handle on this.

I sank into despair. Why couldn't I live a normal life? Why couldn't I make my mind up about something and actually stick to it? Who the hell was I?

Getting dressed in the morning became a fiasco. Sometimes she'd open our wardrobe and wonder who on earth had bought all those dreary, conservative clothes? She would grab a garbage bag and pile them into it, then off she'd trot to the op shop for some *real* clothes; something that was more like *her*. It would have to be red, of course, and outrageous! And fun! She'd have a ball shopping and head home loaded with treats.

Sure enough, two days later I'd be gazing at the garish red nightmares in my cupboard thinking, 'Yeah right, like I'd wear *that*.'

I kept swinging out of control. Lost. Desperately searching for something solid to clutch onto. But there was nothing inside me that stayed constant. I'd climb into bed, pull the covers over my head and beg, 'Please someone; get me off this planet. I can't do it anymore.'

Phil was wonderful. No matter who came trouncing into his office, he was more than up to it. Though I think we were both ill-prepared for the one who turned up one session while Phil was discussing the way I dressed.

'I notice you always wear trousers,' he observed. 'Is there a reason for that?'

I shrugged, feeling uncomfortable. I didn't want to talk about clothes. I could feel one of the parts inside me growing stronger by the moment. But this time Phil persisted.

'In fact, I don't think I've ever seen you wear a skirt or dress. Why is that?'

'Well,' I started, feeling a strange change within me, as though there was suddenly a strong, male presence on my left side, 'why would I ever wear a dress?'

Phil frowned. 'Why wouldn't you? Most women wear them at some time or another.'

'They're bloody uncomfortable. You should try wearing one,' he suggested.

'But you've worn trousers ever since you've been coming here,' Phil persisted. 'Do you know why that is?'

The young man scowled in annoyance. 'I'll tell you what; I'll wear a dress if you will.'

'It's generally women who wear dresses, I believe.'

'I'm sure most *women* do,' he answered firmly.

'Aren't you a woman?'

He looked Phil straight in the eye, 'Oh please, don't insult me. I think I'm a little better than *that*.'

And you know what else I think? I think you should fuck these females; I'll make it easier for you, if you'd just ask. I can get them to do anything.

'So how do you see yourself?'

'Well,' he told Phil, pleased to finally have a say, 'I have a sword. A very big sword. But I put it down a few months ago. I got tired of fighting with you.'

'I see. I wasn't aware of the fact that we had been fighting.'

'Oh yes, I had my sword up for weeks. But I didn't want to hurt you.'

Phil smiled gently. 'You won't hurt me. I'm big enough to take care of myself.'

He nodded, envying him his big, solid body. 'I know, but I thought it would be safer to put the sword down.'

167

Phil was quiet for a few moments, then leant forward and said very gently, 'You know, you don't have a sword.'

The young fellow frowned. 'Yes I do. And it's really big too.'

Phil was shaking his head, but continued on in a gentle manner. 'You don't have a sword. Only men have swords.'

His frown deepened. 'So what do I have?'

Phil paused, searching for words. 'You have a sheath. Something that the sword goes into.'

He looked at him in disgust. 'Oh no I don't. That's what little girls have. That's useless!'

'It's not useless at all. You've just been raised to see it that way.'

This was totally unacceptable. 'But girls are pathetic. And weak. I'm not that. I'm really strong! And I do have a sword, only I've laid it down now.'

'You probably wanted very much to be strong when those men were abusing you. But girls can be strong too.'

'Ugh! I'm not one of them. Never.'

'After what's been done to you I'm not surprised that you wish you were anything but a girl. But girls can be powerful, and strong, and in control too.'

He wouldn't have a bar of it. He had a sword. He knew it.

'Women aren't powerful,' he told Phil firmly.

'I guess it could look that way, especially where sex is concerned. They lay on their backs, open their legs, and the man penetrates them. That would appear to be pretty submissive.'

It was an exciting picture, exactly where women belonged. 'I hate that part of a woman.'

'The vagina?'

'Even the name sucks.'

'Why do you hate it?'

'Because it's useless.'

Phil said nothing. The young male was suddenly hit with a

memory, in that tiny room in Ireland. His mother naked, washing herself, crouched over a bowl of soapy water. His face screwed up with disgust at the recollection.

'What are you thinking?' Phil asked.

'I can still smell it.'

'Tell me what you're remembering.'

'The awful smell,' he answered, feeling nauseated. 'Mum washing herself, it stinks, like a mixture of soap and sperm.' Something else then flashed across his eyes. 'That's why Jo and I have got these matching scars,' he continued, holding out his wrist so Phil could see it.

'How did that happen?'

The memory was vivid. 'The only sink we could use was down a flight of stairs, in a room next to our toilet. Mum or Roger would boil a saucepan of water and we'd carry it downstairs so that we could wash. There was no light, so at night times it got pretty scary. Jo fell first and was rushed to hospital. I think I fell down about two or three months later. I remember being at the bottom of the stairs in the pitch black, peeling off what I thought was tissue paper from my arm. But it was skin.'

Phil was frowning. 'But your mother washed upstairs, using a bowl. Why didn't you girls do the same thing?'

He had no idea. The thought had never even occurred to him. 'I don't know,' he answered, feeling mystified, 'Roger was quite obsessed with cleanliness. He used to make us hold out our hands after we had been to the toilet, so that he could smell them. You know, make sure we had washed.'

'What else went on in that room?'

He sighed. It was so humiliating to talk about. 'I used to lie in bed at night, with my sisters, and hear Mum saying all sorts of things to Roger.'

'Like what?'

He looked down at his feet. 'I don't like repeating them.'

'I know. But I'd like you to tell me, if you can.'

'She used to talk in a little girl's voice.' He stared out of the window, squirming with shame.

'What was she saying to Roger?'

'I don't think I can tell you.'

'Try,' he said softly.

He felt suddenly small and confused. He didn't like what he was feeling; he wanted to be tougher and at the same time he wished he could find somewhere to hide. 'It's not very nice,' he told Phil, hating himself for being so weak.

'I know. But you can tell me, you'll feel better when you do.'

He looked up, seeing the gentleness in Phil's eyes. How could he say the awful words? He looked down at his feet again. 'She used to say . . .'

'Yes?'

'She used to ask him . . . would he like her to . . .'

'You're doing very well, Deb.'

I'm not her. Can't you see that?

The young fellow shook his head, feeling awful, trying to let the words out. 'Would he like her,' he stammered, 'to . . . suck his cock.'

'And she said it in a little girl's voice?'

'Yep.'

'What else did you hear?'

'Lots of noises. And . . . groans from Roger.'

'How old were you?'

'About seven, I think.'

Phil just shook his head.

They sat in silence for a while, and the young fellow let the memories flood in. 'You know what though,' he added proudly, 'I've always liked this scar. It was like finally having some proof,

170

you know? Something on my body that people could see. It would let them know, somehow.'

'Let them know that everything wasn't all right?'

'Exactly.' He stroked the scar, comforted by its ugly reality.

'You should never have had to live like that.'

The young man could feel his eyes watering, and swiftly brushed them dry. 'We were so scared of him. He'd fly off the handle and belt us around the head. We didn't know how to calm him down.'

'That was never your job,' Phil said gently, shaking his head.

But the youngster sat back in the couch, unable to get a scene out of his mind. It was like it was only yesterday; Roger's face twisted and white with rage, his mouth spitting. Mum screaming, pinned to the floor with Roger's hands around her throat. And all he could do was stand there, shaking and utterly inadequate. He had even wet himself, like a stupid baby. He closed his young eyes, not wanting to relive the terror.

'Is it pretty vivid for you, right now?' Phil asked.

He nodded.

'You were very strong to have survived that, you know.'

He felt a lump in his throat again. 'I never knew what to *do*. I felt so useless. I wanted to help Mum, to stop him from hurting her. But I couldn't. I didn't know *how*.'

'You were seven,' Phil said, softly. 'There was nothing you could have done.'

But the young one shook his head, feeling his sense of failure like a giant weight upon his shoulders. 'I didn't know what to *do*.'

'There was nothing you could have done,' Phil repeated gently. 'You were a child in an impossible situation.'

He hung his head, unable any longer to stop the tears from flowing. 'But I wanted to help my mum.'

Chapter Twelve

'I know I'm not like Sybil,' I started, in our next session. 'I don't wake up and find myself in strange places or bump into strangers who know me. And I have an awareness all the time of those different parts, but it's like I'm in the background, watching. Unable to stop whatever is going on.'

'I think you were about that close,' he said, holding his hands two inches apart, 'to developing a multiple personality disorder. What you do have is a very fractured sense of self. We need to somehow glue all those bits together.'

I shuddered at the thought. 'But what on earth would that look like? We're nothing like each other. Is there one of us that is the *real* one?'

'I guess that's what you're exploring at the moment.'

'I'd just like to get rid of them, you know? Then everything would be fine.'

Phil didn't look convinced.

'Do you think that *I'm* the one causing all the problems?'

He said nothing.

'But that's not fair. It's me who keeps everything in some sort of order. Without me, there'd be chaos.'

I was waiting for Phil to agree, but he remained silent, frustrating the hell out of me.

'I don't want to be glued to the teenager. She wreaks havoc.

And the others, God, I don't think one of them is over seven years old.'

'What do you think that's all about?' he finally asked.

'Well ... obviously they've got problems, but what do they want me to do about it?'

'Maybe they're too young to be carrying such a load.'

'And I should be taking it off them, are you saying?'

Once again, he didn't reply.

Was that true? Were they there because I wouldn't look at anything? Was I treating those young ones the same way that my mother treated me? What an awful thought. But what about the teenager, who the hell was she? I was starting to get confused.

'What are you thinking?' Phil asked.

I shook my head. 'In some awful way, that teenager is a lot like my mother. Always flirting and highly sexual, she's got Mum's confidence too.'

'What were you like as a teenager?'

'Oh goodness, all over the place. I got work in a massage parlour in Kings Cross for about nine months when I was sixteen. I was constantly stoned. And relationships with men were frequent and brief.'

'Were you having mood swings during your teens?'

I grimaced with the memory. 'All the time. Awful depressions when I couldn't get out of bed for days. And constant job changes. One day I'd be aspiring to great heights in the clerical world and then just as quickly I'd resign and look for more "meaningful" employment as a masseuse.'

'What were your relationships like?'

'Weird. I usually chose men who were twenty, thirty years older than myself. It was always just about sex. Eventually I'd get bored and move on.'

'When did you meet your husband?'

'When I was seventeen. He was an accountant who wore suits and I was a hippie without a care in the world. I always think he saved me.'

'How so?'

'I hate to think how I would have ended up. Marrying him was like being lifted out of a sordid world and into something more stable, predictable. I think that's why I stayed with him for eleven years. He looked after everything, you know?'

It seemed a lifetime ago. Here I was, back in chaotic disorder. Maybe I should never have left?

'Why did you leave?'

I told Phil about the seven-day groups and their ultimate lack of success.

'So the therapists had sex with the group members?' he asked, obviously taken aback.

I nodded. 'I even slept with one of them. They said it was natural; healthy.'

'How did they reach that conclusion?'

'Well, Renee told us that sex between the therapist and group participants prevented any sense of hierarchy developing and also helped break down barriers.'

He shook his head. 'And you had sex while on these groups?'

Once again I nodded, feeling a little ashamed of myself. 'It seemed the done thing; I got tired of being treated like the "English Snob". They told me I was too inhibited, a result of my British inheritance. Within a year or so I was joining in on all the orgies.'

'Orgies?' he asked, his eyebrows arching.

'Yep. After two or three days into the group it was nothing to all end up having sex together in the main room.'

Phil sighed. 'And are they still operating?'

'No. A lot of them were charged and given jail sentences. Even

Renee spent eighteen months inside. The place eventually got closed down.'

'What were they charged with?'

I looked down at my feet. It all looked so sordid now. 'Sex with minors. And they'd become involved with illicit drugs. They were distributing them around the community,' I answered quietly.

'Sex with minors? How did that come about?'

'There were scores of families living in the community. The teenagers, and I think even those who were quite a bit younger, were encouraged to explore sex.'

Phil looked disgusted. 'It's pretty scary, isn't it, how anyone can hang up a shingle and set themselves up as a therapist?'

'I was desperate for answers. I thought they were wonderful at the time.'

'There's a lot of that out there,' he said sadly. 'Everyone seems to have a quick fix. But it's not that easy, is it?'

I shook my head. 'They seem so promising though. And convincing.'

'I agree. But they can do a lot of damage too. Personally I don't believe that any real change can be effected in the short term. But it's up to the individual, I guess. Ultimately they'll keep searching till they find something that works. Or they give up.'

'Are there a lot of damaged people out there?' I asked.

'More than you can imagine.'

I drove home thinking about what Phil had said. So many damaged people, so many supposed remedies. I wondered if there were women like me who had tried everything. Were they watching Oprah, like I had, and beating themselves up for not 'getting with the programme'? Had they bought every book on self-help and personal development, religiously practised the techniques, and still found themselves back where they started? It was such a sad thought. And cruel too, in a way. For those like me, who were fractured, spaced out and lost, they were simply an additional failure to add to an already long list.

I rang Jo in New Zealand. We talked to each other at least twice a week. Like me, she had explored every avenue for help. We had done the Course in Miracles together, both spiralling out so much that we had to keep taking breaks. She wasn't able to live in the same country as my mother. They hadn't talked for years. She was fascinated by my sessions with Phil and I made a point of keeping her up-to-date.

'How'd it go?' she asked.

'Neat. He's like no one I've ever met before. I so wish you'd find someone like him, Jo. It's just an awesome experience.'

She sighed. 'Maybe I will. Things here are getting out of hand again.'

'How so?' I asked, already knowing the answer. Unlike myself, Jo didn't space out, she went what we called 'loopy'. Her mind would just switch off and she'd speak in an airy-fairy sort of voice. Nothing touched her in that space. It was usually followed by a drastic decision. She would leave her husband, set herself up in a flat with her children, then ultimately 'come down' and wonder what on earth had gone on.

'I don't know,' she answered wistfully, 'I wonder if I should stay here? Warren and I are barely speaking to each other and I've moved into the spare room again. I can't stand him near me and everything about him is driving me crazy. Even the way he breathes!'

I laughed. I remembered feeling exactly the same way about my ex-husband. 'You thinking of leaving again?'

'I don't know. Maybe I should. Maybe I'm meant to leave him. How am I to know though? Sometimes I feel so sure that we're meant to stay together and everything goes well but that's only because I push everything down. It always comes up again. I don't know.'

My heart went out to her. She and I had gone through all the sexual abuse together. She had done her best to look after my little sister and I when we were small and Mum was out working. I wished so much that I could make everything right for her.

'How's your study going?'

'It's about the only thing that's keeping me glued together. I love it. Only six more months and I'll be a midwife. Isn't that an incredible thought? No more awful office jobs.'

'Don't you curse the day we learnt how to type?'

She laughed. 'And what about you, Deb. Have you got any plans yet?'

'God only knows. Seeing Phil is my main priority. As to the future, I haven't got a clue. I'm too scared to find another office job, after my last two debacles.'

'Give it some time. Things change.'

'Something will come up,' I told her, not feeling at all convinced. 'I so wish I could be at your graduation ceremony.' I paused, wondering how best to continue. 'You know Jo, I'm learning that a lot of our damage came from Mum, it wasn't only the men.'

'What does Phil say about her?'

'I don't think he's too impressed with me still being close to her.'

'I don't know how you do it, Deb. I only need to be in a room with her for five minutes and I freeze up.'

'I know I should get away from her, but it's like I'm obsessed with trying to understand. I still can't accept her total lack of response. I want to shake her or yell at her.'

'That will do nothing, Deb. Remember, she hasn't bothered with Mark or Cheryl for thirty years. I don't think she's going to change now. And look at my kids, she doesn't even know the date of their birthdays, or how old they are.'

I sighed. 'Can you imagine leaving your children, like Mum did?'

'Not ever. I think of that all the time when I look at Jamie. He's the same age now as Mark was, when Mum took off. They must have been shattered.'

'Well something must have been different for her. I just wish I knew what it was.'

'Have you told Phil about Roger yet?'

'Yep. Bloody hard, though. And the Frank Feeney thing came up too.'

'God he was a creep. Do you feel any better having told Phil?'

'Oh Jo, it was magic. After all the crazy responses I've got from Mum, and even some of the crap you read in books, it was like hearing something normal for the first time in my life.'

'What did he say?'

I filled her in on all the details, wishing again that she lived closer and could see Phil too.

'He sounds nice, Deb. Is he attractive?'

I laughed. 'Unfortunately, yes, in a cosy sort of way. He's the type you want to snuggle into.'

'He's married?'

'Yep, loads of children too.'

'I'd leave that well alone if I were you.'

'Don't worry Jo, he's drawn a line so thick you almost bump into it.'

We both laughed. 'One day we'll get to live in the same city. Maybe when you're finished with Mum?' she asked, hopefully.

'Maybe when I'm finished with Phil.'

I hung up the phone wishing with all my heart that I had my big sister with me. But I wondered how I would really feel if Jo was seeing Phil? She was far more attractive than me, and feminine too. Maybe Phil would fall for her in an instant. How awful would that be? How would I feel if Jo started relaying her sessions to me, telling me things that Phil had said, things that he might never have said to me? It was a gruesome thought. Then I wondered about my little sister, too. Would I want her to see Phil? Absolutely not. She was vivacious and sexy; men were drawn to her like flies. Phil could fall head over heels in an instant and he'd come to realise what a dreary thing I truly was. Suddenly I didn't want anyone to see Phil except me. Maybe for once I could have someone all for myself.

Chapter Thirteen

'I think I may be a lesbian.'

Phil nodded, waiting for me to expand.

'Well it would make sense of a lot of things,' I explained. 'Why I haven't had sex for nearly five years now. And I've been attracted to women before. Once I even had a short affair in New Zealand.' I slipped this last bit in quickly, imagining Phil wondering about the extent of my activities.

'When did this happen?' he asked, forever unruffled.

I cast my mind back. 'I was about twenty-two. My husband was out of town. I met her at work and within minutes I was actually flirting with her. She was lovely. We went out together one night, ended up back at my place and et cetera, et cetera.'

'Et cetera?' Phil asked, amused. 'Is that shorthand for something?'

'No,' I squirmed, 'I just hate going into details on that sort of stuff. It's all pretty obvious anyway.'

'By "that sort of stuff", I take it you mean sex?'

'Yes, I mean sex. Anyway, it only lasted about a week; I became confused. I couldn't figure out how it was all meant to work, you know, with a woman and that.'

Phil just continued to nod, listening intently and allowing me to explore the thoughts. I was wondering if I looked like a lesbian. Maybe Phil thought I did. Perhaps he had known all along and had been waiting for me to discover it for myself. He *had* brought up the fact that I always wore trousers. But as usual, he was giving nothing away.

'Anyway,' I continued, 'I've decided to explore it all, see what happens.'

'What will that involve?'

'I've found this organisation for women "coming out". They set you up with a lesbian friend. She is someone to talk to and maybe take you to visit lesbian hang-outs, you know, that sort of thing.'

'I see. Is that like a lonely hearts club for women?'

I shook my head, irritated. 'No. You don't form a relationship or anything; it's just about being hooked up with a friend, someone to introduce you into the lesbian world. I think it might be good for me.'

'So what brought this about?'

I thought for a few moments, trying to figure out how to explain it. 'I guess I'm wondering if maybe that's why I'm having so much trouble finding my identity. And why my relationships with men have always been so complicated. Maybe it's because all my life I should have been a lesbian.'

Phil said nothing. I sighed. 'I don't suppose you're going to be much help here, are you?'

'How would you like me to help?' he asked, smiling.

'Well, I don't know! You've been seeing me for quite a while now, do I come across, you know, like a lesbian?'

'I'm not quite sure what you mean by that?'

I scowled at him. 'Another extraordinarily complex question, is it?'

He laughed. 'Well you do have a habit of throwing things in front of me and then expecting me to dissect it all.' He was right, of course. I was hoping he'd have all the answers.

'Oh well, I'll just leap in and have a look. This friend hook-up appears relatively harmless.'

'I'll be interested to hear how it goes.'

We sat in silence for a few moments. I was slightly irritable and didn't know why. Obviously I had wanted to hear something different, I just wasn't able to figure out what.

'Do I drive you potty sometimes?' I finally asked.

He laughed again. 'Not at all. Why would you think that?'

I shrugged. 'I always seem to be changing my mind. Like I don't think it was that long ago I was exploring brothels.'

'It's good. It means you want to redefine yourself. I don't think there's any harm in that at all, as long as it's healthy.'

I narrowed my eyes. 'Are you saying that this lesbian business isn't healthy?'

'I don't think I said anything like that.'

'But you wouldn't be thrilled if I came in next week and told you that I'd converted?'

He was shaking his head. 'I feel like you're needing me to judge you in some way, and I'm not going to do that. What I think about this is irrelevant.'

'So you'd be happy for me?' I persisted.

He smiled. 'I'll be happy for you when my view, or anybody else's, plays little part in your decisions.'

'God you're a squirmy bugger, you've got a loop out of every-thing.'

He laughed. 'I think I'm being very consistent with you.'

'Oh you're definitely *that*,' I answered sarcastically.

'So when does this hook-up take place?'

'I'll call them when I get home, make an appointment. I'm actually quite looking forward to it.'

'Good for you!'

I looked in his eyes for any hint of sarcasm, but he seemed to be genuine.

I was given a link-up with a woman called Sally. She was in her forties and had only come out two years previously. We met for a coffee and hit it off immediately. I asked her a million questions and unlike Phil, she was more than happy to respond.

'So you didn't know that you were a lesbian till your late thirties?' I asked.

'Oh, I think I always had my suspicions. I had been attracted to a couple of women over the years, but just put it aside somewhere.'

'What was it like once you made your mind up?'

Her face lit up like a Christmas tree. 'Absolute heaven! It was like finally fitting into my skin. I only wish that I had taken the leap a lot earlier.'

I sighed. Sally looked so confident in herself and her body. She was a tall, strapping woman but had none of that awkwardness that many larger ladies often do. Her hair was cropped short around a face that was animated and vibrant. I swear her eyes sparkled with life.

'You don't miss men?' I asked, watching her response carefully.

She laughed. 'I still have men in my life, just not sexually. I'd spent twenty years in a marriage that was stale, flat and unprofitable. I don't hate men though. I just love women!'

Once again I sighed, envying her certainty.

'What about you?' she asked excitedly, 'I take it you've only just come out as a lesbian?'

'God no!' I assured her, quickly. 'I'm just looking, trying to work things out.'

'I see. And what's made you ask the question?'

I stirred my cup of tea slowly, unsure of how much to divulge. 'I did have a brief relationship with a woman years ago. I had really enjoyed it, but it raised too many questions. I guess I'm taking a look at it again.'

She nodded. 'It's certainly a difficult transition for a lot of women. I think it's great that you're taking it slowly.'

'Did much change for you?'

She rolled her eyes. 'Absolutely everything! Up until then I felt like I had been living someone else's life. I had hardly any confidence and kept searching for explanations, wondering what was so wrong with me.'

I was nodding my head. 'I sure know what that feels like.'

'Hey,' she said, smiling encouragingly, 'give it some time. As long as you're searching you will ultimately find the answer.'

'I know,' I sighed, 'sometimes it gets tough though. I'm so afraid of leaping in and discovering I've made yet another mistake.'

'So what if you do?' she asked, laughing. 'Leap in! Make a mistake! What's there to lose?'

I smiled, thinking I'd pay a million dollars for that enthusiasm towards life.

'I'm going to leap in,' I told Phil, with determination in my voice.

'I see. And what will that involve?'

'Sally is going to throw a party for me, she's inviting all her lesbian friends over. It should be fun.'

Phil was nodding slowly, but said nothing.

'I think I *am* a lesbian,' I continued strongly. 'The more I think about it the more sense it makes. I haven't wanted anything to do with men for years.'

'True,' he said slowly, 'you haven't. And you think that may be because you're a lesbian.'

'That's right,' I answered eagerly.

'So you're telling me that you don't need a man in your life?'

My alarm signals all went off at once. 'I don't think I said that,' I answered slowly.

'Well, I take it that being a lesbian means that all your future relationships would be with women. Isn't that saying you have no need for men?'

'I don't know,' I stammered, 'I don't see the connection.'

He was looking baffled. 'I'm not making a judgement here. But aren't lesbians by definition saying that they have chosen women as their partners? They don't feel any need or desire for a man in their life?'

I was starting to feel nervous. Was Phil saying that he wouldn't see me if I became a lesbian? Was he implying that I didn't need him anymore? 'I'm still not making that connection,' I repeated. 'This hasn't got anything to do with men, or you, it's just about women.'

He went quiet and my anxiety increased. This had nothing to do with Phil. Surely he didn't think that I was rejecting him. 'I'd still see you,' I insisted strongly. 'Just because I may have something to do with a woman doesn't mean that I don't need you in my life.'

He just nodded. I left the session in turmoil. What had I done wrong? I hadn't meant to imply that I no longer wanted to see Phil. Maybe he didn't like lesbians. A slow, gnawing sense of terror was growing inside me. Had I lost Phil? He had gone so quiet. Was he already drawing back from me, believing us to be finished? I wanted to rush back to his office and undo everything that I had told him. I couldn't bear the thought of having to wait four days till our next session. He'd gotten it all wrong! I drove home in a state of high anxiety, wondering if I should call him and leave a message, or make an early appointment. I started to cry and couldn't stop. I didn't want to lose Phil.

I did the only thing that I knew how; I spaced out into the ether. If I had lost Phil, then so be it. I had a party to go to in two day's time. I was going to enjoy it no matter what.

Feeling inspired with this new quest for identity I went to the hairdressers and had my hair chopped off and cut into a short-back-and-sides. I loved it! I would catch sight of myself in a shop window and stop dead in my tracks. So this was who I was? A tall, strong lesbian. I would need to change my wardrobe though; it was far too conservative. Being short on cash I ducked into my local op shop and searched for something radical and outlandish. I wanted to look bohemian; confident and unconcerned by the opinions of others. Everything was about to change.

Sally's garden was lit with fairy lights and a bonfire. Women milled around, drinks in hand, talking excitedly about the up-coming Mardi Gras. I stuck close to Sally and quickly swigged back a couple of glasses of wine. I was already light-headed and it was only eight o'clock.

'This is Natasha, Deb. She works with me. Natasha, meet Debra, a new lady in the midst of exploration.' A tall, blonde woman of about thirty-five gave me a quick look-over.

'Is that right?' she purred. 'Nice to have some new blood around.'

Sally laughed. 'Now be nice, Nat. Debra's pretty new to all this and I'm looking after her. Don't you go and frighten her away.' I watched Sally leave us and join a group of women by the barbeque. I suddenly felt extremely uncomfortable.

'So. Only recently a lesbian, huh? How long?' Natasha asked, peering into my eyes.

'I'm not a lesbian,' I snapped, rather too quickly.

'Well,' she slurred, 'sorry if I offended you.'

'I'm sorry,' I offered, realising how that must have sounded, 'I mean, I'm not sure what I am right now, I'm sort of exploring.'

'Hmm, so what do you do?'

'I'm actually in therapy. I had to drop out of the workforce a while ago, all hell broke loose.' Why on earth was I telling her all this?

'Therapy? Interesting. A woman, I hope?'

I shook my head.

'A man?' She grimaced. 'I would never let a man inside my head.'

I shrugged, suddenly not caring. I wanted another drink, and quickly. I don't think Natasha even noticed my departure.

I poured myself a wine and hastily rejoined Sally. She draped an arm over my shoulders, gave me a wink and pulled me into the conversation. I started to thoroughly enjoy myself. They were an energetic, fiery group of women who seemed confident with themselves and successful in their various careers. The conversation was lively and sometimes hilarious. It was lovely to laugh again and feel so at ease. By nine o'clock I was rather tipsy and found myself in the lounge room cuddled happily into Sally on the couch. I became aware that someone was discussing breasts. 'I'm a leg woman myself,' Natasha responded, 'big tits do nothing for me. But I do believe that Sally leans a bit that way.' I started to feel increasingly uncomfortable. I swear I was the only woman there with large breasts. And I was snuggled into Sally!

The conversation grew bawdier. I drank yet another wine and wished that everyone would go away and let me just continue my cuddle in peace. Sally was so warm and soft and safe. I felt like a little girl.

'So why were you uncomfortable when the conversation turned to sex?' Phil asked.

'Well I wasn't there for *that*,' I snapped, 'I was just really enjoying being with women. It was wonderful.'

'But they were lesbians,' he said, looking a little confused. 'Didn't you think that one of the women might have been attracted to you?'

I shook my head strongly. 'It wasn't about that,' I repeated. 'It was a lovely change to be at a party, with no men, and know that I could just enjoy being a female.'

'But these women are attracted to women,' he persisted. 'That doesn't make them non-sexual.'

'No,' I answered, somewhat confused, 'but it was good to see women being sexual and it didn't have anything to do with men. Don't you see what I mean? I've always felt that my body and my sexuality belonged to men. It was neat to be at a party and have my sexuality all to myself.' Surely he understood.

But he continued to look mystified. 'I guess I'm trying to understand your response to Natasha.'

I shuddered. 'She was so blatantly sexual,' I told him. 'It made me feel uncomfortable.'

'What were you expecting?'

'I just wanted an innocent night out with women. That's all. It had nothing to do with sex.'

Phil wouldn't let it go. 'But they're lesbians. They sleep with women. They're attracted to women. It is only natural that one of them might find you sexually appealing. So why were you un-comfortable with the idea that Sally liked big breasts?'

I was wishing that I hadn't told him. 'Because,' I said with irritation, 'I obviously have big breasts.'

'And?'

'*And*,' I continued, wondering why he was acting so thick, 'I didn't like attention drawn to them. It felt *uncomfortable*. I wasn't even thinking about sex.'

'I'm obviously not making myself clear here. Let's try another tack, huh?'

I nodded begrudgingly. Why was he finding it all so complicated?

'It's perfectly understandable that you were enjoying the company of women. It also makes sense that you felt safe in a male-free environment. The thing I do not understand is that you appear to be annoyed that these women viewed you as a possible sexual partner. Now, given that they are lesbians, I'm a little confused by this.'

When he put it that way I had to agree. 'I was so enjoying being cuddled up to Sally,' I explained, trying to make sense of that evening.

'You said you felt like a little girl?'

'Yep. It was lovely. She was so soft, and protective too. She had her arm around my shoulder for most of the evening. It was neat.'

'Your mother never hugged you, did she?'

I shook my head. 'She got all prickly.'

'So, maybe what you are looking for is a mother replacement?'

'Please don't say that,' I groaned.

He smiled. 'There's nothing bad about that. It's perfectly natural, given that you're in the process of redefining yourself. Little girls need a mother that they can learn from and develop a sense of their own femaleness, as it were. You hardly had a good example to go by. The only confusing thing here is why you've chosen lesbians.'

I thought on that for a while, trying to make sense of it. And then it hit me like a brick. I moaned in dismay. 'It's that fucking sexual crap again. I can't imagine closeness with anyone without sex being involved, even with a bloody woman!'

'Well it's hardly surprising, given your background.'

'So I'm not a lesbian after all?' I asked, feeling disappointed and confused.

Phil shook his head. 'I'm not saying that. It could well be that you are sexually attracted to women. But at the moment you

189

appear to be combining your desire to be mothered with the need to define your own sexuality. I guess that's pretty natural.'

'Well now I'm utterly confused,' I wailed.

He smiled. 'You'll work it out. You're on the right track.'

I continued to meet Sally for coffee. I loved the fact that there were no men in her life. And she wasn't miserable or pining away for them. There was an important key for me here; I just couldn't put my finger on what it was. I did my usual thing and went to the library. Armed with a dozen books on feminism, lesbianism and sexual identity, I headed home determined to find answers.

'What are they all for?' Ty asked.

I dumped the pile of books onto the dining-room table. What was I going to say? I smiled sheepishly. 'Just a little exploration.'

He flicked through the titles. 'Interesting reading, Mum.'

I opened my mouth to say something but he was already heading into the kitchen in search of food.

'Do you know what I hate?' I asked Phil, as soon as I had made myself comfortable.

He shook his head.

'I'm always so bloody *nice*. I get everywhere on time, I make sure I do everything right, no matter how unreasonable it might be. And I'll grind my teeth to a powder rather than speak my mind.'

'And why do you think you do that?'

'I think I was bloody born nice. And I doubt whether the elocution lessons helped either, I sound *so* polite.'

Phil smiled. 'What were the elocution lessons for?'

'After three years in Ireland, my sisters and I had accents that made Mum's hair curl. She couldn't stand the thought of her daughters sounding so "common"; that was the word she used. So it was "how now brown cow" once a week for quite a while. And the three of us still sound like bloody snobs. That's why it was such a surprise to hear how Dad and Mark and Cheryl spoke.'

'That must have been odd for you.'

'It was. I kept wondering if I'd talk like that if I'd stayed with them? I know they were a little mystified by my accent. You'd think we'd all attended private boarding schools.'

'Does your mother talk the same way?'

'Absolutely. But that came from my gramps. He was very particular about how he spoke, he said some people "strangled" the English language and he wouldn't have a bar of it in his house. There's so much snobbishness, which is weird, considering we're all bloody working class. It's all about being *nice*, though, and being seen to be *nice*. It drives me crazy.'

'It's about being seductive too, though, isn't it?'

I frowned. 'How is it seductive?'

'Well, it's like you're trying to be the perfect patient in some way, never being late, always paying on time, isn't that a form of seduction?'

I groaned. 'What an awful thought.'

Phil said nothing.

'We weren't allowed to swear when we were little, either. Not even words like "sod", or "damn".' I suddenly laughed, remembering an incident in Ireland with my sisters.

'What's so funny?' Phil asked.

'One afternoon, when Mum and Roger were out, the three of us had to wait outside the flat, on the stairs, until they came home with a key. I think it was Jo who came up with the suggestion that we take it in turns and say all of the swear words. We started off pretty tame, you know, "sod" this and "damn" that, but in no time we got right into the swing of it. We were all shocked and giggling at the same time. If Mum had heard us, she would have washed our mouths out with soap. But it was fun.'

Phil smiled. 'A bit strange, isn't it, that you had to be such nice little girls, considering what else was going on in that flat?'

I grimaced. 'Yes. That is weird. You know for most of my life whenever I'd be getting dressed or showering, I could hear a voice inside telling me not to waste my time; that shit can't look good.'

'That's pretty sad, isn't it?'

I nodded. 'I guess I'm just going to have to keep an eye out for this "being nice" racket; it's certainly starting to wear pretty thin with me. But, I don't think I could just start running late, or letting people down. I'd get myself in a hell of a knot. And why would I do that anyway? Isn't that just being rude?'

'I think it's more about being who you are, and not doing or saying things just to please other people.'

I shook my head. 'I worry sometimes that the real me is something too awful to show, like it lurks in the background somewhere, waiting to pounce.'

'That must use up a lot of energy for you, pretending to be something that you aren't?'

I nodded. 'Sometimes I'm weary to the very core, you know?'

'I understand that. But we're working on changing this for you; it won't always be this way.'

I looked in his eyes, wanting to believe him. 'Are you sure there is a real me? What if we discover that there's nothing there?'

'There's somebody there, believe me.'

'And she won't be awful?'

'I somehow doubt that very much.'

Chapter Fourteen

I was starting to feel a difference, but couldn't quite put my finger on it. When I needed to make a decision, or respond to someone or an event, I was able to go inside and imagine talking it over with Phil. That familiar rabble of conflicting voices had quietened down. I was using him as a measure for everything that went on around me, seeing people through his eyes, and trying to work out what he would say or do in any given situation. It was quite a new experience for me.

I couldn't believe this therapy was actually *changing* me. After all the years that I had spent grappling with tasks and techniques, affirmations and self-talk, somehow just talking to Phil was making an extraordinary difference. It was what I had been searching for and never found. Why was this working when nothing else did? I couldn't work it out.

'How is this happening?' I asked him.

He shrugged. 'It's all quite strange really,' he explained, 'no one knows exactly how it works, but it does. That "solidness" that you're experiencing is what most people with relatively normal childhoods take for granted.'

'But what is it?'

'It's what I meant when I told you that you would ultimately need to internalise me. That's what happens between a child and its parents. In your case that didn't occur, so you were left, in a sense, with having to create your own reference point. And as you are learning, a child has a very primitive way of processing material.'

I was shaking my head. 'It sounds like some sort of magic to me.'

'I guess it would. But some of it is quite simple. For example, look at the things you were going through as a child, the losses and the sexual abuse. Normally a child could take that to the parent, all the doubts and the questions and dump it, as it were, into the parent's lap. In a healthy relationship, the parent re-arranges that material and hands it back to the child in a form that makes sense. That's how it's meant to work.'

'Like monsters under the bed?'

'Exactly. Now from what I've heard about your mother, in the first instance it sounds like you weren't even permitted to question her, and secondly, if you did manage to ask her something, her answers were often bizarre. And in some cases, even more confusing. So you were left having to create your own explanations for the world around you.'

I sighed. 'So you're like a parent for me?'

'It will vary from time to time. But right now you're using me as a parent figure. And I have no problem with that at all. It's the only way you're going to be able to repair the damage.'

'I'm beginning to see why it takes so long.' I looked around the room, noticing for the first time that Phil had knick-knacks on his desk: some little metal contraption with silver balls hanging on threads, a large bottle of olive oil (I could only imagine where that had come from, maybe an adoring patient bearing gifts) and various packets and brochures from drug companies.

'You still think two years is a long time?' Phil asked, interrupting my explorations.

I nodded. 'In my life, two years is forever.'

'I guess so. You've covered a lot of ground already. But we've still got some things to glue together. The danger will be that you'll sabotage this process and quit therapy. That happens often.'

I shook my head vehemently. 'No way. This is the first thing in my life that actually *works*. I'm not about to throw that away.'

'That's precisely *why* people quit. It's too unfamiliar. It scares them. Unfortunately we're a lot safer with what we know, no matter how unpleasant or unhealthy that may be.'

'I wouldn't go back to that crap for anything.'

He smiled gently. 'We'll see, huh? You may start skipping sessions or turning up late. There are many ways to sabotage this process and I think I've seen all of them.'

'Doesn't that frustrate you?' I asked. 'Getting so far then having the patient walk out on you?'

He shrugged. 'Not at all. Everyone has his or her own process. I figure that the timing couldn't have been right for them.'

'Doesn't *anything* bother you?' I asked, marvelling at his ability to accept.

He laughed. 'I've been doing this work for years. When I first started I let a lot of things get to me, but you soon learn not to. Most of the time it's a very satisfying process, or else I wouldn't do it.'

I shook my head in wonder. 'Whatever it is you've got, I want it,' I said enviously.

'It's all yours,' he answered, 'you take whatever you need.'

I looked up at him, startled. 'Really?'

He nodded.

All that substance, his earthiness, that wonderful acceptance, I could have all of that? Something warm rippled through my being.

'You deserve it,' he said, softly.

I could only shake my head. I was flooded with gratitude.

Despite the steady progress, I was continuing to gamble, often blowing my entire income in one day. I had never really understood money. I knew I never had enough of it, but I couldn't seem to let myself hang on to the stuff. I got fidgety if I knew there were twenty dollars in my purse. I'd start thinking about how I could get rid of it. Before my money even came in I would have made up a list of everything that needed to be covered; I was always forty of fifty dollars short. Feeling despondent I'd tell myself that I was going to be broke anyway and I'd go out and blow the lot. I would hate myself afterwards, thinking that Phil would be disgusted with me, or worse, disappointed. I'd promise myself that as soon as my next cheque arrived I would budget it carefully and steer clear of the casino. But it never happened. My mother was also a compulsive gambler and when I visited her on weekends we both 'treated' ourselves to a night out at the local pub. We wouldn't leave until neither of us had a cent left in our purses. It was a constant source of shame to me and I didn't like to bring it up in my sessions.

Living on the edge financially also kept me in a high state of anxiety. I was borrowing money from friends just to enable me to eat. My bank account was in overdraft and the bills were piling up. I figured that the only way out of this mess was by getting a job or having a big win. The latter looked far more probable.

Phil was aware that I blew money, but not of how frequently or how seriously it was affecting my living conditions. I soon found myself living in two worlds. I was steadily making progress with Phil, reducing the mood swings and the episodes of dissociation, and in that other outside arena I was blowing every cent I had and increasing the time spent with my mother. Something was bound to crack.

Chapter Fifteen

It was that time again. Phil would be away for two weeks. I had geared myself up for it, determined not to go gallivanting around Australia. Ty was on school holidays, which helped, despite the fact that our routine got blown to pieces. I needed a distraction of some kind, something to keep my mind occupied and away from the niggling fears about Phil's disappearance. It arrived in a totally unexpected form.

Ty had asked me to do a final reading of one of his assignments. I sat next to him at his computer and we worked together.

'Why don't you go on the internet Mum, see if you can find a site that interests you?'

I scowled. 'I hate bloody computers, Ty, you know that.'

'I know, but I'll get it all set up, so that all you have to do is key in a word of interest, and the computer will do the rest.'

'I don't know,' I said warily, 'what if it gets stuck or something?'

Ty laughed. 'If it gets stuck, just leave it. I'll fix it up when I get home later.'

'All right,' I agreed, somewhat anxiously, 'I'll give it a shot.'

Ty pressed a lot of buttons and left me alone with a blank box to key in my word of interest. I sat in front of the screen for a while, wondering where I would like to go. I decided to type in the words 'sexual abuse' and see if I could find some information on psychotherapy. After an hour of visiting some pretty weird and wonderful places, I finally happened upon an American website for sexual abuse healing. I was riveted. It had so many fascinating topics for discussion. And a notice board where you could write in a question and within moments a dozen or more responses from fellow survivors were flashing in front of you. I signed myself up for membership immediately, then commenced to read through pages of debate on therapists and their techniques. It was fantastic! Women were writing about absolutely everything that I had been through with Phil, all their doubts and insecurities, their fears and hopes. There was even a section for dissociative disorders. I felt as though I had stumbled upon a smorgasbord of information.

'You still in here?' asked Ty in disbelief.

I looked up from the screen, surprised to see that it had turned dark outside. 'I've found something amazing!' I told him excitedly.

He laughed. 'Just as well we've got unlimited hours. I don't suppose you've started dinner?'

'Oops.'

'It's all right, I only came in to tell you that I'll be staying at Adam's tonight. We'll just grab take-outs.'

'You sure? I can whip up a meal in no time.'

Ty shook his head. 'You stay there. I'll catch you in the morning.'

I gave him a grateful smile and returned to the screen. I had nervously typed a question, asking how long most of them had been in therapy. Within half an hour I was flooded with replies. I couldn't believe my eyes. The time frame ranged from five to fourteen years. I sat back in shock. Fourteen years! Phil had assured me we would only need two. Had he been humouring me? Or was he just easing me in slowly to a lifetime of therapy? I hastily wrote another question. By midnight I had already come to know quite a few of the contributors. They shared their experiences with me, everything from the nature of their therapist to the range of their symptoms. I was hooked.

Because of the time difference, the website was at its liveliest between 4 am and 2 pm. Within days my sleep pattern went out the window. I couldn't get enough. I was further intrigued when one of the women invited me into their chat room. 'You'll get to talk with all of us,' she enthused, 'and you don't have to wait for a reply. It's like having a normal conversation.' I hastily wrote back a note and asked for directions. She guided me to the site and within minutes I was in. I had found heaven!

Hours later I was completely absorbed. I sat there at times, laughing till I wet myself or crying like a baby. These women were my soul mates. We shared everything: a history of sexual abuse, the search for answers, and weekly sessions with a therapist. I told them all about Phil and we chatted long into the night on just about every topic under the sun.

The days went by unnoticed. Ty checked in once in a while, still amused by my latest obsession, but generally pleased to see me having so much fun. I had to remind myself sometimes to get dressed. Having a pee was bad enough; it meant missing out on an entire discussion. I was learning so much. I realised how lucky I was. There were women out there battling with drug or alcohol addictions while others fought daily with the desire to cut themselves. Despite everything though, the main ingredient in that chat room was humour; wonderful, gut wrenching, belly-aching humour.

I made friends with a woman from Maine who called herself Squirrel. She showed me how to go into Private Chat and soon it was her I came looking for the moment I went on-line. She made me laugh so hard sometimes that I couldn't type or see a word on the screen. I gave myself the name of Traveller. It seemed fitting. We got to know each other's therapists intimately. She commiserated with me when she heard that Phil was away, sharing her own experiences whenever her therapist took leave. By the time my two weeks were over, we had drawn closer, sharing the more scary things about our past and our symptoms. I had found a friend.

'Mum?'

I looked up from the screen, surprised to see Ty at the door in his pyjamas.

'What time is it?' I asked, quickly typing to Squirrel that I'd be back in a tick.

'Seven. Have you been up all night?'

I nodded. 'I'll get some sleep during the day.'

'Okay, make sure you do though.' He headed into the bathroom and I reluctantly told Squirrel that I would need to leave for a while; it was time to make breakfast.

'I've found the most incredible internet site,' I told Phil, the moment we sat down.

He smiled. 'Tell me all about it.'

I filled him in, all about Squirrel and how different the therapists are in America. 'Her therapist rings her once a week, to check how she is,' I told him, '*and* she gets emails from him.'

Phil laughed. 'Feeling a little gypped, are you?'

'Well, it would be nice.'

'I don't know how they find time for it,' he answered. 'If I had to go home, read all my emails and send a reply back to everyone, it would take me all night.'

'Another thing,' I continued eagerly, prepared to let that one go, 'most of them have been in therapy for over five years, some of them even *ten* years.'

Phil frowned. 'That is a little surprising. But maybe they have a different process over there.'

'So we should still be finished in two years, you're not just saying that?'

'No,' he assured me, 'in fact, if we hadn't completed therapy in about that time, I would think something was wrong.'

'So there's no way I'll still be seeing you in five years.'

'Absolutely not. Of course I do have patients that I have seen on and off for much longer than that, but they're an exception, and usually they've taken long breaks from therapy.'

I felt reassured and went on to describe some of the more fascinating aspects of my newly found adventure. 'It's remarkable, you know, talking to people who are just like me. And hearing about how awful it is for some of them.'

'In what way?'

'A lot of them have drug or alcohol problems, most of them are on medication. And quite a few of them cut themselves too.'

Phil looked concerned. 'I'd go a bit cautiously, if I were you.'

'Why?' I asked, feeling a little annoyed by his doubts.

'Just a suggestion.'

I flicked it aside. 'This is the first time in ages that I've found people who I can really talk to. I don't need to explain myself to them, it's like we all speak the same language.'

Phil just nodded. I rolled my eyes and changed the subject.

The moment I got home I turned on the computer and located Squirrel. She had been eagerly awaiting my return.

'How'd your session go, Trav?' she typed.

'So so. I don't think Phil was too keen about this site.'

'Anthony wasn't either, when I first told him. He was worried about all the weirdos in here, especially the slashers.'

'Slashers?'

'The women who cut themselves.'

'I did that a couple of times, scared me though.'

'I'm glad to hear you quit. Freaks me out a bit.'

'So you tell Anthony everything that goes on in here.'

'Just about. It's the only world I have outside of my sessions with him.'

'Really?'

'Yep. I can't go outside much, I don't like crowds.'

'Has it always been like that, though?'

'No, as I got older I think I started to lose my confidence.'

'Maybe I should visit you. We could have a blast.'

'I could make you cookies and warm milk.'

I smiled, trying to imagine what she looked like. 'Hey Squirrel, are you tall or short or what?'

☺ 'I'm absolutely beautiful, of course.'

'Come on, the truth now.'

'Aw shucks, spoil my little fantasy why don't you. Okay, I'm almost totally grey, am carrying at least five kilos that I don't need, and I'm five feet tall.'

'Five feet? You're the same height as my mum, yikes!'

'What are you? Some sort of giant?'

☺ 'Nope, I just feel that way next to shrimps like you. I'm five-seven.'

'Old and wrinkled too?'

'Ha Ha. Wrinkled yes, but only forty-two.'

'Still a baby. I'm fifty-six.'

'Oh God, I've found myself another surrogate mother.'

'Fuck off! Inside I swear I'm still a trapped and tortured five-year-old.'

'Hey, don't say that, Squirrel. It sounds too sad.'

☹ 'Feels pretty sad too.'

'You and me are going to get all fixed up you know, and then I'm going to fly over there and we'll go explore Maine together.'

'You could meet Anthony! We'll have therapy sessions together. If that doesn't scare him off, nothing will.'

'I'm going to be way done with therapy by then, Squirrel.'

'I won't ever finish with Anthony.'

I read that line carefully, not knowing what to say. She had been seeing Anthony twice a week for nine years.

'Cat got your tongue?' she typed.

'Sorry, ma'am, just thinking.'

'About?'

'About therapy.'

'You still figuring the whole thing will only take two years?'

'I'm banking on it, Squirrel. I've been working on this stuff for most of my life. I intend to move on eventually.'

'It's different for me. I won't ever leave Anthony.'

'Well, we'll just have to plan our adventure around him.'

☺ 'I'll take you fishing. But you have to cook it, I'm a peanut-butter-sandwich girl myself.'

'Let's just throw the fish back and I'll join you in that sandwich.'

☺ 'I like you, Trav.'

☺ 'Ditto.'

'You're in that spooky place again, aren't you?' Phil asked.

I nodded. I had spent the day with my mother.

'I can feel it,' he continued, 'it's a bit like being stoned, isn't it?'

'You can feel it?' I asked incredulously.

'Yep. Makes it hard to think straight. Sort of like floating in a vacuum.'

I was stunned. But also charmed. No one had ever entered my spaciness. It had been a lonely place where only I existed.

'How come you can feel it?'

He shrugged. 'Because you're letting me,' he said slowly, struggling as I normally did, to find words in the ether.

I was still amazed. He looked like I felt, miles away from everything and trying to stay focussed. I had to laugh. 'This is really bizarre.'

'Quite unpleasant, isn't it?' he managed.

'I'm probably more accustomed to it than you are. I still can't believe it though. No one's ever been in here with me. It's quite odd.'

He just nodded, letting himself soak up the experience.

Moments passed. He looked quite drowsy. I thought he was going to fall asleep. Soon his eyes did eventually close and I sat there quietly, just watching him. He was dozing off. The whole thing entranced me.

He must have slept for about five minutes. It was glorious to sit across from him and see him so vulnerable, slouched in his chair and dead to the world. I felt that warmth spread through me again. God, I loved this man.

His eyes opened and I smiled. 'Welcome back.'

He shook his head, trying to bring himself to. 'Hmm, must have dozed off there.'

'That was neat,' I told him, still beaming. 'Like you trusted me.'

'How so?'

'To let yourself fall asleep with me here. That felt really nice.'

'Why wouldn't I trust you?'

I didn't know the answer to that. But for now it didn't matter. I was enjoying the glow too much to analyse it.

'I don't know how you cope in that spaciness. It must make life very difficult.' He was starting to come back down to earth.

'I've just spent the day with Mum so I guess it was predictable.'

'How's that going?'

'Oh, I don't know,' I sighed, frustrated by my inability to change things. 'When I'm with her I start believing that her world is my world. Like I'm just pretending that I don't belong in her environment.'

'You're not your mother.'

'I know. But sometimes we seem so alike. When I've been with her for a few hours it's like I lose touch with myself again. Things she says start making sense.'

'Give me an example?'

'Well, she's just finished reading this God book. It said that we choose everything that happens to us. And I knew that she was referring to the sexual abuse, without actually saying it. Soon I found myself wondering if that could actually be true. Maybe I did choose it?'

'That's a pretty horrific thing for her to suggest, and a nice out too.'

'How so?' I asked, starting to sound like him.

'Your mother had choices too. It was her decisions which placed you and your sisters in such an unsafe environment.'

'But maybe it was all meant to happen?' I persisted, desperately trying to make sense of it all.

He looked unconvinced. 'Bad things do happen in this world. Horrible things. There are thousands of people out there living sad and desperate lives. But we all have choices. You make choices every day. For whatever reason, your mother made decisions that were entirely selfish and took no one else into account. You and your sisters paid the price for that. Was it meant to happen? What does that question even mean?'

'Well,' I said, trying to put my mother's point across, 'Mum said that if it wasn't meant to happen then it wouldn't have.'

He let out a long sigh. 'Your mother is in denial. That means she never has to take responsibility for her actions.'

I thought of my lost brother and sister, over there in England, who hadn't been given a second thought. I recalled Jo, in New Zealand, with children who my mother barely knew. Mum wasn't pining away or agonising over her decisions. Nothing ever got brought up about any of them. I was still hopelessly confused. 'Is it just that she doesn't care?' I asked, searching for an explanation.

'Your mother obviously has some sort of pathology. I can't say what that is because I haven't met her. But from what you've told me she lives moment to moment. Her choices are more like impulses and a desire for instant gratification. I doubt she has ever grown up.'

I considered that for a moment. 'She is a lot like a child, especially when she doesn't get her own way. Not surprising though, her own mother was pretty frightening.'

'It usually works that way,' Phil explained sadly.

'You know what I wish? That I could bring her in here, sit her down next to me and you could tell me what she's all about.'

'How would that work?'

I thought about it, getting quite excited. 'Well, you could bring up the sexual abuse stuff and watch her reaction. Then you could tell her what it was really like.'

Phil shook his head. 'So you want me to do your work, do you?'

'No,' I said slowly. 'It's just that you'd be able to see her, to watch her responses. Then you could tell me what's wrong with her.'

'I don't think that would achieve anything. Ultimately you're going to have to come to your own conclusions.'

'Why can't I let it go, though? Why do I keep persisting so much?'

'You've still got a fantasy of how it should have been with her. That's why you get angry or frustrated. The child in you is still desperately hoping that a perfect mother will appear. Letting go of that fantasy can be very painful.'

I sat there and let his words sink in. I knew that something had to change; my life was still chaotic. I was continuing to recreate the same events that I lived through in my childhood: the shortage of money, living on the edge, the shame of having dirty secrets; I was still keeping my gambling from Phil. I left the session resolved to do something. I just didn't know what.

The sleeping pills were lined up on my dining table. They had been there for weeks, providing an odd sort of comfort to me. I sat looking at them and thinking of my mother. Were they an easier option than confronting her? Was I really that frightened of losing her? My thoughts were interrupted by the telephone.

'Deb? How's it going?' It was my weekly call from Jo.

'You've called at an odd time. I was miles away, thinking about Mum again. You okay?'

'I've found a psychologist, Deb. I've got a session on Thursday.'

'A psychologist? What made you go that way?'

'My doctor referred me to her. Her name is Cherry. I'm already quite nervous.'

A dozen doubts raced through my mind. A woman? A psychologist? I'd wanted her to find a male psychiatrist, like Phil.

'Couldn't you find a psychiatrist?' I asked, hoping not to douse her enthusiasm.

'I found two in our area. Neither of them are taking new patients. I had to do something; things are getting pretty bad over here.'

Maybe we each had to find our own solution. I decided to drop my doubts and trust Jo's judgement. No one was going to get one past her; she had tried too many things already.

'It's quite exciting, isn't it?' I said. 'I can't wait to hear how your first session goes.'

'Me neither. Don't worry, I'll call you the minute I get home. So, what's all this about Mum?'

I sighed. 'I think I'm going to have to do something.'

'Like what?'

'Maybe confront her once and for all.'

Jo groaned. 'What's that going to achieve?'

'I don't know. But I can't keep going the way I am. It's like I undo all the good work that I've done with Phil.'

'You going to tell her to fuck off?' I had relayed that conversation to her some weeks ago.

'Maybe I will.'

'Better you than me. I'm still too scared to even contact her.'

'We've made her so powerful, Jo. It's crazy, given that we're both in our forties.'

'I know. Let me know how you go, huh?'

'I will. Wish me luck.'

'Just look after yourself for goodness sake.'

'And hey, good luck with Thursday,' I added.

I hung up the phone and looked at the sleeping pills again. It was now or never.

The ten-minute drive to my mother's house was nerve-wracking. I kept rehearsing the conversation only to realise that I was saying nothing new. I thought of what Phil had told me, that it wasn't about her response. I needed to speak from the heart, to tell my truth and not hold anything back. Her blank expression kept floating before me and twice I pulled the car over thinking it was a pointless exercise. Then the sleeping pills would flash into my head. I had to do this.

My mother beamed when she opened the front door. 'Hello, dear, what a lovely surprise!'

Gee thanks God. Make it just that little bit easier for me.

'I don't think you'll find this visit lovely, Mum,' I started, taking a deep breath and heading into the lounge room.

Mum caught the tone in my voice and her facial expression changed immediately. 'I'll make a cup of tea,' she said quietly, making her way into the kitchen.

'No thanks, Mum, I won't be here that long.' She turned around and looked at me. My body was shaking. 'Just sit down here with me for a moment, if that's okay?'

'Okay. What's this all about?' She was already cutting off.

I took a deep breath. Then all at once I felt the little child inside of me. She was standing there alone, carrying all the memories, the fear and the years of shame.

Stand up for me, she pleaded. *Just say it for me.*

I was flooded with her pain. I looked at my mother, her eyes already challenging me, as they had done for years. But I owed it to that little girl. She'd carried this for way too long. I took another deep breath, scrambling for courage. 'Do you know, Mum, that for over a month now, I've had five bottles of sleeping pills lined up in my dining room? And I've been preparing to take them rather than face you with the truth?'

She said nothing. Just stared directly at me, her eyes blank.

It's not about her, Debra. Don't get hooked into her.

'And what I've learned from Phil,' I continued, 'is that I'm actually worth more than that.'

Where is this going? Get to the truth. Quit being nice and reasonable. That's how she's trained you.

I thought of the thousands of times that I had pushed down the anger, making myself ill rather than hurt her feelings. I could feel that rage inside me now. I couldn't stop shaking.

'So Phil has sent you here, has he dear?' she asked curtly.

I shook my head. 'This has nothing to do with Phil. It's about me, and Jo. And those fucking filthy *creeps* that you called your friends.' I had to hold my hands together to stop them from trembling. Still my mother stared blankly back at me. I stood up and looked down at her. 'You know what I've never told you?' I asked, my voice shaking. 'That you were an awful fucking mother. You never thought once about us, not *once*. You knew exactly what Roger was doing. There was no way you couldn't have. And there's something very wrong with you, very wrong, that no matter how much it hurt Jo and me, you still stand up and justify yourself.'

'I don't think that's quite fair, dear,' my mother interrupted. 'I did my best.'

'*Fuck your best!*' I roared. 'I wish you could have said you were sorry, just once. But you had an answer for everything. And I don't care anymore about what you've got to say. That's all that ever fucking mattered in my childhood. What *you* wanted! What *you* thought! This is all I want to say to you right now, fuck off, fuck the hell out of my life and leave me alone.' I headed quickly to the front door, shaking from top to toe, determined not to be pulled back into her craziness.

'Look dear,' she said quietly, 'why don't you come back in and we'll have a cup of tea? It doesn't have to be like this, you know, come on, come back inside.'

I looked back at her in horror. A cup of tea? Had she even heard a word?

'Leave me alone, Mum. I mean it. Don't visit. Don't call me. I want you out of my life!'

I got into my car feeling as though I was disintegrating. My hands were shaking so badly that I could hardly put the key in the ignition. I backed out of the driveway. I was three streets away when I had to pull over. The rage had vanished but there was a pain inside that I thought would rip me apart. I started to moan, then wail. I couldn't stop it. It felt like my heart was breaking. 'Oh God, I've lost my mum. I've lost my mum.'

Chapter Sixteen

'So how do you feel now?' Phil asked.

I shook my head. 'Strange. She hasn't called, which is good. I guess I feel a bit guilty. But I know that's ridiculous. I don't know what I feel really. Drained, mainly. That stuff that came out of me in the car was frightening.'

Phil nodded. 'You've been carrying that for years.'

'But why did I feel like I'd lost her? That doesn't make sense.'

'My guess is that you let go of the fantasy. That's a very painful process.'

'I don't think anything has ever hurt that much.'

'I wouldn't doubt that. So what's your plan, do you intend to see her again?'

I looked up at him in surprise. 'Hardly, after all that ghastly stuff. Why? Are you saying I should?' I was suddenly confused.

'Not at all. I'm just trying to see where you are with it.'

'I like not having her in my life. I want to keep it that way.'

Phil just nodded and I couldn't work out what he was trying to get at. Had he thought I'd been too harsh with Mum? Was I meant to go back now and apologise? My head started to spin. 'I don't understand your questions,' I insisted. 'What do you mean?'

He shrugged, 'I told you, I'm just exploring the lie of the land.'

I was getting frustrated. 'I suppose now you're going to say that I should forgive her? Isn't that what all the books say?'

'Do you want to forgive her?'

'No,' I snapped. 'But now that makes me a nasty piece of work, doesn't it?'

'Not at all. You do what you need to do.'

I was suddenly furious with him. 'Can't you for once offer a bloody opinion?'

'Why does my opinion matter?'

'Oh great, answer a question with a question. What page are we on now, two-hundred-and-sixty-eight of the bloody psychotherapy manual?'

He looked straight into my eyes. 'Why are you angry with me?'

I stared out of the window, fuming. I didn't know why I was angry with him. I seemed to be angry with everyone lately. Neither of us said anything and the clock ticked on. I wanted something badly from him but didn't know what it was. 'I've run out of things to say,' I finally managed.

'Something's going on for you, I think it's important for us to explore that.'

I shook my head, feeling pretty hopeless. 'I don't know what it is. Let's just change the subject. Talk about football instead. I've had enough of this crap.'

'Okay,' he agreed, 'it's your call.' We discussed the possibilities of our teams making the finals. I was glad for once, when the session came to an end.

Despite the absence of my mother, I continued to blow money on a regular basis. But I had finally thrown away the sleeping pills. I used the time chatting on-line with Squirrel and trying to work out what position to take with my mother. Should I never see her again? Normal people have relationships with their mothers; shouldn't I be working towards that? My own thoughts were taking me around in circles. I decided to go to the library and do some reading on the subject.

I found a book on sexual abuse and healing. After flicking through the self-help techniques I finally came across the chapter on parents, particularly mothers. The author discussed the various problems that arose from a mother who may have turned her head while the abuse took place, or who stayed in a position of denial despite confrontation. A number of suggestions were offered, but paramount to all of them was the notion of forgiveness. The only way to move on in life, the author proposed, was to ultimately forgive the mother. She had done her best and could do no more than that. After all, she was only human, and as such, should be allowed to make mistakes. Failure to forgive was a sign of immaturity.

Likewise, the author continued, the survivor of sexual abuse needed to forgive the abusers. Holding onto anger and bitterness would bring no healing to the survivor. She suggested writing a letter if direct confrontation with the abuser was too threatening or not possible. In this letter the abused should acknowledge what happened, express their feelings and let the abuser know that they intended to move on. I put the book down and thought it all over.

There were so many people that I would need to forgive; my mother, for a start, then Roger and the other molesters, Frank, Ray and Terry. My dad. The list was endless. I imagined all of them standing in front of me. Every one of them with their perfect justifications for why they had acted as they had. Not one of them had said sorry. I thought of Jo and I, the years we had spent trying to fix ourselves, to find some sort of normality. Was it my job to forgive them? Did I even want to?

I talked it over with Squirrel. She hadn't seen or spoken to her parents in years. 'I'm not going to be much help to you, Trav,' she wrote, 'I guess we all have to make that decision by ourselves.' I looked at her words on the screen, knowing that she was right.

'I've been thinking about forgiving Mum.' I brought Phil up-to-date with my reading.

'On what basis are we forgiving her?'

'That she didn't know better. If she'd known better she would have done better.'

Phil was nodding slowly. 'And you're happy with that conclusion?'

'I hate it when you ask questions like that. I start to doubt myself all over again.'

He smiled. 'Then maybe you're not completely clear on it yet.'

'Yes I am,' I insisted. 'Just don't ask me any more questions.'

He laughed. 'I'm your psychiatrist! I'm *meant* to ask you questions.'

I rolled my eyes. 'It's been two months since I've seen Mum. She's respected my request and hasn't telephoned once. I want to close the book on this subject, once and for all.'

'So you're planning to see her?'

I nodded. 'Yep. Just a short visit.'

'And you'll resume contact again?'

'Yep, but not so frequently. It's been quite nice having my own space.'

'I see. Well, I'll be interested to hear how it goes.'

I felt a familiar feeling of frustration. Couldn't he just *once* let something be? I decided to change subjects. 'You know, I've been thinking about what it's going to be like when I'm all fixed up. No more fantastic highs, no more confusion, and I wondered if life would be sort of dull? Flat?'

Phil smiled. 'Is that how the rest of us live, you mean?'

I nodded. 'Yeah. What makes it all worthwhile for you lot?'

'We just get on with it, I guess. You find areas in your life where you can have some sort of control, but generally you deal with the ups and downs and find enjoyment where you can.'

'That sounds ghastly!'

He laughed. 'Those highs starting to look good, are they? Why do you think so many people drink, or take drugs? They're all looking for some form of escape. Life isn't easy, you know.'

'That's just dreadful,' I moaned. 'What's the bloody point of going on if it's so miserable?'

'I'm not saying it's all bad, but certainly life can be tough.'

'So why bother? Why don't you all just top yourselves?'

'I don't think we're wired for that. The survival instinct is very strong. No matter how hard it gets, the majority of us struggle on through it.'

I was shaking my head in dismay. 'So I'm going to get better, after all these years of being fucked-up, and discover that life is dull, tough and generally a struggle? Well, fuck that!'

He threw back his head and laughed. 'Welcome to planet earth.'

'I won't accept that,' I told him strongly. 'There's got to be more to it than that. Otherwise it's all just too absurd.'

'Well, now you're getting on to the metaphysical. Maybe God has a plan?'

I eyed him carefully. 'We don't talk about God here.'

'No, we haven't. I'm just following your train of thought.'

'Do you believe in God?' I asked, not sure that I wanted to know the answer.

'Yes, I do.'

'Hmmm.'

'Does that bother you?'

'I'm not sure. I've had a problem with God for most of my life. When I was little I must have prayed to him a thousand times, but he never answered. As I got older I tried everything to make some sort of meaningful contact, but all I got back was silence. If He does exist, I don't think I like Him. He sits back and lets all this shit happen. What sort of a loving God is that?'

'Maybe we need to spend more time on this question. I've

actually had a cancellation this afternoon, would you like to come back and we'll continue it then?'

I was delighted. 'Absolutely.'

I had two hours to kill. I decided to head into the city and find myself somewhere nice to eat lunch. I needed to think this God stuff through.

I sat stirring my cappuccino and watching the lunchtime crowds rushing through their precious hour of freedom. Did they really just struggle through with little joy in their life? Where did they find meaning? I thought back to my years in Ireland, to St Maries of the Isle, the Catholic convent school that my sisters and I attended for three years. I had loved the nuns. But more than anything I was captivated by the rituals of confession and communion. I loved the idea that if I had been bad and covered my soul with the black dots of sin, the simple act of confession washed them away and left me sparkling clean again. It was like magic. Jo and I swore that we would become nuns when we grew up.

We stopped going to church for some reason when we arrived in Australia. I remember thinking that my soul must have become pitch black. By the time I had become a teenager I no longer prayed or asked for forgiveness. I decided that God was for the good people. And that certainly left me out.

Later, in my thirties, I felt myself pulled into the world of God again as my mother embraced religion. She had joined her local church of born-again Christians and had thrown herself into it completely. Everything became God-driven. For three years she read the bible almost fanatically, finding an answer for all of her questions. I tried to believe again. I started praying and even went to church with her a couple of times. Was God watching me? Did he love me? Was it simply a matter of handing Him all of my problems, as my mother did, and letting Him show the way? I tried, but something felt wrong. It reminded me of waiting for my dad to rescue me. Isn't that all I was doing now? Asking God to save me, to make me happy? After turning my mind inside out, I decided to let it go. If there was a God, so be it, He didn't need me to believe in Him. But Phil believing in God? Now *that* was a shock to the system.

'So,' I asked, smiling, 'have you been swatting up on the meaning of life?'

'I flicked through some of the Dalai Lama's works, but didn't have time to finish it,' he joked.

'I've been thinking you know, about this God stuff. You don't really believe in heaven and hell, do you?'

He shook his head. 'I certainly think there's something much bigger than me. And there has to be more to life than this.'

'Like a prize at the end, you mean?'

'Who knows? I think we could be doing so much better, and certainly many are trying, but you look at the state of the world and it makes you wonder. It's in quite a mess, isn't it?'

'Hmmm, but maybe there isn't any meaning to it? Maybe we just get born, live a while and die. Does there have to be some great purpose?'

'For a lot of people that's the only way they can make sense of what's around them.'

I was still confused. 'I don't like it. It reminds me of Mum too much, handing over responsibility and leaving it to God. Dad did the same thing. I picture God standing up in heaven looking totally baffled and saying to both of them, "But I gave those children to *you*, why do you keep giving them back?"'

Phil smiled. 'I can understand you feeling that way. In the end though it comes down to finding meaning in your life. In one form or another you'll need to come up with an answer that satisfies you.'

I sat back in the couch, knowing that there was something that I wanted from this conversation, but still not quite sure what it was. 'Obviously the material stuff isn't going to do it for me, I've learnt how easily that just comes and goes. But what else is there?'

Phil smiled, saying nothing.

'Come on,' I urged, 'you're going to have to give me a clue here, I'm obviously missing something.'

'Well, I guess that leaves you with the things that aren't material.'

I frowned. 'Like what?'

'Like love, trust, respect, you know, those ethereal sort of things.'

I thought on that for a moment. 'Good Lord,' I said, suddenly seeing the irony. 'You mean to say, that I come to see you because I'm living in the clouds and *way* out of touch with reality, and I'm going to eventually realise that the only things that are real and meaningful are *ethereal*?'

He nodded, smiling.

'Well why didn't you just tell me that in the first place?'

'Because in the first place, we needed to bring you back down to earth.'

I laughed. 'That's quite bizarre, isn't it?'

'It works the same way as independence, I guess. You need to become dependent before you can attain it.'

I shook my head. 'Do the paradoxes never end?'

We sat in silence for a while, as I let myself absorb this new idea.

'I'll tell you one thing,' I said strongly, 'if there is a God, I've certainly got a thing or two to say to Him.'

'Like what?'

'Like, "Hey, what the fuck was that all about? You send me

down to this rotten planet, hook me up with weirdo parents, send every creep and lowlife my way and then turn your back on me?" I think he owes me an explanation.'

Phil laughed. 'What else would you say to Him?'

'I think I'd ask Him what his great plan is. And maybe He should reassess it. This planet is falling down around our ears, it needs help, and quickly.'

'I agree. But what do you do?'

I thought on that for a while, too. 'Maybe it isn't about God, perhaps it's up to us to do something?'

'Could be. There are people out there trying to shift the balance. We certainly could do with more compassion, more caring. But I'm not convinced that we're winning the war just yet.'

I wondered how I was contributing. Up until then I had been too busy with my own chaos. 'It's like I've spent my whole life trying to sort out what's right and wrong, you know? I think I've gotten a handle on it, then some part of me rebels like fury. It's the subject that Mum and I argue most about. She doesn't see anything as "wrong" or "bad". When we talk about it my head feels like it's going to split apart.'

Phil just nodded, saying nothing.

'But is she right? Who am I to make judgements? Isn't forgiveness about accepting somebody for who they are?' I was once again drowning in a sea of confusion. 'It was a darn sight easier before I met you.'

He smiled. 'Why is that?'

'Because I take you everywhere I go now. So when I'm listening to Mum, I imagine that you're sitting with me, listening too. And I don't think for a moment that you'd respond the way that I do. It's like I see her through your eyes now, and that's pretty unsettling.'

'What do you imagine I would do, or say?'

I rolled my eyes, not liking the truth. 'You wouldn't be sitting there in the first place.'

Phil stayed quiet and left my sentence dangling in midair.

I lay in bed that night thinking over our conversation. What was God? Was He really someone you could talk to? Did He talk back? I'd read so much and heard so much about this supposedly loving God and yet He still remained absent to me. I thought of all the times I'd tried to reach Him, how desperate I'd been for an answer, any answer. I remembered roaring at Him once and calling Him a nasty piece of work. The little Catholic in me had quailed, waiting for retribution to crash upon my head. But still nothing. I decided to try again.

I closed my eyes and thought of Phil, letting the warmth flood through me. 'Hey God,' I asked, 'is this what it would feel like if I made contact with you? Is this what you feel for me?'

After a couple of minutes silence I tried again. 'How come you don't say anything? I know you can hear me.'

I imagined Him thinking, 'Oh goodness, it's that Debra again, whatever is she wanting me to say?'

I laughed. That's just what Phil would have asked. 'It's okay, God,' I told Him, 'You don't have to say a word. But hey, thanks for Phil. I mean that.'

I fell asleep bathed in gratitude.

Chapter Seventeen

The following morning I eagerly went on-line to tell Squirrel of my decision. 'I'm going to forgive Mum,' I wrote. 'I think I'm ready to move on.'

'Good for you. Have you talked it over with Phil?'

'Yep. As usual he doesn't say much.'

'Do they ever?'

I laughed. 'Hey, Squirrel, do you have different parts?'

'Yep, but I don't like to talk about it, Trav. It can start all sorts of trouble.'

'Okay, sorry. We'll change the subject.'

'Do you?'

'Yep.'

'Do they have different names?'

'Not really, but I do have a rampant teenager.'

'What does Phil think about it?'

'He just talks to me as he always does.'

'I lose time.' ☹

'Oh Squirrel, I'm so sorry. That must be awful for you.'

'That's why I won't go out, except to see Anthony. I'm too afraid of what might happen.'

'Does the medication help?'

'I think that just keeps me on the planet.'

I sat in quietness for a while, reflecting on all the damage.

'Hey, Trav, you nodding off there?'

'Nope, still here. Just thinking about stuff.'

'Don't you go getting all down now, ya hear?'

'I'm not, honestly. I spent so many years trying to minimise everything, it's only now that I'm beginning to understand the enormity of it all.'

'They fucked us up good, huh?'

'Squirrel? Can I ask you something?'

'Anything.'

'Who did it to you? You've never told me. And, hey, I'll understand if you tell me to mind my own bloody business.'

'No, it's okay. I think I trust you enough now. It was both of them. The egg and the sperm donor.'

Jesus. 'I'm sorry, Squirrel.'

'It started when I was two.'

I read the words in horror. 'God, Squirrel, that's just too bloody awful for words.'

'Hey, I'm here though. And I'm tough. That's got to count for something, hasn't it?'

'I think you're amazing, madam.'

'You and me both, girl.'

'Hey Squirrel, I *love* having you to talk to.' ☺

'Ditto, Trav.' ☺

My mother greeted me as if nothing had happened. And neither of us said a word about our last meeting. We filled each other in on the previous two months and I left feeling pleased with myself. This forgiveness stuff didn't look so hard after all.

Jo was intrigued. 'She didn't say anything?'

'Nope. Maybe that's one area where denial can be useful,' I joked.

'I don't know, Deb. Isn't everything back to where it used to be?'

'Oh don't you start, Jo,' I groaned. 'It's bad enough listening to Phil's questions.'

'Does he think it's a good idea, you being back with Mum?'

'Yeah right, like he's going to offer an opinion! Anyway, enough of me, how's it going with your lady?'

'I'm not sure, really. It's odd, like I'm always about two steps ahead of her. It's good to be able to unload though. I go in once a week and everything just gushes out of me.'

'You covered anything about the past yet?'

'No. By the time I've told her everything that's gone on in the last seven days we've usually run out of time.'

'Has she got the history, though?' Something didn't feel right.

'No, she seems to be quite different to Phil. I've told her about Roger and a little bit about Mum, but she's more interested in the present. She said that's where we need to keep our focus.'

My doubts were increasing. 'How do you feel about that?' I swear I was sounding more like Phil as each day passed.

'Oh, I don't know, Deb. In a way it's a relief, but I know that nearly all of my problems are because of what went on back then. But whenever I bring any of it up it's like it overwhelms *her*. I start saying things to try and make her feel better. She actually *cries*, Deb.'

'That doesn't sound right, Jo. That's like the crap we did with Mum, trying to make *her* feel better.'

'I know. That's what I'm afraid of. I guess for now I'll keep going and see how it pans out. It's good just having someone to talk to, if nothing else.'

'Well, keep me posted.'

'You too. And good luck with Mum.'

I groaned and hung up the phone. Had I made a mistake? I didn't want to think about it anymore, it was all just too hard.

'Are psychologists very different to psychiatrists?' I asked Phil, still unsettled by my conversation with Jo.

'Why do you ask?'

'Because Jo has started seeing one in New Zealand.'

'How's it going for her?'

'Funny. Not anything like my sessions with you. She says she wants Jo to stay focussed on the present. That doesn't seem right to me.'

Phil sighed. 'I guess we all have our own methods. Different things work for different people.'

'I don't accept that,' I told him strongly. 'I've tried things that didn't have a hope of working. If I'd known better I wouldn't have gone near them.'

'But maybe they do work for some people,' he persisted.

I shook my head. 'I wish someone had referred me to a psychiatrist decades ago. It would have saved me *years*.'

Phil was dubious, 'But maybe you weren't ready for it decades ago.'

'Not good enough. That would only make sense if I had tried it and ditched it. I didn't know a thing about psychiatrists. I thought you lot just doped people up or had them committed. You ought to bloody advertise, or something.'

Phil laughed. 'Well, you're here now. And if this psychologist doesn't work out for Jo, maybe she'll move on. From what you've told me about her, she's pretty determined.'

I nodded, still not satisfied. 'You were my last shot, you know. I had nothing left to try.'

'That's what most of my patient's say. Psychiatrists are often the last resort.'

'Why is that?'

He shrugged. 'We've got some pretty bad publicity over the years. Some of it justified. Most people associate psychiatrists with mental institutions. That can be pretty scary.'

'I thought you'd commit me,' I admitted, remembering my initial terror.

'There you go. It's a common misconception. A patient has to be in very real danger of hurting him or herself before I'd step in like that.'

'But what about my sleeping pills? Were you worried then?'

'Of course I was.'

'Did you think about committing me?'

'No. I trusted your inner resources. You have a very strong survival instinct.'

'I'm terrified of mental hospitals,' I admitted, shuddering. 'Always have been.'

'They can be pretty scary places. I worked in one for two years.'

'Really? What was it like?' I couldn't imagine him in that role.

He shrugged. 'It had its good and its bad points.'

He wasn't going to say anything further on the topic. I rather begrudgingly let it go.

'Oh, by the way,' I said, suddenly remembering, 'I've decided that I'm not a lesbian.'

'Right,' he said slowly, 'so what happened there?'

'I read a thousand books, and talked to Sally for hours, trying to figure it all out. In the end I realised that I was searching for a new concept of women, something totally different to Mum. I needed to be around women who were proud of who they were. It hadn't been about sex at all. I think I'll stick to men. I'm not going to explore the possibility any further.'

'So you've stopped seeing Sally?'

I nodded. 'Yep. She was neat, though, and a real help. But I needed to stop seeing her, it was just adding to my confusion.'

'Fair enough,' he answered. 'I guess you can always change your mind.'

'I don't think so,' I said honestly. 'I like men. Despite everything.'

Phil smiled. 'It's a good place to start.'

I was back to visiting my mother on weekends and still gambling. It was driving me crazy. I wondered how come I was feeling so good in myself, for the first time ever, and yet continued with behaviour that was self-defeating? I wanted to get out of that habit. I wanted a life that was successful and something I could be proud of. Gambling made me feel like a failure. I was ashamed of myself for being so weak. But no matter how many promises I made, I still ended up sitting in front of the poker machine, pouring in my money like there was no tomorrow.

'Squirrel, do you ever gamble?'

'Yeah right, on the five bucks I have left over from my pension.'

'Ah.'

'Have you got a problem with it?'

'Yep. Pretty bad too.'

'Have you told Phil?'

'Not everything, I'm too ashamed to admit it.'

'Tell him, Trav.'

'Easily said, Squirrel.'

'Bullshit. Just tell him.'

'I'm telling *you*, madam!'

'I'm not a shrink, what do you think I'm going to say?'

'I don't know, what about, gee, that's awful.'

'Fuck off! Sympathy is the last thing you need. Don't you think we've both kept enough secrets for one lifetime?'

'I'm not keeping a secret.'

'Bullshit.'

'Gee, don't hold back there, Squirrel.'

'Get outta here, you knew what I was going to say.'

☺ 'Did I ever tell you that I'm glad I met you?'

☺ 'I hate to be the one that breaks this to you, Trav, but we haven't actually met.'

I laughed out loud. 'A reality check. I love it.'

'Sod off and go to bed, isn't it some ungodly hour over there?'

'Oh no, Squirrel is getting all maternal on me.'

I entered the session feeling distant and irritable.

As usual Phil sat there quietly. Waiting.

'I need you to clarify something for me,' I started.

'Go ahead.'

'Am I *meant* to feel close to you?'

He frowned. 'How do you mean?'

'You know what I mean,' I said, irritably. 'That wasn't a complex question. Am I meant to feel close to you? Is that normal?'

Phil just looked back at me, saying nothing.

A familiar anger swept through me. 'Is it against the rules to answer that question?' I snapped.

He shook his head back and forth slowly, still saying nothing.

'Oh, fuck you. Can't you for once answer something without making a big deal out of it?'

'I think I answer quite a few of your questions, at least those that I can. But I'm wondering where all this anger is coming from.'

I huffed. 'I hate this relationship shit! It's too hard to work out.'

'That's pretty predictable, given your history.'

'Oh fuck my history,' I snapped. 'I'm talking about *now*, with *you*.'

'Yes?' he asked slowly.

'Is this relationship just about me?' I continued, still struggling for the words.

'Not that I'm aware of. There are two of us here.'

I shook my head with irritation. 'I know that! But you don't want or need anything from me, do you?'

'That's right,' he nodded. 'And I imagine you find that very difficult to believe.'

'It's not about whether I believe it or not. I can't stand it! It makes it such a one-sided affair.'

Phil was looking at me intently. 'So what do you want?'

What the fuck *did* I want? I know I wanted something badly, but couldn't for the life of me work out what it was.

'Maybe you need me to treat you like a thing, like a sexual object? Would that feel more familiar? Why don't you offer me what you've got?'

I glared at him. 'Oh fuck off with that shit again.'

He laughed. 'Why? Obviously you're telling me that you need to be used to feel like you have any value in this relationship. So what's on offer, give me your best shot.'

'I haven't said that at all!'

'That's exactly what you're saying. You asked me don't I want or need anything from you? It's making you angry that I don't. Maybe you don't even believe it? Are you still waiting for me to turn into a creep, like all those other men did?'

I was shaking my head in annoyance. 'This just isn't fair! All I've done is ask you a simple question and you're taking it to some place entirely different.'

'Okay,' he said gently, 'maybe you're right. Let's start all over again and you tell me what it is you want to know.'

I groaned. 'What I have been trying to say,' I said slowly, still thoroughly annoyed with him, 'is that this relationship feels like a one-way street. That I'm the one coming here with a million needs, riddled with dependency, while you just sit there comfortably, totally uninvolved.'

'Ouch,' he said quietly.

I suddenly felt awful and raced in to try and make it sound better. 'I don't mean that, obviously you're involved, it's just …' I was way out of my depth and gave up in total frustration.

'Don't give up,' he encouraged. 'This is important, and I do realise that it's not easy for you. Just keep trying, we'll get there eventually.'

I sighed. What the hell did I want to say? I searched my mind, looking for another tack. 'Okay,' I started, 'let's try this. I feel like you're giving everything and I'm the one doing the taking. It doesn't seem right.'

He was nodding slowly, waiting for me to elaborate. I struggled on, hoping that I would eventually hit upon the right words. 'I feel useless. Like I'm not doing my part.' In that instant I knew exactly what this was about. I groaned in dismay.

Phil waited quietly while I let it all sink in.

'You were dead right,' I admitted miserably. 'It's the sex crap again. I think that sex is all I've got to offer. You not wanting me in that way feels like a slap in the face.' I sank into despair. When would it ever fucking end!

Phil was watching me. I was back to feeling dirty again.

'This isn't your fault,' he said gently. 'This is what they did to you.'

'I know,' I moaned. 'But I thought I'd got past that shit with you. Here I am wanting to fucking service you so that I feel I'm doing my part.'

He smiled. 'This will change, you just need to be patient.'

I shook my head. 'I'm too fucking damaged. You really ought to give up.'

'Never. You're worth way more than that.'

'But don't you get pissed off with me? How long is it going to be before you tell me that you can't work with me anymore?'

'You haven't even come close to that.'

I shook my head in denial. 'But what if I do? There must come a time when you eventually give up.'

'Look,' he explained, 'there are some patients who are very emotionally draining. But you're not like that. We're a long, long way from that point, believe me. I doubt in fact that it will ever even happen. We'll see this through to the end, I promise you.'

I drove the long way home. I needed time to think. It was true. I couldn't place Phil anywhere because there was no sex involved. A relationship without sex made me feel inadequate, but even worse than that, I felt as though I was completely powerless, with nothing to fall back on. I kept picturing him with his wife, seeing them both cuddled up on a couch together. He was obviously close to her. I couldn't stand the thought of them, but I couldn't get the picture out of my mind. How could I keep him interested if I couldn't use my body to hook him in, if all my clever tricks were useless? Why would he continue seeing me? How could I ever get really close to him if there was no touch involved? I suddenly thought of Roger and all those other paedophiles. Fuck, I had let them off lightly.

As soon as I got home I rang Jo and filled her in on the session.

'You know what's really awful though,' I continued, 'I can suddenly understand what all my other relationships were about.

I offered my body to anyone and everyone. It was the only way that I felt useful. There was never anything else, Jo. No closeness, no intimacy, it's just too scary to think about. What on earth *were* those relationships?'

'I don't think I'm quite the right person to ask, Deb,' she said sadly. 'I'm the one still sleeping in the spare room, remember?'

My anger flared again. 'You know what we ought to do, Jo? We should find Roger and kill him.'

'Nice thought. I don't know how we'd ever find him though. And would he still be alive?'

'Well, he was twenty-eight in the nineteen-sixties. What would that make him now? Late fifties, or sixty? He could easily still be alive.'

'And probably still fucking up some child's life,' Jo added.

'I don't know where we'd start. Is he even still in England?' I sighed. 'Maybe for now I'll just enjoy the thought of cutting him into a million pieces.'

'Don't forget the others, Deb. That's a lot of hacking up to do.'

When Ty had gone to bed, I went on-line to visit Squirrel. I entered the chat room but couldn't see her name on the list. It took a few moments for it to dawn on me that this was her day for therapy. There was nobody else in the room that I felt like talking to so I decided to flip through the notice boards instead. I entered the section on therapists and started to read through the discussions.

My eye was caught by a question headed: Relationships with Therapists. I couldn't believe what I was reading. The writer was asking for advice on a development that had started six months into her therapy. Her therapist had told her that he was growing very close to her and wanted to bring touch into their relationship. At first she had been wary, herself a survivor of sexual abuse, but soon she got to enjoy his hugs. He told her that she was a very special patient and that he felt there was a 'spiritual connection' between the two of them. Soon the hugs turned into passionate embraces and her therapist was suggesting 'outside' meetings. The writer wanted to know was this common for others in therapy?

I was mesmerised. I hastily read through the responses. Ninety per cent of the women writing back advised her to get the hell out of therapy and find herself a decent psychiatrist. Some suggested she sue him, while others proposed a more gentle approach. Despite my shock, I felt incredibly envious. I wondered what she had that I didn't have. How had she managed to get so close to her therapist where I had failed? Was there a 'special' patient for Phil too? I imagined him passionately embracing her and wanting to sleep with her. I felt green with envy.

My mind wouldn't let go of the picture. I was conflicted all over again. On one hand I *knew* that Phil was trying to offer me something different, something better. But I couldn't help wondering if that was because he simply didn't fancy me. Maybe if I were younger or more attractive it would be altogether different. I re-read the letter over and over again, each time imagining that it was Phil and me. I almost felt ill with confusion. I finally managed to tear myself away from the site and go looking for Squirrel.

'How are you?' she typed.

'What's wrong?'

'Oh Squirrel, I've just been reading the notice boards, and now I'm totally confused again.'

'Why do you go there, I told you they can be full of shit.'

'I know, I just popped in while I was waiting for you to come back.'

'So what happened?'

'A woman has become involved with her therapist.'

'And?'

'And,' I typed furiously, 'I wish it was *me*.'

'No you don't, Trav.'

'Yes I do. I'm green with envy.'

'Envious of some fucked-up psychiatrist who can't control his dick?'

I had to laugh. 'Well, now you put it that way . . .'

'Well, really, what other way is there to see it?'

I sighed, and then remembered she was waiting for an answer. 'Don't you ever dream about become involved with Anthony?'

'Of course I do, and then I wake up.'

'Okay, you're right, I'll let it go. How was your session today?'

'Don't change the subject. Tell me what came up for you?'

'I felt that she must be better than me if she managed to hook her therapist in.'

'Jesus, Trav, how great an accomplishment is it to give a man a hard-on? Do you really think that's some sort of an achievement?'

God, I guess I did.

'Trav? Would you mind if I offered you an alternative view of the situation?'

'Shoot.'

'Try to imagine how hard it was for that woman to find the courage to seek out a psychiatrist. Then recall what those first six months were like: the confusion, fear and doubts, the first glimmer of hope. Now picture that psychiatrist becoming exactly like every man that's ever come near her, thinking only of his wants and his needs. How's that for a new perspective?'

I read her words slowly, letting them sink in. 'You're right, I know.'

'Doesn't it give you a greater appreciation for Phil?'

'I know, he's a good man.'

'So don't fuck it up, madam.'

I had to laugh. 'I love your bedside manner.'

☺ 'I never said I'd be sweet. So tell me what's been going on, has something happened with Phil to bring all this about?'

'Oh Squirrel, it's the sex crap. Doesn't it ever turn up in your sessions?'

'Do you mean like suddenly wanting to unzip him and give him a blowjob?'

I nearly fell out of my chair. 'You have that with Anthony?'

'All the time.'

'What does he say?'

'Yeah right, like I tell him.'

I laughed. 'We're useless, Squirrel.'

'Speak for yourself. It's only been the last six months that I've admitted it to myself. Telling Anthony? That should take me at least five more years.'

'I can't wait till it passes. It's driving me crazy.'

'Do you tell Phil about it?'

'Not all the gory details. Just the fact that I can't imagine getting close to him without sex being involved in some way.'

'You actually *say* that?'

'Yep.'

'Well, aren't you coming along in leaps and bounds?'

'I told you, I'm going to get all fixed up then I'm going to start some sort of a life.'

☹ 'This *is* my life.'

'Things change, Squirrel. Anything can happen.'

'I don't want them to change, though.'

I didn't know how to respond to that so I quickly changed the topic. We talked away into the night, alone in our rooms with the company of computers.

I decided to be honest with Phil and tell him what had happened.

'So the therapist developed an intimate relationship with his patient?' he asked.

I nodded. 'It sent me into a sea of confusion again.'

'About what?'

I squirmed. 'I felt that she had succeeded where I had failed. But,' I added quickly, before he leapt in, 'I did eventually change my mind.'

'Well, that's certainly encouraging.'

I smiled. 'It was just a short detour into doubt again.'

'I did have some qualms about you visiting that site.'

'I know. I can get thrown pretty easily.'

'It's not just that, I wonder how healthy some of those people are. And what good it might be doing you.'

'A lot of them are just like me.'

'But are they?'

I recalled some of the conversations about cutting, and drugs. But it wasn't like that with Squirrel. 'I'll be a bit more selective next time. I think I learnt my lesson.'

Phil said nothing.

'Are we close?' I asked him, suddenly.

He nodded slowly. 'I think so.'

'Could we be closer?'

He smiled and nodded again.

'Am I getting in the way of that?'

'In a way, yes.'

'What do I do that stops us being really close?'

He thought for a moment. 'I guess your spaciness is the main way that you keep a distance, and we're working on that. Another method is not telling me the truth or keeping things from me.'

'Sometimes it's hard to know what to tell you and what to keep to myself.'

'I know. It's a learning process. But just having this conversation is a good sign. I wish we could somehow take a hold of this part of you and give her some more substance.'

I sighed. 'I know, it's like for brief moments in time I can see things quite clearly, there's no interference or competing thoughts. I like this feeling.'

He smiled gently. 'Gradually there'll be more of it. We'll just keep on with what we're doing.'

'Something else I'd like to know,' I continued, 'what *is* this spaciness?'

'Hmmm. That's a more difficult question. It's very common for children who have been sexually abused. The mind is faced with too many conflicting things. It's certainly a result of trauma.'

'Yes but what is it?'

'I think it's a coping mechanism for the mind. It creates another room, as it were, where it can escape the trauma.'

'Does everyone call it spaciness, or do they have other words for it?'

'Each person uses their own word, but the sensation is generally the same. They feel cut-off and detached from everything around them.'

'And eventually I'll lose that?' I asked, not able to even imagine what that would be like.

'I think so. The more honest you're able to be with who you are, the less likely you'll need to escape into that space.'

I sighed. 'That's a nice thought.'

'You're beginning to see how much damage sexual abuse actually causes.'

I shook my head. 'It's so far reaching. Do you know, one counsellor told me that all I needed to do was accept that the abuse had been a pleasant experience? She believed that guilt was the only factor that stopped survivors from getting on with their lives.'

'Frightening, isn't it?' he agreed. 'Another common theory is the idea that you should just "get over it". As if you could. You look at how much that abuse has infiltrated into virtually every area of your life.'

'I know. I always thought that I was managing to keep it in the background somewhere.'

'Not possible, is it?' he asked gently.

'Nope. Not even remotely.'

We sat there quietly for a few moments when another thought occurred to me, 'One more question. If you're doing the job that a parent would have done, does that mean when I'm fixed up that I'll be a bit like you?'

He smiled. 'In a way, yes.'

'So, if I got together with a number of the women who had been treated by you, would we see some similarities?'

'I guess you would.'

I laughed. 'That's weird. So we'd be like siblings in a way, with you being the common father?'

'In a strange sort of way, I guess so.'

For some reason, the idea delighted me.

Chapter Eighteen

Twelve months had passed since I had started therapy. My moods had finally stabilised. And the internal racket of conflicting voices was slowly quietening down. It was an extraordinary feeling to wake up and be the same person I had been the previous day. I began to think that maybe I could make some plans. I knew it was imperative to get some distance between my mother and me. Even if it just meant moving closer to the city. Ty had started university and was making noises about finding a place to live with his girlfriend. He was eighteen now and itching for some independence. I knew it was only a matter of time before he moved out. I would need to do something; our house was much too big for one person to live in. I started to check the accommodation columns.

More pressing, however, was my relationship with Mum. We'd had a row on my last weekend visit. Unable to keep quiet about it any longer, I had broached the topic of her choice in friends.

'He's a paedophile, Mum, for God's sake!' I'd said. 'How can you even let him in your home, yet alone be friends with him?'

She smiled. 'Look darling, I don't believe it's my job to judge him. He's had a hard time. And he's done his two years in jail. Doesn't that earn him the right to another chance?'

'But he's the third one you've met in the last three years. This house is crawling with the creeps. Why is that?'

It was bizarre. I had just spent half an hour in the garden while she struggled to entertain an alcoholic who had been slumped on the couch, too drunk to even make conversation. She had made him coffee and tried to fill the awkward silences. I had watched in disgust till I couldn't stand it any longer. When he did finally leave, the telephone rang and from the look on Mum's face, I knew who was on the other end; a paedophile friend only recently out of jail. I had rolled my eyes and headed into the garden. I sat there feeling a mixture of confusion and despair. My mother had read every personal-growth book ever written. She was an expert on the subject. Yet she never asked herself the important questions. Added to this knowledge was her relationship with God. He was, she told me, her closest friend. He took care of everything. We'd had numerous heated discussions about responsibility. Mum believed that whatever happened in her life was 'meant' to happen. If she gambled her money away, that had been what God had wanted. If drunks took advantage of her hospitality, then so be it. It was all a part of God's plan. It made me want to scream.

'But where does *your* responsibility come into it?' I would ask, wriggling with frustration.

'My choices are God's choices, dear.'

'So He chooses your friends, does He? He wants you to be surrounded by drunks and paedophiles?'

She smiled. 'Obviously He does, or it wouldn't happen, would it?'

'Haven't you ever wondered why paedophiles play such a big role in your life? They've been in your home ever since I can remember.'

She shrugged. 'It's only a big deal to you, dear. I don't see what all the fuss is about.'

'I know you've told me that there was no sexual abuse in your childhood, Mum, but don't you think it might be a vague possibility?'

'We've been over that, dear. I don't have a recollection of anything like that.'

'But it would make sense, wouldn't it? It would explain why you've had so many paedophiles in your world.'

She shook her head. 'I don't think so, darling.'

I was writhing in frustration, and aware that my mother was tiring of the conversation. But I wouldn't let it go. 'Mum,' I started quietly, 'do you realise that when Ty has children, I'll be warning him to never bring them to your house, or leave them with you for the weekend? Doesn't that tell you something?'

She shook her head. 'I know they'd be perfectly safe with me, dear. But I can't stop you doing whatever you're going to do.'

'How could they be safe with you, Mum? You've got paedophiles crawling through every crack in this house.'

'That's a little exaggeration, I think.'

I took a deep breath, trying to calm myself down. 'So, it's not wrong, Mum, that men sexually interfere with children?'

'Of course they shouldn't, dear.'

'But you're happy to be friends with them?'

'They haven't harmed me in any way. So why should I judge them?'

I looked her straight in the eye, searching for something, *anything*. She stared right back at me, a trace of amusement in her eyes. I felt a shudder run through me. 'You're actually enjoying this, aren't you?' I asked her slowly.

She smiled. 'Enjoying what, dear?'

The hairs on the back of my neck were standing up. 'You *know* what I'm talking about, what I'm trying to get from you, and there's just no way that you're going to give it, is there?'

She laughed, getting up and heading for the kitchen. 'I'm going to make a cup of tea, darling, would you like one?'

'No,' I answered quietly, 'I think I'll go for a walk.'

'What's wrong with my mum?' I asked Phil.

He shrugged. 'What do you think it is?'

'Sometimes I'd like to think she was just insane. That would make sense of everything. But she's not crazy. It's something else, I just can't put my finger on it.'

'It seems very important for you to understand your relationship with her.'

'It is. It drives me crazy. Like I try so hard and always end up giving in.'

'What are you trying to achieve with her?'

'I want to understand. There's so much missing information. Like how could she leave two of her children and never have contact with them again? Not even to write to them. She hasn't spoken to Jo for three years and she's not remotely bothered by it. I sometimes get the awful feeling that I could vanish out of her life and she wouldn't give it a second thought. We're all so disposable.' I shuddered, reliving the cold, blank expression in her eyes.

'But she was all you had. The thought of losing her would have been terrifying for you.'

I nodded. 'But I wouldn't be losing anything, would I? She doesn't care, does she?'

Phil took a slow, deep breath. 'In her own strange way, she loves you.'

'That's what she says, but she doesn't *feel* anything towards us. When I'm with her now I compare it to what it's like being with you. That's pretty scary, you know.'

'How so?' he asked, leaning forward.

'Well, it's like I'm not really there, like I don't exist for her. She has a picture in her head about who I am and she talks to that. It's like a play, or something. When I say something to you, you not only hear it, but you then respond in a way that actually makes sense. It's not like that with Mum though. I tell her something and it's weird, as though she takes it, distorts it horribly, and hands back something that isn't even recognisable. It's scary.'

'That would explain your spacing out, wouldn't it?'

His words struck a chord. 'I hadn't thought of that. But that's exactly what happens. Whenever I visit her it only takes about an hour and I start disappearing into that weird space again.' An awful thought occurred to me.

'Oh Christ. Is that because she sees me as a thing, not a real person?'

Phil stayed quiet. I felt the hairs on my neck stand up again.

'She doesn't see anyone as real, does she?' I asked quietly. 'That's why she could leave Mark and Cheryl behind and never make contact again. That's why the paedophile subject makes no sense to her.' The horror of it was dawning on me slowly. 'We were her precious "things". She was so keen to show us off to her visitors.'

Phil remained quiet, letting me place the jigsaw pieces together by myself. It was too, too awful. 'And I've been trying so bloody hard to get close to her. There's nothing to get close to, is there?' I asked in disbelief.

'You were a little girl with no one else. If you lost her there would have been nothing.'

I shook my head. 'But there *was* nothing. I've been pretending all these years that we actually had a relationship. It's bullshit. And there's something even worse,' I added, remembering the amused look in my mother's eyes. 'I think Mum *does* know what's right and wrong; she's known all along. That's why she gets that funny look on her face whenever I bring the sexual abuse up.'

'What funny look?'

I shuddered. 'It's like she's challenging me, and enjoying the fact that I squirm around in frustration. She knows I'm not going to point out the obvious to her.'

'And what would that be?'

I grimaced. Was it true? I still didn't want to believe it. I looked at Phil, wishing he could make it something else. 'There's something very wrong with my mother, isn't there?'

'In what way?'

'I'm not entirely sure, yet. But it feels almost ... evil.' I said the last word quietly, not even wanting to hear it.

Phil just nodded.

'I thought all this time that maybe she simply didn't understand me, you know? But this is far worse. Surely my mother hasn't known all along, hasn't sat there listening to me, seeing me struggling and desperate for an explanation, and she's actually *enjoyed* it?' It was too awful to comprehend.

I was stunned. All those weekends at her place, the constant phone calls and hours of conversation. What if I had done nothing? Said nothing? Would we still have a 'relationship'? Or would I be discarded too? I knew in that instant that I had to test it out.

The following day I was sitting in her lounge room again. She had been thrilled to see me, as usual. 'It's so *boring* around here without you, dear. I don't know what I'd do without your visits.'

I was once again taken aback. She did look pleased to see me. And she'd prepared my favourite meal. I prattled away about my week, about all the new things I was learning with Phil. She listened raptly.

Of course we're close, I told myself again. Obviously I hadn't told Phil enough. I decided I'd need to cover it in more detail during our next session. The weekend had been fun, despite the fact that I spaced out within an hour.

'I've written a letter to Mum, Deb.'

I was shocked; Jo hadn't made contact with her for years. 'What for?'

'I'm not too sure, it's a lot of things really. I realised that up until now, you're the one who's had to confront her with every-thing, and I've never said a word. I decided that it was about time she heard my side of the story. Do you want me to read it to you?'

I was fascinated. 'Sure. Go ahead.'

Jo cleared her throat. 'Mum, I've been listening to everything that Deb has been going through lately, all her sessions with a psychiatrist and her attempts to get things through to you. I figure it's time I told you what being your daughter was like for me. I have never said a word; I've been too scared of you. On those few times I did try to tell you what was happening, when I was only about nine years old, you glared at me like it was me who had committed the crime. You didn't want to know. And you still choose paedophiles over the company of Deb. How can you do that? Over seven men molested me, Mum. Some of it took place while you were at home. Most of it was from your pathetic boy-friends. I kept so many of your dirty secrets, knowing that you were seeing other men when we were with Dad, and Roger. You knew I knew, making me promise never to tell. And I didn't. I just carried the secrets around for you, feeling that it was me who was doing something wrong. You knew I hated it. That's why we could never be alone together without the air getting thick with tension. I stopped calling you three years ago to see what would happen. I should have known. You couldn't have cared less. I have children, you know. Your grandchildren. You know nothing about them and are probably disinterested anyway. I'm working my way through all this muck, as Deb is, and I want you to know that we'll be fine without you. We always have been. Jo.'

'Whew!' I didn't know what to say.

'What do you think?'

'Gosh, I don't know. How did you feel after writing it?'

'I was shaking. I guess it brought everything up again for me.'

'Hey Jo, do you remember how old you were when it started with Roger?'

'I think it was in Southampton, that would have made me about ten.'

'But why did he wait till then? Why didn't he start when we were living in Ireland?'

'Because Mum was around, remember? And we were all in the one room.'

'Stuff went on with me in Ireland.'

'Like what?'

'When Roger was washing me. He put things inside me.'

'Really?' Jo asked, sounding horrified. 'What sort of things?'

'I can't remember, something metal, though.'

'Jesus, no, he didn't do that with me. What a sick prick.'

'I can't get the times right, though, they all seem mixed up. Was Frank the first time we were in Ireland, or the second?' I asked.

'Both, I think. I'm not quite sure.'

'And what about Ray and Terry?'

'That was in England, during the day, while Mum and Roger were at work,' Jo replied.

'After school?'

'Yep. They'd send you and Kim out to play while they molested me, then they'd call you in.'

I remembered one of those days. 'It was like you and I both knew what was going to happen.'

'I know. And I couldn't do anything to stop it,' said Jo.

'You tried though, once, didn't you? I seem to remember something about you yelling at the front door.'

'Yep, I called out for help, but Terry told me to shut the hell up or else. I just had to stand outside and wait till he was done.'

I could hear the guilt in her voice. 'Hey Jo, what else could you have done? It's not like Mum would have come running.'

'That's for sure.'

I thought of Jo's letter. 'Jo? Are you hoping for some kind of response from Mum?'

'I know she probably won't write anything back. But maybe it will make her think.'

I sighed. 'I've got an awful feeling it will just go over her head.'

'I'll post it straight after talking to you, Deb. Otherwise I'll change my mind, I know it.'

'Are you nervous?'

'I feel a bit sick, actually. Do you think I should send it?'

My heart went out to her. 'I think you've got a right to tell your truth, Jo. Who cares what happens afterwards? It's not like you've got much to lose.'

She laughed. 'That's right, it's hardly going to spoil a perfectly good relationship.'

I sighed. 'Bloody sad, isn't it?'

'Yep. But I'll hang up now and go post it. Let me know what happens, okay?'

I agreed to call her, but knew deep down in my heart that the only response she would receive would be the familiar racket of Mum's deadly silence.

'What do you think Jo is hoping for?' Phil asked.

I shook my head. 'The same bloody thing that I've kept trying to get from Mum; some sort of response. She knows it's not going to happen though.'

'No, but Jo had a right to tell her side of the story.'

'I know,' I said, still feeling confused, 'I just imagine Mum receiving it and thinking she has another daughter dumping on her.'

'Maybe it's time your mother heard all of the truth.'

I was shaking my head. 'I know. Mum's never heard a word about what happened to Jo. But why do I feel so sorry for her now?'

'In your own way you've always been protective towards her. That's how you're able to still be in her company. You've made a silent agreement with her to treat it the same way she does.'

'There's no other way,' I answered irritably, 'can't Jo see that?'

'You don't sound like you have much compassion for your sister?'

'Of course I do! But I feel torn.'

'So what are you going to do if your mother brings it up?'

'I don't know. The letter's pretty harsh, you know.'

'Your childhood was pretty harsh. There's nothing in there that isn't the truth, is there? You're still trying to protect her, as if she was the child and you were the mother.'

'She *is* a bloody child.'

Phil leant forward. 'No, she is not. She may act like a child, but your mother is an adult. It's about time you realised that. You've been mothering her for most of your life.'

It only took five days for the letter to reach my mother's house. I had spent that time nervously pondering her response. I was so accustomed to being the only daughter who gave Mum a hard time. It felt strange to have Jo enter the fray. I continued to feel sorry for Mum, and then felt guilty as hell, knowing how hard it had been for Jo to write that letter. When Mum finally broached the subject, I was awash with conflicting emotions.

'Did you know Jo had written to me, dear?' Mum had phoned me immediately.

'Yes, Mum, she read it out to me.'

'Well, I can't say it was very nice. Quite unnecessary, I think. I just put it straight into the bin. Anyway darling, how was your weekend?' So that was that. I continued on with the conversation but felt awful for Jo. What could I tell her?

I dialled the New Zealand number feeling a million years old.

'Hey Jo.'

'Hey you. Did she receive it?'

'Yep.'

'And?'

I sighed. 'She threw it in the bin.'

'What did she say?'

I could feel the hope in Jo's voice. In that instant I hated Mum with all my heart. 'She just asked me had I known you'd written it and I told her that you'd read it out to me on the phone. Then she said it wasn't very nice.'

'Wasn't very nice?' Jo repeated. 'Is that all?'

'And that it was unnecessary. I'm sorry, Jo,' I said, feeling awful. 'But the most important thing is that you wrote it. That was a huge shift for you.'

'I know, I know. I guess I was expecting something after all. Was she angry?'

'More like self-righteous.'

Jo sighed.

'Bit disappointed, Jo?'

'Just deflated.'

'I don't blame you. That's how I always feel after talking to her.'

'I think I'll hang up and get back to you later, Deb. I need to take it all in.'

She sounded miserable. 'Well, don't take too long. Ring me soon, okay?'

'You seem a bit down,' Phil observed.

'I guess I am. It's all this family crap. I just don't get it.'

'What part are you having difficulty with?'

'I keep thinking that we ought to all just forgive each other. There's so much anger and resentment between us, so many unsaid things. Why can't we just agree to let it go?'

'It's pretty difficult to make peace with something if it's kept hidden, or if some of the family members still choose to deny it.'

'So is denial the thing that's causing most of the trouble?'

'I think so. Obviously there's a lot of pain as well. You girls suffered a great deal. But you're unlikely to ever feel validated by your mother if the sexual abuse remains an unspoken topic.'

I sighed. 'I get so confused. Sometimes I think I'm so much like Mum. We can go out and have a ball together. We see things the same way, you know?'

'How's that?'

'Well, there's ...' My mind suddenly went blank. 'Hang on, I'll get to it.'

'I'll be interested to hear this.'

I thought of how my mother treated her boyfriends, as if they were the scum of the earth; I certainly wasn't like that. And her views on God and responsibility; we couldn't even *talk* about that.

Phil was waiting patiently.

'I've just gone blank for now, but I'll think of something eventually. We're a lot alike, Mum and I, otherwise why would we get on?'

Much to my annoyance, he simply shrugged.

I sighed. 'You know what is good, though?' I started, wanting to change the subject. 'I don't feel so fractured these days. It's like I wake up now and am the same person as I was the day before. Those parts don't seem to be active.'

'What do you put that down to?'

I shook my head. 'I've been in therapy for over a year and maybe they've said all they need to say. Or maybe they've finally left.' Now there was a lovely thought.

'It's possible.'

'Well that certainly sounds convincing.'

He smiled. 'It's you who needs to be convinced, not me.'

'Well at least I'm not sitting here with a dozen conflicting desires going on in the background. It's a lot more peaceful.'

'That's good. It shows we're making progress.'

I nodded, but I was aware that he was holding back.

It must have been the season for writing. I drafted a letter to my dad, deciding to tell him the truth about the years that followed my mother's departure. It was a tough letter to write. I would find myself minimising the sexual abuse and the violence, eager to reassure him. But each time I did so I thought of Phil's words. Was I doing the same as my mother, sweetening it all up and putting a nice face on it? I would tear up the paper and start again. In the end I simply told the truth. I ended the letter with a request that he write back to me if he felt able. I wanted to set up some form of communication with him.

I had his response in my hand as I entered my session with Phil.

'I need you to read this,' I said, handing it over.

'What is it?'

'It's from my dad.'

Phil nodded and started to read through it. I think I knew all of it off by heart, I had read it that many times. My father had written that it filled him with sadness to hear what had happened to his daughters. He had asked where the blame should lay. For many paragraphs he spoke of the trouble he had gone through when Mum was in his life, how she had never been responsible, and had left him in a sea of debt. He ended by telling me that he had always loved me and we would forever be his precious little girls.

'Hmmm, how did you feel when you read it?' Phil asked, handing me back the pages.

I shook my head. 'I think I'd like you to keep it.'

He frowned. 'Why?'

'I'm not sure. I was in bed last night thinking about it. It's odd really, but when I look back at the last twelve months with you, everything we've been through and how you've been there for me, then I read this letter from my so-called father, it's like I see a gap. A gap between what *was* and what should have been.'

'That's very perceptive of you.'

'I know he's trying his best, and at least he wrote back, which is more than Mum would have done. It's just all this talk about love, it's so bloody empty.'

'Go on.'

'Well, if you ask Mum or Dad, both of them wax lyrical about their precious little princesses, how much they adored us. We were loved so *much*.' I could feel a familiar anger rising. 'Yet somehow seven men were able to molest two of these supposedly adored princesses. And how come Dad gave up looking after three months? He could have found us, even if it was to send a fucking birthday card! But he let the three of us go, the same way Mum was able to forget Mark and Cheryl. Where's the fucking love in that! It would break my *heart* to lose Ty. I'd spend every bloody waking moment searching for him. I would never give up. Even if it took my whole life, I'd find him!' I had started to cry, overwhelmed with the injustice of it all.

Phil waited for me to let it all out. 'It's tragic, what happened to your family.'

I nodded, still hurting. 'Were we that easy to let go of?' I asked.

Phil shook his head, his eyes filled with sadness. 'This was never about you. It was about your parents. Try to see that.'

I felt weighted down with sorrow.

'Will you write back to your father?'

I sighed. 'I don't think so. I guess he and Mum will live their fantasies forever, who am I to change them?'

'Take your time with this; it's a lot to take in.'

I looked up at him, seeing his tenderness and encouragement. 'I don't think I could do it without you.'

He smiled. 'See it as a joint effort.'

After a couple of weeks had passed, I wrote a letter to my father thanking him for taking the time to respond. I wished him all the best. I couldn't think of anything else to add.

Chapter Nineteen

Ty had found a flat and was due to move out in a fortnight. I helped him pack but could only just look on as my young man took his first steps out of my life. He and his girlfriend went shopping for dinner sets and bedding, lounge suites and tea towels, coming home weighted down with packages and bristling with excitement. I was so proud of him as he dealt with each hurdle, learning the basics of bonds, rent, electricity and leases. He took it all in his stride, enjoying the learning curve and not wanting or needing too much of my assistance. He was growing up quickly.

I went on-line with a heavy heart.

'Squirrel, I need to tell you something.'

'Fire away.'

'Ty has found somewhere to live.'

☹ 'That must be hard for you.'

'It's not just that, Squirrel,' I typed, feeling overwhelmed with sadness. 'This is his computer.'

The screen remained still.

'Squirrel?'

The message came up that Squirrel had exited the chat room. I waited for over an hour. But she didn't come back.

The following morning I tried again.

'Squirrel? Talk to me?'

☹

'I'm so sorry, Squirrel.'

'Go out and buy yourself a new computer, or a second-hand one.'

'I would if I could, Squirrel. But you know I'm broke.'

'So visit your local library, use their computers.'

'I'll try, I promise, but you know we have a shocking time difference. And the library only lets you go on-line for one hour at a time.'

'Don't want to lose you.'

'Ditto.'

'You're my best friend.'

I felt like my heart was breaking. 'Give me your address, for God's sake, at least I can write to you.'

We exchanged addresses, but knew it could never be the same. We had been in each other's private worlds for months.

'I'm going to miss you so much, Squirrel.'

'Don't want you to leave!'

My eyes were streaming. 'Say goodbye, Squirrel. Please?'

'You take care, girl, and tell Phil that he better be good to you.'

'I will. And you be gentle on yourself, madam. Thank you for everything.'

'Bye.'

'Bye.'

I exited the chat room for the last time, feeling I had lost a precious friend. But another parting was looming large. Ty had organised a trailer and a couple of his friends to help cart his belongings away. I watched them load up his electric guitar and amplifier, his wrestling figures and computer, and saw his and my years together, piled into a trailer. I helped where I could, but knew that Ty wanted to do this on his own. It was important for him that his girlfriend saw him in charge. The last few things were loaded and it was time to say goodbye. He looked at me awkwardly. 'Well, I think that's everything.'

I smiled. 'You've done a good job, Ty.'

He walked over and gave me a hug. 'I'll call you tonight, Mum.'

'You do that, gorgeous.'

I watched him drive away then I walked into his empty bedroom. He was gone. My son had actually left home.

I stood there for a long time, noticing that he had left some of his drawings on the wall. He was such a creative lad, always had been. I remembered his ability to draw in three dimensions when he was only six or seven. Now he was in university, making his way through a difficult four-year course in software engineering. I was so incredibly proud of him.

I eventually closed the door to his room and walked around the quiet, empty house. However would I get used to him not being there? Who was there to cook for? Or shop for? He would no longer come flying through the door, desperate for a pee and something to eat. I sat down in the lounge room and tried to let it sink in. For eighteen years my world had revolved around him. I had adored being his mother, despite the terror of getting it wrong, despite the doubts and the uncertainties; it had been a delight and honour to raise him. So who was I now?

He rang me as soon as he had settled in. I knew he was concerned about me and I didn't want him to worry, he had enough on his plate already. So I stuck to my decision about moving and renewed my efforts to find new accommodation.

Over the next two weeks, I visited three libraries, and for one reason or another found it impossible to gain access to the chat room. Some days I sat in front of their computers, desperately wanting to talk to Squirrel, and feeling as though she was only inches away from me. But no matter how many times I tried, the same frustrating 'disconnected' message followed each of my attempts. I would leave the library heavy-hearted and hating the idea that Squirrel would be thinking I hadn't even bothered. Finally I asked Ty to send her a farewell email.

'How's it going without Ty?'

I shook my head. 'Odd. I rattle around that house, trying to make myself feel useful. I hadn't realised how strong that structure had been. Now I eat when I feel like it and try to keep myself occupied.'

'It will take some time to get accustomed to, I imagine.'

'That's for sure. Other than that, I'm feeling good. Solid. It's quite a novel feeling. I'm even excited about finding a new place to live. I'm playing around with the idea of going back to university. It's about time I got involved in the world again.'

Phil just listened while I explored my options.

'You seem very grounded, that must feel good.'

I nodded, smiling. 'It's magic. I can't remember when I last spun out, it was that long ago.'

'So what's planned for the weekend?'

'Heaps! Football, of course, and I'm going to get the paper first thing and see if there's anything interesting. I guess too that I'll need to start packing.'

'How do you feel about that?' he asked, fully aware of my history of moves.

'Okay I think. I'll take it slowly, just in case. You know what,'

I added, 'it's a nice change to be talking about the future and not wallowing in past muck. Maybe we're over the worst of it?'

'We've certainly covered a lot of ground together. And you've come a long way since our first meeting.'

I grimaced. 'God, I look back and don't even recognise that person now.'

'Do you remember it all?' he asked.

'Yep. She was so incredibly lost.' The memory brought tears to my eyes. I hadn't realised how far I had come since then.

'What would you say to her?'

I thought about that, picturing her sitting at the desk, answering Phil's questions and terrified of his response. I remembered her spaciness, floating in the ether with nothing to hold on to. 'I think I'd tell her,' I started, feeling a lump in my throat, 'to just hang in there, she's doing fine.'

I found an ideal flat just off The Parade in Norwood, only five minutes from the city. I so wished that Phil could see it. It was very small, only one-bedroom, but it had everything I needed and was in a wonderful location. I spent the next three weeks doing an enormous chuck-out. I got rid of everything that was old or broken and determined that this new life of mine was going to be different. I was single again. I had never really experienced being alone. I would make it fun.

Mum helped me move in. We filled the flat with all my lovely, clean, new things; I wouldn't let anything enter that wasn't fault-less. After hours of unpacking and organising the furniture so that it looked just right, Mum headed home and I sat on my new couch and surveyed the apartment. It was perfect! Not an ornament out of place. The walls had been freshly painted and were sparkling white. Everything smelled so new and fresh; so much so that I felt guilty lighting up my first cigarette. Suddenly I was imagining my lovely new home going brown and smelly with nicotine. Despite the fact that it was freezing cold outside, I opened the front door and all the windows, hoping the smoke would escape and leave the newness intact.

It was no good though. I could smell the nicotine.

I shouldn't smoke. A smoker doesn't belong in this pristine environment. I imagined Phil visiting and seeing his nose turn up. My spirits were deflating by the minute. I decided to go out and explore my new environment.

The Parade was only a five-minute walk from my flat. It was filled with restaurants, outdoor cafes, boutiques and exotic delicatessens. My spirits lifted immediately.

This is wonderful.

I vowed to come down at least once a week and treat myself to a cappuccino.

I spotted the neon lights of the pokies flashing ahead of me. I wandered inside just to take a look and was hit with the enticing aroma of freshly brewed coffee. I could see the poker machines in the back of the cafe.

I won't play. I'll have a hot drink and enjoy watching the passers-by.

I got back to my flat three hours later with eighty cents in my purse. I had gambled away my rent, food money and Phil's fee. I felt sick and ashamed of myself. On opening my front door I was hit by an icy draught. But at least it smelled clean.

Phil was pleased that I had moved and enjoyed listening to my stories about the new area and how much pleasure I was getting from living so close to the city. I didn't tell him about my gambling.

Or the fact that I seemed unable to stay in my flat for more than an hour or so before becoming restless. I'd eventually settle, I assured myself. And there were other things that I needed to clarify.

'What are relationships all about?' I asked him.

'Now there's a big question. Try and be a bit more specific for me.'

'I'll give it a shot, but I have so many questions. Okay, first thing; if my goal here is to finish therapy with you, and not need you anymore, why would I want to get involved with a man again?'

He thought for a moment. 'Well, you may not, for a while. But eventually you might find that you want someone to be close to, a man you can share your world with.'

'But why would someone want to live with me?' I asked, still not quite grasping it.

He smiled warmly. 'Why wouldn't someone want to get close to you? You're very likeable, you know.'

I frowned. 'I don't understand it.'

'I think maybe you're analysing this one too much. Who knows what it is about us that attracts someone? Take you and me. What's that all about?'

I looked up at him in surprise. 'What do you mean?'

'Well, I like you. Why is that?'

'You're paid to like me.'

He arched his eyebrows. 'I don't think so. I could have told you right from the start that I didn't want to work with you.'

I shook my head. 'But that would be ludicrous. You can't refuse to see someone just because they're weird. How many patients would that leave you with?'

He laughed. 'I'm not talking about weirdness, as you like to call it. Sometimes a person will come to see me and I'll know that I won't be able to work with them.'

'So you turn them away?' I asked, imagining how awful that would have been.

'I refer them to someone else.'

'And you like me?' I repeated, still unable to digest it. 'Why?'

He smiled. 'Who knows? Isn't it a whole mixture of things that contribute to why we may like a person or not? Maybe it can't be analysed.'

He liked me? How neat was that? I was going to take that home with me and cradle it for hours. 'But a relationship won't be anything like this, will it?' I asked, referring to him and me.

'Why can't it be?'

'Well,' I began, trying to make sense of my befuddled thoughts, 'when I next meet a man, he's not going to be like you, is he? He's going to have all sorts of wants and needs, and expectations?'

'Yes, like you will also. But I don't see any reason why it can't be like this for you.'

How wonderful would that be? Being able to feel this close to someone. Not being afraid of showing them who I was. Feeling safe, heard and cared for, now wouldn't that be a whole new experience? 'I think I'd like that.'

Phil smiled warmly. 'I think you deserve it.'

I let myself *hear* that for once, and actually believe it. 'This is such an odd relationship, isn't it?'

He nodded. 'You know that we will never be friends, though?'

It was an odd question and I was thrown.

'It's not like we can get together for a coffee,' he continued, 'or take the relationship outside of these four walls.'

I frowned, not understanding where he was coming from. 'Well … yes,' I stammered, 'I know that.' But I could feel a familiar sinking feeling inside. Wouldn't he want to be my friend? Was that what he was trying to make clear? Did he need to put me back in my place? I was, after all, just one of his loopy patients. Suddenly I was no longer basking in a warm glow.

'What's going on?' he asked softly.

I looked out the window, feeling annoyed with myself. 'Ah, it doesn't really matter, does it?'

'Yes, it does. I'd like to know.'

I was sinking fast. 'Those rules you've got,' I started bitterly, 'about no sex, no meeting outside the office, and now I hear, no friendships; that's not about protecting the patient at all, is it?'

'I believe it is.'

I shook my head, thoroughly disillusioned. 'It's because you psychiatrists want to keep well away from the patients. So you never get tarnished. The truth is that you'd have nothing to do with me on the outside, would you? I'm not like your *normal* friends, and you just want to make that clear to me.'

'I don't think you're being fair. It's not the way I see it at all.'

I didn't want to hear anymore. I was sure he would somehow find a way to put a nice spin on it, and I really wasn't interested. 'Don't worry about it,' I told him. 'I think I get the message loud and clear.'

Luckily the session had only five more minutes to run. I chose to leave early.

I couldn't shake off the bitterness. So was it all rubbish? Phil talking about us being close, and liking me, telling me that I would one day be all fixed up, was that just crap that they told all of their patients? The truth was that I would always be sullied in some way and people like Phil wouldn't want a bar of me. I felt totally betrayed. And a little ridiculous, too. All those times I had thought I was getting better, believing that I was in some sort of *normal* relationship with Phil. How stupid was I? He had his own normal wife and his own normal friends. I was a patient with a mental illness and that's what I'd always be to him. Well, fuck him, and fuck all those other normal pricks out there. I didn't need them.

Chapter Twenty

For the next two months I did everything I could to make my new flat work. But I knew something was wrong. I decided to enrol at university. I hoped that it would give me something positive to sink my teeth into and also get me out of the flat. Ty rang constantly, offering his encouragement and helping me wade through the mountain of university literature.

I signed up for classes that looked interesting and offered a challenge. I had always loved studying and regretted leaving school at fifteen. I kept Phil informed about my new classmates, the lecturers and the course content. However, I would arrive home and start pacing, no matter how tiring the day might have been. I felt flat, as if I was simply going through the motions. My sex drive was non-existent and I couldn't remember the last time I felt really excited about anything. Except this bloody flat.

Things got worse. I found it almost impossible to feel comfortable in my own home. Within an hour of waking I was pacing, picking up stray hairs from the carpet, making sure there were no dirty dishes or stains on the kitchen bench. I still felt guilty smoking and was perpetually cold with the windows wide open.

The pokies opened at 9 am. I imagined the warmth, the coffee, and the freedom to smoke.

Just play carefully, and leave your bankcard at home. That way you'll leave your rent and living expenses intact.

But I didn't want to leave it behind. That meant I'd only have the twenty dollars in my pocket. It wouldn't last for more than half an hour. I put my bankcard into my purse, and told myself that I probably wouldn't need it; I would be bound to win something.

It became a daily routine. If I didn't have any classes I went straight to the pokies. I started to feel out of control, and scared. I had barely enough money to buy food. I was in the supermarket writing out a cheque for twelve dollars, when the cashier asked me, 'Would you like any cash with that?'

I was surprised. 'Cash? How does that work?'

'You have a frequent-shopper card with us. That means you can withdraw cash, you just add the amount you want onto the balance of the cheque.'

My adrenalin soared. I knew that my bank account was empty, but maybe I could take out fifty dollars and have a win. I could put it straight back that day before the cheque even hit my account. I asked for one hundred dollars, which would cover my session with Phil and give me enough gambling money.

I left the supermarket charged with excitement. It was so lovely to know that I could spend hours at the pokies and not run out of money. I ordered my coffee, sat at my favourite machine with a cup full of coins and lit up a smoke.

Yes, this must be heaven!

I didn't win anything. The next morning I was at the supermarket as soon as it opened. I cashed one hundred and fifty dollars. I was going to the casino in the city. I knew I could win big there. As soon as my lecture was over I walked through the mall and entered the casino.

Somewhere in the far recess of my mind there was a growing sense of terror. But I just kept pushing it back, assuring myself that any day now I would get a hold of things and fix it all up. But I couldn't seem to stop myself. Some days I was visiting the supermarket two to three times, each visit increasing the amount of my withdrawals.

It had been two months since I moved, and I was happily chatting to Phil about my successful move and my lovely new apartment. We continued to discuss my progress and any problems that may have arisen from studying full-time. I didn't mention the sickness in my stomach or the waves of fear that greeted me each morning. I was still convinced that I could get a handle on it.

Three months passed. I knew I had written cheques for something close to two-thousand dollars. I had no way of honouring them. I was too scared to answer the phone. I knew it would be my bank and I had no answers, no explanation. I spent more and more time at my mother's house. I felt I was safer there. That no one could catch up with me.

Letters arrived, threatening letters saying that I would be taken to court for fraud if I don't make contact. I was too scared, though. I didn't know what to do. I hated my flat. It was cold and the phone kept ringing. I started to skip classes. I was spending five days out of seven at my mother's house.

'You sound awful, Deb. What's the matter?'
    'Oh, Jo, I'm in such a bloody mess.'
    'What have you done?'
    'I can't tell you, it's too awful.'
    'Deb? Come on now, tell me. Is it to do with a man?'

'No, I wish it was though. That would be easy to deal with.'

'Is it money?'

'Yep. But don't ask me to tell you because I can't. I only have to think about it and I feel sick.'

'What does Phil say about it?'

'He doesn't know.'

'What? You haven't told him?'

'No, I *can't*. He thinks I'm doing so well. If I could just find a way to handle this, I'll be fine. But I don't think there's a solution, you know? I'm getting so scared.'

'Slow down, Deb. You'll be fine. There's always an answer to these things.'

I was shaking my head. 'Not this time, Jo. I'm in such big trouble.'

Jo sighed. 'So what are you going to do?'

'I don't know yet, but I can't keep this up much longer.'

'Why don't you just leave that place and come over here, Deb? I've got a spare room.'

'I can't, Jo. I'm so incredibly short of money. I've had to eat noodles for the past week; that's all I can afford.'

'Jesus, Deb, speak to Phil for goodness sake.'

'No, I'll sort this out, somehow. Sorry to dump it all on you.'

'Don't be silly. You haven't really told me anything. You stay in touch with me, okay? Don't go and do anything stupid.'

I hung up the telephone and looked around my flat. I *hated* it.

Phil was completely unaware. I managed to convince him that everything was going smoothly. I reduced our sessions to once a fortnight. I could not afford more.

I was spacing out badly and trying to stay calm. It was Monday morning and I didn't think I could face another day of terror. I called my mum, burst into tears and told her that I needed to move out, quickly. Could I stay with her? She was delighted. She organised a trailer and within hours we emptied the flat, left a letter for my landlord telling him that he could keep the bond, and I was out, at last. I lay in bed that night in my mother's spare bedroom, allowing the relief to flood through me. No one would find me here. No more phone calls or letters. I was through with university. I was safe.

'I need to give you a change of address.'

Phil arched his eyebrows in surprise. 'What's going on?'

'I'm living with Mum now.'

'I see.' He got up from his chair, walked over to his desk and returned with a pad and pen.

'What's that for?' I asked. 'You haven't taken notes since our first sessions.'

'We haven't had something like this come up before.'

He sat in front of me, pad in hand, waiting. Where would I start? I was having difficulty pulling him into focus.

'You're pretty spaced out, aren't you?'

I nodded. I felt like such a total failure.

'Start from the beginning,' he suggested.

'I've been lying to you. Pretending that everything was fine. It wasn't.' I felt miserable.

'I see. Why would you have done that?'

I shook my head. 'I thought I could handle it myself.'

'Tell me what's been going on.'

I poured it out. It felt like vomiting and once I started I couldn't stop. I told him everything: the cold flat, the gambling, my trouble with the law and my eventual impulsive departure.

Phil was writing rapidly. At last I was drained. There was nothing else to say. I still felt sick but was relieved to have finally come clean.

'I guess I'm rather taken aback by this. You appeared to be doing so well.'

I looked at him guiltily. 'I know, and in one way I was. I felt so much better with you, I'd stopped having those bloody sexual dreams, I wasn't feeling so spacey and my mood swings had virtually stopped. I felt sure that I could handle things.'

'So I'd like to understand why you felt a need to lie to me.'

I felt awful. 'I wasn't lying; I just didn't tell you everything.'

His eyebrows arched.

'I know,' I said, 'that was crap. I don't really have a good excuse. I so wanted everything to work. And I was too ashamed to tell you about the gambling.'

'I wouldn't have judged you for that.'

I sighed. 'I know that. I just kept making everything worse though, till it got so big I felt like I was drowning.'

'What are you planning to do now?'

'I don't know. It's good at Mum's place. I've calmed down a lot.'

'You're also so spaced out that you can hardly see.'

'I know, I know. I don't know what to do about that right now.'

'We'll just take it from here,' he said softly. 'This is simply a little setback. It happens.'

'Have I let you down badly?' I looked at him in dismay.

'Of course you haven't.'

'Are you annoyed with me for blowing it?'

'Not at all. We'll work this out together. You're not alone on this. We've just taken a little detour on our journey, that's all.'

I smiled weakly. 'I think I've taken us into the rapids.'

'That's okay. I've negotiated rapids many times.'

I let out a deep breath. 'I'm so sorry.'

'You haven't done anything wrong. It sounds like something came up to sabotage your move. That's very common.'

'I wanted it to work, real bad.'

'I know you did. Sometimes it's not that easy, is it?'

I shook my head. 'I feel like I'm right back where I started.'

'You never go back,' Phil assured me. 'Those changes are there to stay. They can't be taken away from you. There's obviously more work for us to do. We'll take it one step at a time, okay?'

I nodded. The spaciness was making me feel ill. I felt a million miles away from everything solid or real. I was floating. 'I don't feel too good.'

'No, I can see that. We're going to have to find some way to ground you. Pretty difficult if you're staying at your mother's.'

'I know. But I can't leave there. I've got nowhere else to go.'

'That's not quite true, is it?'

'Yes, it is.' The thought of moving again appalled me. I had no energy left and certainly no desire to find another flat.

'My mother's been given notice on her house. She has to find somewhere else to live in eight weeks time.'

'Is that right?' he asked. 'When did you find that out?'

'A couple of weeks ago. It quite shocked me. She's lived there for about two years.'

'Do you think that had anything to do with ditching your flat?'

I thought about it, it hadn't actually occurred to me.

'Does she know where she's moving to?'

I shook my head. 'She's thinking about moving to the country.'

'Are you planning to go with her?'

'I don't know. Maybe. Right now I'm going to help her pack. She has masses and masses of stuff and doesn't know where to start. I'm going to organise things, make it a bit easier.'

'Like you always did?'

'She doesn't know where to start. I'm there to help, that's all.'

'I see.'

We sat there in silence and let the clock tick by. I was tired to the bone. I didn't want answers anymore.

I became totally immersed in my mother's plans. She had found a house in Eudunda, a small country town about three hours drive from her home in Aldinga. The days were filled with packing, sorting, giving things away and cleaning. It was an enormous task. My mum was a hoarder. When we weren't focussed on the move we went to her local pub and gambled. I was content. The only time I left her was for my sessions with Phil.

Ty called me regularly, aware that something had gone wrong, but not too sure how to approach it with me. I tried to reassure him, but it was hard. I couldn't answer his questions about how long I would stay with Mum or what I was doing about university. Thankfully he stopped asking, and just called to say hello and keep me up-to-date with how he was doing.

As the weeks passed I knew that I wouldn't be going with Mum. I had lost interest in everything. And I was too tired to conjure up yet another plan. I thought of all the times I had moved and knew I couldn't make it through another one. I started to think of suicide again. The only thing that got in my way was Ty. Raising him had been the most important thing in my life. I knew that if I killed myself it would have a dramatic impact on him. And I couldn't bear that idea. I would push him into the back of my mind.

'I'm scared of this spaciness. It's the worst it's ever been.'

'I can see that. For some reason you've taken yourself right back. This must have been exactly how it was for you as a child.'

'But what if I go too far? And can't get back? Could that happen?'

'Not if you keep your appointments with me. Right now I'm the only solid thing you've got.'

I was once again a million miles away, drifting in space, nothing to hold on to. 'I'm not going to move with my mother.'

'Okay. What's your plan?'

'I've had enough. I've sold all my stuff at her garage sales. When she leaves I'm just going to walk away.'

'Where to?'

'Nowhere. I don't want to go anywhere. I'm just going to start walking, maybe find a big tree somewhere.'

Phil smiled gently. 'Then what?'

'Nothing. I just want to get away. I want to be where no one can find me, and no one can touch me.' My heart was hurting.

'Is that what it felt like when you were little?'

I nodded my head, trying not to cry. 'Yep.'

'It must have felt like there was nowhere safe. Nowhere to hide?'

I nodded again, feeling the tears well up.

'I can't do this anymore,' I told him, letting the tears fall. 'I don't know where to go from here. It's too hard.'

Phil leant forward. 'You're not alone, Deb. I'm here, remember. You don't have to do this by yourself.'

I shook my head. 'I know, but I'm all out of ideas. I can't seem to ever get it right.'

'You don't have to come up with ideas. We'll do this together.'

'Why won't you give up on me? Can't you see that it's hopeless?'

'It only looks like that now. You're simply reliving something from your childhood. For whatever reason, you've chosen to go back to your mother's to sort something out.'

'I want out,' I told him. 'I've got a right to end all this crap, haven't I? Can't I for once give up?'

'You could,' he answered gently. 'I take it you're talking about suicide?'

I nodded helplessly.

'That's a pretty desperate remedy, don't you think?'

'I'm just weary to my bones. I've had enough.'

'And what would I tell Ty when he comes to see me?'

I shook my head. Why did he bring Ty into it? That wasn't fair. 'Ty wouldn't come to see you,' I said quietly.

'Of course he would, this would be the first place he'd come looking for answers.'

'Don't make me think of him,' I pleaded.

His eyes held mine. 'I don't want you to die.'

'*Why*?' I asked, couldn't he see that I'd reached the end?

'Because I know there are lots of good things in front of you.'

I shook my head. 'You're wrong!' I insisted. 'You're seeing something that isn't there. I'm done. In fact, I've been thinking we should probably end our sessions together. It's going to be pretty hard to see you when I'm under my tree.'

He smiled. 'Well, let's take it one step at a time, huh? Do you want to make another appointment? Are you doing anything tomorrow?'

I shook my head. Why wouldn't he give up? Couldn't he see the obvious? I dragged myself off of the couch and stood tiredly in front of his desk. Phil handed me a card with the session date and time written clearly on the back.

He knows I've lost track of the days. I thanked him quietly, put his card in my bag and left.

I was back to three sessions a week. Phil waived his fee, aware of my financial circumstances. Everything became a blur. I would keep planning my final departure only to find a card in my bag with another Phil appointment in place.

The packing was in full swing. Mum's house was piled with boxes and crates. Visitors came and went. I sat with the drunks and paedophiles feeling completely untouched. Nothing mattered anymore. I had lost my fight. It felt a relief to let Mum just be who she was. It didn't matter that she spoke no sense nor seemed at all concerned about my own future plans. I had let go. I didn't care.

'What's wrong with me?' I asked him, scared again about how unreal my world was feeling.

'You've regressed, particularly since you've been back with your mother.'

'I've changed my mind about medication. I want you to put me on drugs.'

Phil looked surprised. 'That's a radical departure for you. I thought you hated taking pills.'

'I did. But that was then. I can't stand this anymore. Can't you just give me something?' I pleaded.

He shook his head slowly. 'I don't think there's a pill that can fix this.'

'There must be! Just write me out a script and I'll take the drugs.'

He smiled softly. 'We're going to work through this. I know that looks hard for you right now, but trust me okay?'

I looked into his eyes. So warm, so reassuring. How could I not trust him?

'I'm so scared.'

'I know you are. There's a lot going on for you, it's bound to feel overwhelming at times.'

'I can't seem to stop it though.'

'I know. We'll just have to ride it out for now.'

'But where are we?' I asked, feeling desperate. 'Why can't you tell me what to do? I feel like we're both floating around going nowhere.'

He shook his head. 'We're not going nowhere. But yes, right now our boat does appear to have lost direction. We're sort of stranded in the ocean. We'll have to wait and see what happens.'

'You're not even *in* the bloody boat,' I complained.

'Is that right?' he asked, smiling broadly. 'Has there been a mutiny? You've dumped me overboard.'

I couldn't help but laugh. But it was still true. 'You aren't doing anything! It's like you're as useless as I am right now.'

'What do you want me to do?'

I felt an inner roar of frustration. 'You're no different than my bloody mother. She's just as clueless.'

'I'm still unclear about what you think I can do?' he persisted.

'I don't know, for God's sake! You're meant to be navigating this fucking boat. How come we're spinning round in circles?'

He said nothing for a while. We sat there in silence.

Finally he leant forward. 'I'll tell you why we're spinning in circles. It's because this is how it must have been for you as a child. You were lost. Confused. There was no adult to turn to for help. The only contact you had was from sick men who took dreadful advantage of you. It must have been hell for you. And that's where we are right now. In the middle of that hell.'

'But when do we get out of here? When will it end?' I asked, desperate for a solution.

'That's sort of up to you. This will take however long it needs to take. But I have been here before; trust me. We'll get through it.'

'I need help though. It's getting worse.'

Phil paused for a moment and then said something that shocked me to the core. 'Maybe you need to book in to Glenside for a few weeks?'

It was our major mental institution. I looked at him in horror. 'Glenside? What sort of a suggestion is that?'

He shrugged. 'You said you needed help. Maybe it wouldn't do you any harm to get looked after for a short while?'

I was still in shock. 'Well, thank you very much. That's exactly what I'd say to my son too, if he came to me with a problem: "Go book yourself into the mental asylum." That's just lovely of you.'

'I'm not your parent, though,' Phil gently reminded me.

I was still bristling. 'Well, fuck that for a good idea.'

'It was just a suggestion.'

'Thanks but no thanks.' Bloody prick. So okay, he wasn't my dad, but he should have been able to offer more than that. 'I can't believe that you would say that.'

'You asked me for my advice.'

'Jesus, remind me not to do that again.'

'You obviously want something from me.'

'I *know*,' I wailed, frustrated by my inability to name it. 'I keep thinking, for God's sake somebody, step in and stop me. Surely I can't go on this way without someone intervening.'

'But how can I?'

'I don't know,' I answered, terrified that this was going to be left in my hands. How far would I take it?

'We'll get through this, you know,' he offered again.

I shook my head. That wasn't good enough. I was spiralling out of control.

Chapter Twenty-one

I felt that I had fractured into pieces again. The teenager within turned up to my next session with Phil. She was relentless. 'I'm not afraid of you,' she challenged.

'I would hope not,' he answered, unruffled.

She crossed her legs. 'I don't intend to sit here harping about the dreary past, you know. I'm *way* over that.'

He smiled. 'What would you like to do?'

'What are the options?'

'It's your call. Your time.'

She glared at him. 'That's right, I forgot. You never come up with anything, do you?'

'What would you like me to do?'

'God only knows. Something different would be a good start.' She stared out of the window feeling bored and restless.

'How's it going with your mother?' he tried, changing the subject.

'Fuck my mother. It's like a lunatic asylum there. If it wasn't for me everything would be falling apart.'

'You keep it all together, do you? That must be quite a strain.'

She shrugged. 'I've done it all my life. Better than watching everything disintegrate around you. Anyway, enough about me, that's all we ever talk about. Let's focus on you for a change.'

He smiled. 'What would you like to know?'

She twirled her hair. 'Let me see. I know, there's something I've always wanted to ask you. Do you find me difficult?'

He frowned. 'Difficult in what way?'

'Oh come on,' she groaned, 'that's a pretty simple question. Am I difficult?'

He shook his head slowly. 'You may be unpredictable, in a predictable sort of way, but no, I don't find you difficult.'

'Don't you get tired of just sitting there listening?'

'Not at all. But I'm not only listening, my mind is also keeping track of what's going on.'

'Is that right? So what's going on now?' she teased.

'Seems to me like I'm being tested again.'

She sighed. '*Wrong*. I'm through with testing you; it's a total waste of time. I'm wondering if some fun could still be had though.'

He laughed. 'You're flirting with me again.'

'My oh my, whatever next?'

'Where are you planning to go when you leave here?'

'I'm going to find me some serious fun.'

'Really? And what might that entail?'

She laughed. 'Do you realise that I haven't had sex in over five years?'

'Yes, I'm aware of that.'

'Well, I think it's time to put an end to this enforced state of celibacy. It's completely boring, I feel like a bloody nun.'

'Are you sure that's a good idea?'

'I think it's an excellent idea.'

'So who's the lucky man this time?'

'Ah,' she smiled, 'there's still one or two floating around. Hopefully I'll be able to track someone down. I'm so incredibly horny.'

'You know what you remind me of at the moment?'

'No, but I'm sure you're going to tell me.'

'A bed warmer,' he said slowly. 'Did you ever read Roots?'

She knew the book well. 'Yes, they put the slave-girls at the bottom of their beds to keep their feet warm.'

'Exactly.'

'I'd like you to even make a hint at that sort of a suggestion. I'd tell you where to get off in no uncertain terms.'

'I'm not too sure of that. You're sending me some pretty strong signals.'

Maybe you need a bed warmer.

'Well, should I just get this over with and ask you if you want to fuck? Is that what you're saying?' she demanded.

'Maybe you should.'

For just a moment, she was tempted. 'I think not. Your answer is so bloody predictable.'

'Are you so sure of that?'

She rolled her eyes. 'Yes, I am sure. I'm not completely thick, you know.'

'You know what I think you ought to do?' he offered.

'Pray tell. I'm sure it's bound to be enthralling.'

He laughed. 'Go home and masturbate.'

That pulled her up short. 'Masturbate? Why would I do that?'

'Because I don't think this is a good time for you to be out and about.'

'I'm sure you don't. But if you don't mind I think my idea sounds like a hell of a lot more fun.'

'I see.'

'And another thing,' she went on, 'I've been thinking that maybe I should find myself another psychiatrist. Maybe one who's a little more willing? Now that would be exciting!'

'How so?'

'Well, for a start, it would be wonderful to be with a man who actually *wanted* me. And secondly, it would provide me with an opportunity to have some *real* fun.'

Phil shrugged. 'Is that right? Well, it's your choice of course. But I think I'll stick to my original suggestion.'

Masturbate? He wishes.

She left the session determined to find some trouble. In her little yellow book was the phone number of a man she had fancied years ago. Within hours she was sitting at a dining-room table, drinking wine with him and his buddy.

I'm going to have them both, maybe at the same time.

She pictured herself lying naked between the two of them, doing their bidding; she was getting hornier by the minute. Their conversation got bawdier as she made it clear to the men exactly what was on offer. She could feel their excitement growing.

'So why don't we play strip poker?' she teased. 'Time for a bit of fun, huh?'

'Sounds good to me,' said Brian, rising from his chair to go looking for the cards.

'More wine?' Graham asked, filling her glass and peering down her top at the same time.

Yes, look. Look all you want, because soon it will be all yours.

Brian was rifling through the cupboard for a deck of cards. 'I know they're here, for God's sake, I only used them a week ago.'

She stood up to go to the toilet and immediately needed to grab the side of the table for support. The wine had gone straight to her head and she was starting to feel ill.

'Let me have a lie down?' she asked them. 'I'll be back in about an hour, I promise.' She headed into the spare room and collapsed onto the single bed, spinning but still horny. Phil's words entered her brain: 'Go home and masturbate.' What did he know? He never wanted to have any fun. But his words persisted.

Maybe I will.

She felt the room spinning around her. Within minutes she was up again and asking Graham to drive her home. 'I'll be vomiting all over the place if I hang around much longer,' she warned.

Reluctantly he agreed. An hour later she climbed into bed, masturbated, and fell fast asleep.

'I don't want to sit on that couch,' the little girl told him.

'That's okay,' Phil said gently, 'where would you like to sit?'

She shook her head, pouting. 'I don't like this office.'

'I'll tell you what,' he suggested. 'I've got another room. It's like a playroom. Would you like to go in there?'

Her face lit up. 'Really? A playroom? Neat!'

She followed him into the corridor and they entered a room that she had never seen before. It had a huge yellow couch. 'Can I sit on this?' she asked excitedly.

'Of course you can. You can even lie down if you like.'

She lay back onto the couch, rolling around blissfully.

Phil sat on a chair close by. 'What are you feeling?' he asked.

She beamed up at him. 'I think you're neat!'

He smiled warmly. 'Thank you.'

'Can we play a game?'

'What sort of game?'

'I don't know. Do you know any?'

His face went serious. 'Well, I have one patient whose father used to play a game with her; he used his thumb. Can you guess what that game was?'

She frowned. 'No.'

'He told her to close her eyes and he put his thumb up to her mouth. Only it wasn't his thumb at all.'

She started shaking her head. 'I don't want to play a game like that!'

'Tell me what you want to play.'

'Well,' she said, 'I guess we do wonder why you never take your trousers off. Why is that?'

'Why do you think I don't?'

She suddenly felt sad. 'Because you don't want me.'

'Why don't you take *your* trousers off? Isn't that what usually happens?'

She shook her head. 'It doesn't work like that. You have to tell me what you want, and I'll do it.'

'I see. That's the rule, is it?'

'Yep. But you never want to play.'

Phil stayed quiet and the little girl lay there, wondering for the thousandth time why this man didn't want to touch her and racking her brains for some new game.

'I drew you a picture!' she suddenly remembered, reaching into her bag and pulling out a folded piece of paper.

Phil took it out of her hands and looked at it for a few moments. 'Tell me what it is.'

'It's all of *us*,' she explained slowly. 'We thought it might help you out, you know, it's like a map of all of us, and where we are in the body. See!' she said, pointing to the little girl on the left, 'that's *me*!'

'And who is this one on the right?'

She rolled her eyes skyward. 'That's the teenager, the one who causes all the trouble.'

'Oh yes,' he said, smiling, 'I'm definitely acquainted with her.'

'It's her job to deal with the men.'

'That must be hard for her. What does she have to do?'

'Oh, you know, she gives the blowjobs and anything else they might want. That's her job.'

'And what about you?'

'Me? I'm here to make the men happy and to look after Mum.'

'How do you make the men happy?'

She squirmed a little, feeling embarrassed. 'I let them do what they want to me.'

'I see. And who's this one?' he asked, pointing to the largest person on the page.

'She's the main one, the biggest. She's the one who wants us all to go away.'

'And what do you want to do?'

'I want to play with you,' she repeated. 'Can't we play a game together? That would be so neat?'

'I'm waiting to hear what sort of game you'd like to play.'

She wished so bad that he would ask her to do something for him, but she knew he wouldn't. What could they play instead? She continued to search her brain for an answer. 'I know!' she said, suddenly excited. 'Let's play a word game. Like hangman. That would be fun?'

Phil smiled. 'Okay, I'll go find us a pen and paper. You wait here for me.'

She sat up in the couch feeling delighted with herself. This was going to be so neat! Phil returned and for the rest of the session they took it in turns thinking up words and trying to beat each other. The little one was over the moon with joy. She left his office feeling warm and safe and completely satisfied.

I arrived at my next session totally deflated. 'What's going on? Am I right back where I started?'

Phil shook his head. 'Not at all. You've just regressed as a result of being with your mother. Obviously there are still a few things you need to sort out.'

'But I've got all those parts floating around again,' I wailed.

'I know. But don't give up hope. This will turn around again.'

I shook my head. 'Thank God you told the teenager to go home and masturbate. I got *that* close to getting myself into trouble.'

'What happened?'

I filled him in on all the gory details.

'You were lucky that they were happy to drive you home.'

I nodded. 'I know. I always seem to avoid trouble in the nick of time. You know what I've realised though? Despite the trouble that she likes to get into, that teenager has some qualities that I wouldn't mind having?'

'Like what?'

'Her confidence, for a start. And her incredible strength. I guess too that I wouldn't mind that sex drive.'

'She's the only one that feels it, is she?'

I nodded. 'Yep. Maybe I've made a mistake by trying to get rid of her? That could be why all hell broke loose, she just wasn't going to let herself be ignored like that. Maybe we need to make some sort of deal. I like the little one too; I think she's the one who carries all the joy. And she adores you. Life in that flat was pretty darned serious.'

Phil smiled. 'Take your time. Eventually you'll work it out.'

'It's so confusing, though. I mean, could the truth be that I *am* like my mother? And I'm just fighting it all the way?'

'You're not like your mother.'

I shook my head. 'But that rampant part of me, is that the *real* me, or what? Maybe Mum is right when she says that we're two of a kind?'

'You are *not* your mother,' Phil repeated slowly.

I sat back in the couch, trying to let his words sink in. 'We only really get on, you know, when I keep my real thoughts and ideas to myself.'

He nodded, saying nothing.

And that's why I space out. 'It's tricky stuff, this.'

'It is, and you're working through it well.'

'God I hope so. Another thing,' I admitted gingerly, having avoided it for the entire session, 'I've been having some rather violent thoughts towards Mum.'

He arched his brows. 'Tell me about them.'

I grimaced. 'It's usually at night, when I'm in bed. I start thinking about everything, like how many times I've tried to get through to her and the way she refuses to acknowledge what happened to me and Jo. I imagine walking into her bedroom when she's asleep and ...' I couldn't go on, I felt too guilty.

'And what?' Phil asked gently.

I looked down at my feet, trying to decide whether to tell him or not? But what did I have to lose? 'And just plunging a knife into her. It feels like that's the only way I'll ever find any peace.'

'It must seem like that right now. But I doubt you'd ever actually go through with it.'

I looked up at him, for once without a ready answer.

We made our way to the front door. 'Would you visit me in jail?' I asked, hating the thought of not seeing him again.

'Of course I would,' he answered, smiling warmly. 'I'd probably feature rather strongly in your trial too, I imagine.'

How neat. It seemed one of the kindest things he'd ever said to me.

I arrived home still walking on air. Mum looked up as I walked into the lounge room. 'You look pretty pleased with yourself, dear.'

I smiled. 'Phil just said the nicest thing to me.'

'What was that?'

What the hell? 'He said that if I murdered you, he'd not only be at my trial, but he'd visit me in jail, too. How neat is that?'

Mum just looked at me. 'That's charming, dear.'

Chapter Twenty-two

There were two weeks before my mother had to leave. The packing was relentless. We had made little headway into the hordes of her belongings despite our hours of hard labour. It was Monday morning. I had woken up tired and slightly irritable. The moment I walked into the lounge room I knew that something was wrong. My mother's moods were almost palpable. I looked at her face and saw the familiar closed, hard expression. I went to do my usual thing and ask her what the problem was, but something stopped me dead. I headed into the kitchen to make myself a cup of tea.

Say nothing. For once in your life, say nothing and see what happens.

I filled my cup and walked back into the lounge room, sitting in my usual chair, opposite her. I knew she was waiting. But I just sipped my tea and flipped through the morning paper. Minutes passed in silence. She hadn't even said good morning yet. A tension started to build inside me. The air felt thick and I desperately wanted to say something, anything to break that awful empty atmosphere.

No, say nothing. Just wait and see.

An hour passed. I had read the paper and had two cups of tea. And still there was not a word from my mother, who sat only feet away gazing into the flame of a candle. My stomach was churning in discomfort. Everything in me wanted to speak out, to ask her what was wrong, and to offer her assurances. But I managed to keep quiet. It dawned on me that I didn't have to stay in the lounge room. I could get up if I wanted and find something to do. I exhaled in relief and leapt up from my chair. I would start emptying out my room; I still had boxes of stuff left over from my flat that needed sorting.

Hours and hours passed and still my mother didn't speak to me. It was eerie. I wondered how she could do it. How long could she keep this up for? Surely she was as uncomfortable as I was. This was unnatural. Two people in a house and not a single word. I kept waiting for her to break the silence, but nothing happened. Not the next day, nor the next.

'How's it going?' Phil asked.

I shook my head. 'I'm trying something different with Mum. It's pretty scary though.' I filled him in on the past few days.

'So she hasn't spoken to you at all?'

'Nope. I keep thinking that she can't go much longer but I'm not so sure now. I guess I'll just wait and see.'

'How are your moods?'

'Pretty good actually, considering. If this had happened a year ago I would have spun out into one of those manic phases, or plunged into depression. But it's different this time, like despite the madness going on in that house I'm managing to keep one step back from it.'

'That sounds good,' Phil said encouragingly. 'It means the work we've done over the last eighteen months is paying off.'

I nodded. 'I know that I have to be there right now, it feels like there's unfinished business, you know?'

'Yes, I get the impression that this is important.'

'It is. I'm starting to realise so many things. I think I disagree with virtually everything that my mother lives by. I bury so much of it, though. I must bite my tongue a hundred times a day. And you know what's *really* odd?'

'What's that?'

I answered slowly. 'I don't think she likes me at all.'

'It's very important to her to keep you in her world, though.'

'I know, but the real me, the one she hardly ever gets to see, I think she hates her, you know?'

'That must be a pretty difficult thing for you to accept.'

I nodded. 'But I think in some way, that I've always known that. That's why I've kept myself hidden.'

'There's a lot that you're sorting through right now.'

'Yep. But I still intend to find that tree.'

He smiled warmly. 'I know you do. But maybe that tree is inside you, waiting for you to find it.'

I looked up at him in surprise. 'Hey, now that's a nice thought. Find somewhere that I can go to, sit down, be alone and soak up the stillness.'

He nodded. 'It's there inside you, somewhere. You'll find it.'

By the fourth day it finally dawned on me. My mother wasn't uncomfortable at all. She was fine. She could go for months without saying a word to me. I didn't exist for her.

I sat in my bedroom in shock. All those years that I had filled the silences, I needn't have bothered. All that song and dance I created to make it look like we were having a relationship. Now I knew why. I hadn't wanted to see the truth. It was too horrifying.

I got up from my bed and started to pack a suitcase. I didn't know where I was going but I knew I had to get out of that house. I phoned a friend and asked if I could come over for a few days. My mother sat two feet away while I made the call. Still she said nothing, but this time I wasn't expecting her to. I looked over in her direction. 'I'm going, Mum. I won't be coming back. Take care.'

She didn't even look up. 'Okay dear, you too.'

And that was that.

Chapter Twenty-three

'So where are you now?' Phil asked.

'Staying with Michael and his family. They're friends of mine from way back. He's got a caravan in the back garden. It's nice.'

'What are your plans?'

I shrugged. 'The tree is still looking good.'

'It feels to me like you've got some sort of a plan. You realise that if you continue on this track you'll become a vagrant?'

I nodded. 'In some weird way that's a comforting idea. I want to be homeless. I don't want to be weighted down with responsibilities and bills. It's like I keep setting up a life, doing all the right things like finding somewhere to live, getting a job, only I don't know why I'm doing it. It's always bloody meaningless.'

'And you'll find some meaning by being a vagrant?'

I shook my head. 'No. I'll just have stopped trying. I swear I can't construct one more cardboard lifestyle. I'm through with that.'

'Is that what your flat in Norwood was? A cardboard lifestyle?'

'It was what I thought you wanted,' I told him honestly. 'I figured you'd be proud of me. But it meant nothing to me. I was just going through the motions.'

'You're in the process of learning about who you are. Until now you've been whoever the person you're with wants you to be. It's bound to be difficult, even scary, to create a new sense of identity.'

'But all I know about me is that I love football,' I wailed. 'That's hardly enough to build a life around.'

He smiled. 'It's a start; a good, solid start. You're just going to have to build on that. It takes time.'

I thought back on our time together; in one way it had flown and yet it felt like I had been seeing him for a lifetime. 'Do you know,' I started, suddenly wanting to confide in him, 'at one time there, I absolutely hated your wife.'

He smiled warmly. 'A very normal reaction, believe me.'

'Really?'

'Of course, it's natural to feel possessive, even jealous.'

'Hmmm. I always felt dreadful about it.' What else hadn't I told him? 'Oh, yes, another thing, I couldn't bear thinking about your children; it just hurt too much.'

His eyes softened. 'I know that. I've seen you struggling with it.'

I nodded. 'There was so much to work through. Hardest of all though, was the notion of trust.'

'Do you trust me yet?' he asked gently.

I looked up at him, feeling as though I had known him forever. 'I do now, after all this time. Isn't that incredible?'

We sat together in silence for a while. I brought my mind back to the present, still feeling an emptiness inside, a total lack of interest in anything.

'What do you want?' Phil asked, breaking the quietness.

'Want? In what way?'

'I guess I'd like to know what your soul wants?'

I was totally thrown. It was such a strange question. 'I have no idea,' I answered truthfully.

He nodded. 'We need to find that out.'

'What if I haven't got a soul?' I asked.

'Go inside and take a look. Maybe you'll find something that will surprise you.'

I was mystified. But promised I'd think about it over the next few days.

I knew that I couldn't stay in the caravan forever and that if I continued to see Phil I would need to find some sort of living arrangement. I wanted something temporary though, a place that I could just up and leave when the time was ready. That big tree was still beckoning.

I rang a few caravan parks but their prices were steep. With all the debts I had incurred, my finances were already tightly stretched. I pored through the newspaper, searching out alternative forms of accommodation. There was a section for Rooms and the rates looked quite reasonable. I rang one of the advertisements that offered room and board for ninety dollars a week. The owner seemed friendly enough, assured me that I could have a week-by-week tenancy, and arranged a meeting for the following day.

Ty drove me to Glenelg to view the house. I asked him to wait in the car while I had a quick look around. It looked nice from the outside. In only a couple of moments a car pulled into the drive and a lithe, grey-haired man of about forty-five stepped out.

'Debra? I'm Martin. Thanks for getting here on time; I'm in quite a rush.'

I followed him into the house, immediately hit by its state of disrepair. 'Now don't go by appearances,' he implored, 'by the end of the week I'll have it all freshly painted and new furniture moved in. I'm going to supply everything, bedding, television, kitchen utensils and the laundry will be fully operational.' He sounded keen to keep me interested. I followed him through the rooms, aware of their smallness. 'This will be the communal kitchen,' he continued, as we walked into a large, brightly lit room. 'Everything you need will be supplied.' Having rushed me through the house he looked at me for a response. I felt uncertain. I'd never lived in a communal house before. What would the other tenants be like? What if they were creeps or drunks? I was looking around the kitchen trying to make up my mind.

'Now, another thing,' he went on, speaking rapidly, 'I want someone to act like a caretaker. You know, keep an eye on the kitchen, and make sure everyone is pulling his or her weight. I'll be happy to reduce the rent a little, if we come to that arrangement. You look like a mature, sensible person.'

How the hell does he know what I'm like?

I was annoyed, but tempted by the rent reduction.

'I don't mean to rush you,' he said, obviously rushing me, 'but what do you think?'

I was torn. In one way it was everything I needed. There was no lease, the cost was right and maybe having people around could be a good thing?

'All I'm asking for today is a one-hundred-dollar deposit. We won't finalise things till next Saturday, when the house has been finished and you can pick the room you'd like.'

Christ, I didn't have a cent on me and my money wasn't due in for three days. Once again I was feeling torn. Martin was trying not to look impatient and doing a bad job of it. I suddenly remembered Ty. Maybe he could lend me the hundred dollars. 'Can you give me five minutes?' I asked. 'I need to go to the ATM.'

He looked at his watch. 'Okay, five minutes. But I really will have to get going.'

I nodded and hurried outside to join Ty in his car.

'What's it like?' he asked.

I pulled a face. 'I don't know. It seems fine enough. But I can't seem to make my mind up.'

'What are the doubts?'

I shrugged. 'I'm not sure. Maybe it's just the thought of making a commitment. He needs a hundred dollars too. Can you help me out there, just for a few days?'

'Of course I can, Mum. But are you sure it's what you want?'

'No,' I said, miserably, 'but I'm running a bit short on options.'

Ty handed me the money. 'Well you don't have to say yes, remember that. There'll be somewhere else, there always is.'

I gave him a quick hug. 'I know. But I think I'll take it. I can't really find a good reason not to.'

I hurried back into the house and handed Martin the money. 'I'll take it,' I said, trying to sound confident.

'Excellent. Now when we get together on Saturday I'll give you a copy of the house rules. They're all pretty standard.' He started to write out a receipt.

'House rules?' I asked, suddenly alarmed. 'I haven't lived in this sort of situation before. How does it work?'

'Just the basics.' He rushed on, 'No smoking, and no visitors in your room.'

I stood there horrified.

'But I smoke,' I told him.

'Not a problem. There's always the garden.' It was the middle of winter. And no visitors? For Gods sake, I wasn't a teenager. Martin was handing me the receipt.

I shook my head. 'Hang on a minute, I'm not too sure that this is going to work.'

'Of course it will,' he said flippantly, patting me on the shoulder. 'Maybe it's a good time to quit smoking.' I immediately resented the physical contact.

'I'll take that deposit back!' I said. 'I'm too old for rules and regulations.'

He looked quite annoyed. 'All because of a cigarette?'

'Plus no visitors,' I added. 'That's probably okay for some people. I think I'd feel a bit ridiculous.'

'Oh come on now, you'll be fine, Deb.'

Deb? Where did he get off on this familiarity? 'I mean it,' I told him firmly, 'I've changed my mind and I'd like that deposit back, thank you.'

Martin reluctantly handed me back the hundred dollars. I let out a huge sigh of relief.

Ty was waiting. I jumped into the car and handed him back his money. 'I think that might be the best decision I've made in a long time.'

Ty laughed. 'Don't worry, Mum. Something will come up.'

As we drove back to my caravan, I thought of the teenager. I knew it had been her who had asked for the deposit back. I thought of her confidence and that wonderful ability to hold her ground. I had always given in far too easily, not wanting to offend or upset anyone. She was strong, if not a little wild as well. But maybe we could pool our resources. If she would trust me to make the decisions where sex and men were concerned, couldn't I give her a little more breathing space? I so needed her confidence. She was right there, just about an inch away from me, I could *feel* her.

I don't want to live on this planet without you. I need you. You've done such an incredible job for me.

I recalled how she had stepped in on so many occasions, handling situations that I was too scared to deal with, or too closed off to confront. She had been remarkable. We were almost touching now, her and me, enemies for such a long time. I felt a lump in my throat.

Come home, I asked her softly, *let me take it from here.*

'You all right, Mum?'

I wiped my eyes, feeling better than I had in a long time. 'I'm excellent, Ty. I think things are going to change, you know.'

He smiled. 'Me too.'

'So how long has it been now since you've had any contact with your mother?' Phil asked.

I cast my mind back. 'Gosh, about three weeks, I haven't even thought of her.'

'Is that a new experience for you?'

I nodded. 'Even on that last break-up with her I spent most of my time obsessing about how she was doing. And feeling guilty. I don't have any of that. It's like she doesn't exist anymore.'

'You do seem a lot more grounded.'

I was startled. 'You're right! I haven't been spaced out at all.'

He smiled. 'Well, welcome back to planet earth. It's nice to have you join us again.'

'Thank you,' I answered, returning his smile. 'That was the most frightening time I've been through. I really thought I was going to spin off into the ether and not come back.'

'Have you figured out yet what it was all about?'

I sighed. 'I know it sounds absurd, but it's like I had to go right back into the thick of it. Living with Mum again brought everything up. I think it was the only way I was going to ever understand what our relationship was all about. Once I saw that, in all its frightening clarity, I think I was finally able to let her go.'

'And how are you feeling now?'

'Absolutely liberated! And the weirdest thing of all, is that for the first time in my life I'm feeling safe.'

'That makes sense,' Phil explained. 'Your mother has always been a threat to your well-being. She didn't want you to separate from her.'

'It's a wonderful feeling. I've never lived a moment without an undefined sense of fear somewhere deep inside me. It's not there anymore.'

'Separating from your mother was always going to be an enormous task. It sounds to me that you've finally managed to do that.'

I nodded. She was gone. After forty-three years I had finally let her go.

Chapter Twenty-four

It was funny, in an odd sort of way. I was living in a caravan, riddled with debt and with no plans for the future, and yet I was feeling more solid than I had in my entire life. Things were about to change and I knew it.

I lay back on my bed, enjoying the background sounds of parakeets and Michael's children. This caravan had provided me with a much-needed refuge and I knew my time here was drawing to a close. I thought about Phil; how he had helped when nothing else had. Was it just a matter of timing, as he so often said? Surely it was more than that. He had formed a relationship with me and remained committed. While I spun around in confusion and threw my worst at him, he stayed steadfast and consistent. He had taken my crazy thoughts, my fears and incessant doubts then handed them back to me in a form that my mind, for once, was able to make peace with. And perhaps most awesome of all, he had taught me how to trust. My heart swelled with appreciation. However had he come into my world? And stayed?

'You let me,' he answered softly.

I shook my head. 'I didn't do anything. It's you. I feel like I owe you the world.'

He smiled. 'You owe me nothing.'

'I feel like there should be something I could give you in return.'

He shrugged. 'I guess there's always your body.'

I looked him straight in the eye. 'You know what I think? I think it's time you stopped bringing that stuff up.'

'I thought you brought it up,' he challenged.

I shook my head, feeling a strong determination rise up within me. 'No, I said that I wish I could repay you for what you've done for me. I wasn't referring to sex in any shape or form.'

'Maybe that's all you think you can offer though?' he persisted.

'Look,' I said firmly, 'I really mean this.'

'So what are you saying?'

'I'm saying that's the last time I want you to treat me like that.'

'Like what?'

'You know exactly what I mean.'

'I want you to say it.'

'Okay, fine. I'm not a sexual thing. I don't like you insinuating that that's the only thing that motivates me.'

'You're more than that, are you?'

I looked at him in shock. Had he gone nuts? 'My word I am!' I answered fiercely.

His face broke into a slow, radiant smile. 'Do you know,' he said slowly, 'that I've been waiting for over two years to hear you say that?'

Good Lord, he was right. I would never have said something like that before. Yet it was true. I believed it from my very core. I smiled, 'Hey, what about that, it finally happened.'

'I always knew it would.'

We both sat there quietly, while I marvelled at this new, sparkling truth.

I eventually moved out of the caravan and found myself a cosy bed-sitter. Phil and I reduced my sessions to once a week. The first thing I did was sit down with a pen and paper and work out a budget. My income was meagre, but I was surprised to discover that if I lived carefully, I could afford to cover the basics and still pay off a little bit every week towards my debts. My goal, however, was to get back into the workforce.

I started to write, discovering yet another aspect of myself. Since my early twenties I had wanted to put my childhood down on paper, but each time I tried, I ended up spacing out and manic. I know now that I would never have been able to make sense of my past until the shrouds of denial were lifted, both my mother's and my own. And even at this late a stage, I could only describe the events of my childhood through a dialogue with Phil. Without his compassion, those early years stood too stark and incomprehensible.

And at long last I had finally stopped gambling. In fact, I lost all desire to do so. I could no longer even imagine playing those poker machines; I had gained too much respect for every cent that came my way. Seeing twenty dollars still sitting in my purse at the end of the week made me feel like a millionaire. There was no way in the world that a cent of that would go into a poker machine.

There were a few odd changes that surprised me. I was, at last, able to shop for a whole week's worth of food. I would fill my cupboards, seeing all my breakfasts, lunches and dinners for the next seven days, and feel a glorious sense of satisfaction. I had never been able to do that before.

Sometimes when I was writing this book I would have to stop and cry. I could feel that little girl inside me, resting now, at last trusting me enough to let me make the decisions that would keep her safe. My teenager is at peace and has gifted me with her confidence, her courage and yes, that fiery sexuality. I feel honoured that those fractured pieces stuck out the distance and simply would not let up, no matter how hard I tried to make them disappear.

Chapter Twenty-five

Phil had taken a two-week absence and it was wonderful to let the days go by, neither doubting his return, nor feeling that desperate need to see him. I entered his front door wondering how many more times I would make this journey. I sat in the waiting room, looking around at the familiar surroundings, remembering the times I had sat there feeling furious as the clock had ticked by and still he hadn't come to get me. My impatience had seemed limitless. Funnily enough, he was fifteen minutes late for this session.

'Debra? Come in.'

God, it was good to see him again. I had missed him. But for once I didn't have a mind filled with questions, doubts or the need for reassurances. It was just a pleasure to see his familiar face.

'I've been really well,' I started, getting myself comfortable on the couch.

He smiled warmly. 'You look well.'

'It's been dawning on me that my time with you is coming to an end.'

He nodded slowly. 'And how does that feel?'

'It's strange really. In one way it feels like the saddest thing in the world; you've been everything to me, for over two years now. The thought of not seeing you is almost unimaginable.' I felt a familiar tug in my heart. 'And yet,' I added, 'it's pretty special too. I'm actually going to *feel* this separation. That's never happened before. I've had people go out of my life a million times and haven't felt a thing.'

'This has been quite a journey, hasn't it?'

'God yes.'

We sat there quietly, remembering the past in our own way.

'I'm writing a book about it,' I told him.

'Is that right?' he asked enthusiastically.

I nodded. 'It's like falling in love with you all over again. You've been extraordinary.' I looked at him, with warmth and sadness.

'You did this, Deb,' he said slowly, 'you should be extremely proud of yourself.'

'You know what I wish though?'

'What's that?'

'I wish I could get my sisters and somehow bring them to you. It's so sad to see them still going through their own private hells.'

He suddenly grimaced. 'I don't think I could do it.'

I was completely surprised. 'How come? You've got all the background now. Wouldn't that make it easier?'

He shook his head. 'It's been hard, you know. For me.'

I was totally perplexed. 'How so? You've always been so calm and in charge.'

He smiled. 'It's my job to stay calm. But it has been difficult not getting emotionally involved. In a way I guess I had to. But it's not always easy knowing when to keep back and when to step in. Your childhood was incredibly sad.'

I thought of Jo. 'But,' I persisted, 'wouldn't it be different the second time round? Wouldn't that make it easier?'

He shook his head. 'I don't think I could cope with your mother again,' he answered.

'Gosh. I hadn't realised how difficult it has been for you.' I was thrown. It had not occurred to me that Phil had been impacted in such a way. I presumed it was just old hat to him. Once again I was deeply moved.

'You're always surprising me,' I told him, wondering how had it been for him, listening to all that sordid, revolting history.

I sat there quietly, awash in emotions. How could I feel this *close* to a human and leave him? It didn't make sense. I let out a deep sigh. 'I'm not finishing therapy with you just yet, though,' I told him. 'I want to take this real slow.'

He smiled that wonderful, warm smile again. 'You take all the time you need.'

And I did. There was so much to learn. Now separate from my mother, I was finally able to see who I was, and who I most certainly wasn't. I threw away my little yellow book. Within its tattered pages were the telephone numbers of men that I hope never to see again. I didn't blame them for being in my world; I was selling something and they were willing buyers.

I saw too that almost all my 'friendships', some of them going back years, were a form of compromise for me, much like the relationship with my mother had been. They demanded that I kept my truth to myself and validated behaviour that was downright questionable.

'There's something else that I'd like to talk through with you, regarding our relationship?'

'Sure.'

I was hoping that the words wouldn't fail me this time. 'I think there's a bubble that I might need to burst, where you're concerned, that is.' I needed to take a deep breath; I so wanted to get this right. 'You've been everything to me for over two years now, the most important person in my life. But I'm aware that this is sort of a one-sided relationship, isn't it?'

Phil frowned. 'In what way?'

'In that I don't know you at all, do I? I'm not saying that you haven't been caring, or that we didn't get close, but you know me inside out, like nobody else ever has. And yet, it will always be just this, won't it? You're a psychiatrist and I'm your patient.'

'That's true,' he answered slowly, 'but I'm still not quite sure what you're saying.'

'I think I want more, you know? I'd like to be in a relationship with someone who could share himself with me, someone who I could get to know. I mean,' I searched through my brain for the right words, 'I guess what I'm wanting to clarify is, while I remain in therapy with you, is it getting in the way of me forming new relationships?'

Phil smiled. 'Yes, yes and yes. But ironically, you needed to have this relationship with me before you were going to be able to develop a healthier one outside.'

It was what I needed to hear. 'I think some part of me was always harbouring a little wish, you know, of making this relationship with you into more than it really was, and maybe I needed to do that. But just lately I've been feeling that I might be missing out, and if I continue to see you, you'll sort of be filling the gap. Does that make sense?'

He nodded, smiling warmly. 'It certainly sounds as though you're gearing up to ending your therapy.'

'I think so too,' I answered, suddenly feeling a little deflated.

'So are you saying that this is your last session?'

I looked into his eyes, feeling hesitant. 'Maybe just one more?'

'Okay, you do this whenever it feels right for you.'

The week flew. I was working frantically on my book, eager to complete it and move on to my next project. There were so many things in this new world of mine that I was itching to experience. Before anything could truly begin though, I knew that I needed to say goodbye to Phil.

'This is it, you know,' I started.

Phil nodded, smiling. 'Your last session?'

'Yep.'

'How are you feeling?'

'Good. Ready to get on with it, if you know what I mean.'

'I can see that.'

'I've been thinking a lot this past week. I've been so desperately searching for "normal", for as long as I can remember. I thought at one time that my therapy with you would end when you told me that I'd finally made it, you know, joined the Normal Brigade?'

Phil smiled. 'And?'

'And it just doesn't matter anymore, whether I'm normal or not. I like who I am, and I know that I'm different to everybody else, we all are. God only knows what "normal" actually looks like. I thought for a while that it meant being like you, you were my model for normality.'

'Hmmm, not so sure whether that's a good idea,' he joked. 'I've got my own quirks, you know.'

I smiled. 'I'm well aware of that. And that's what is so neat. I don't want to be like you, or anybody else. This is okay, who I am. Warts and all.'

'That must be a good feeling for you.'

'God yes. I don't feel defensive anymore or have that need to pretend. I'm so much safer, these days, with who I am. It feels solid.'

Phil nodded. 'I can certainly sense that.'

'You know, it was such a long time ago that I sat across from you, yearning for that quality of earthiness that you had. And you told me to take it, take whatever I needed. Do you remember that?'

'I do.'

'Well, I took all of it, and I can feel it inside me now. It's wonderful to be able to sit here, to look at you, and not feel that desperate longing anymore.'

'I was happy for you to do that.'

'I know, that's what has made it so special. I don't feel as though I've taken from you at all.'

'That's right, you haven't. It's quite unique, isn't it?'

'It sure is.' I looked around the room, seeing the paintings on the wall that I had become intimately familiar with, the desk piled with books, the tree outside his window; they were etched indelibly into my brain. And there was Phil, sitting across from me, wearing the jumper that I had once wanted to snuggle into. It felt as though a million years had passed since that day.

'I think I'll end this session early,' I told him, feeling as though there really was nothing left to say.

'I thought as much. I'd like to say thank you, again. It's been an honour getting to know you.'

I smiled, loving him more than ever. 'Likewise.'

I stood up, feeling awkward. 'Thank you' was such a tiny phrase after everything we had been through. We stood at his front door.

'I don't know what to say,' I managed.

He patted his shoulder, indicating that I come in for a hug. I put my arms around him for the first time ever, feeling that lovely earthiness that was now my own. I let myself have that hug and truly feel it before finally pulling away. 'Thank you for everything.'

'You're more than welcome.'

And I walked away.

Epilogue

Two years have passed since I walked out of Phil's office for that final time.

Ty has completed his degree, moved to Melbourne with his girlfriend and is currently working with a computer firm. A few months ago his father and I attended his graduation ceremony. As I stood there watching him stride across the stage to collect his degree, I was filled with wonder at this magnificent young man who is my son.

It took me a while to let him read this book, for although he had known bits and pieces about my childhood, I had wanted to keep him shielded from the details. I needn't have worried. Once Ty became involved in this project he picked it up with his usual enthusiasm and has encouraged me every inch of the way. We are both immensely proud of each other.

Jo is now doing well. Having found herself a new therapist, she too is finding peace in her world and restoring her family with rugged determination. We talk to each other now and then, both of us finding new ways to build our own relationship. It has changed. Once this process of growth begins, everything has to be re-evaluated and it was no different for Jo and me. We eventually did get together, in the same city at the same time, and all hell broke loose. But I have great faith in us, and believe we will establish a healthy and positive relationship.

I still think of those three people in England who are the other half of my strange family. Maybe one day I will make contact again and let my brother and sister know that they will always find a warm welcome at my door. I imagine that the time may come when they begin their own search for answers.

I no longer live in Adelaide. I wanted to start a new life in a place where I wasn't surrounded by memories and broken relationships. I have three part-time jobs, which I thoroughly enjoy, and am slowly building a network of healthy, supportive friends. When I read through this book, I am amazed by how different I feel to the woman I was back then. My world is stable now. One day flows smoothly into the next. I no longer dissociate and I can hardly recall what a mood swing feels like. Now I can make plans and feel confident that the 'I' who made them will be there in the future to carry them out. But I do have my off days, like everybody else. Once in a while I find myself missing those fantastic, magical highs. I miss feeling extraordinary. It's a funny thing being 'normal', some could even say a little dull and predictable. And watching the Mondays roll along one after the other can be pretty underwhelming. I finally understand why folks take holidays or give themselves an alcohol-soaked evening now and then. It breaks the monotony. These days I continue exploring and learning new things about myself. I imagine it will be an ongoing process.

And finally, a few months ago, I fell wonderfully, hopelessly in love. I found myself a fellow who is caring, gorgeous, gentle and more than capable of handling a woman with a past such as mine. Bit by bit I have been able to show him who I am and who I was. Now and then I want to take flight, afraid of the unfamiliar, the risk of loss and the commitment to being open and honest and real. And when I run Mark just waits, offering his patience, letting me know that he will be there when I find the courage to come back to him. And though it may take a day or two, I always do. He is a good man.

So, yes, yet another miracle has arrived in this extraordinary life of mine.

And now I would like to direct my final words to any person out there who may be floating in space and desperately searching for answers. I ask you to not give up. And don't ever believe that where you are now, is where you are destined to stay. It doesn't matter how lost you are, how different you may feel to everyone else around you, or how long you have lived in confusion; there is hope out there.

I had learnt to view the world through the eyes of paedophiles and a mother in denial. It was a bleak and barren landscape, devoid of joy, hope or trust, and committed to destroying any good or decent thing that came my way.

There is another vision; of a world where compassion lives, and goodness. A planet that, thank God, has people upon it who can teach us how to love and trust again. Whichever journey you choose, I trust that you will find your way to this grander vision. There is a Phil out there for everyone, in whatever form that may take. You just have to keep searching. Accept nothing less. You deserve it.

Dear Merilyn

Barbra Leslie

Dear Merilyn is a book about a woman artist and her struggle to keep painting. It is also the story of her search for harmony and release from destructive patterns of behaviour formed early in her life in response to disturbing events.

But *Dear Merilyn* is not merely Barbra Leslie's autobiography. It is an Australian family saga, conveyed with fearless honesty and without the soapie filter on the lens. By turns, the events are shocking, frightening, funny, esoteric and heart-warming.

Reproductions of Barbra Leslie's art illuminate this true story that will pin you to your chair.

'In *Dear Merilyn* Barbra Leslie sweeps a searchlight – some would say a blowtorch – over her own life. It is all-encompassing, all-revealing . . . She exults in moments of intense joy and exhilaration. Her erotica can be as raunchy as Aubrey Beardsley. Dominating the book is that ecstasy out of hell – the vision of the artist.'

Colin Thiele

For more information visit www.wakefieldpress.com.au

Dark Dreams

Australian refugee stories by young writers aged 11–20 years

Edited by Sonja Dechian, Heather Millar and Eva Sallis

Dark Dreams is an anthology of essays, interviews and short stories written by children and young adults aged 11–20 years. These young writers relate or imaginatively recreate the story of someone who came to Australia as a refugee.

This is a unique book in Australia. The stories are the finest of hundreds collected through an unprecedented nationwide schools competition, devised by writer Eva Sallis and run by Australians Against Racism Inc.

The essays and stories represent many different countries. Some focus on survival, some on horrors, some on the experiences and alienation of a new world. Some are stories of refugees still living in detention centres in Australia.

'These stories sear us with their authenticity and their humanity. From Holocaust survivors, Vietnamese boat people on to contemporary refugees fleeing oppression in Afghanistan or Iraq, Sri Lanka or Africa, these are accounts we must heed, and learn from.'

Tom Shapcott

For more information visit www.wakefieldpress.com.au

The House at Number 10

Dorothy Johnston

Sophie Harper is abandoned by her husband, not for another woman, but 'a raft of girls – a floating, open-ended freedom'. Left with a four-year-old daughter to support, Sophie finds work in an old house in Canberra that is being used as a brothel. While the laws governing prostitution are being re-written, and prosecutions temporarily in abeyance, Sophie combines caring for her daughter with working in the house.

The House at Number 10 is a novel about the complex relationships people develop with the buildings they live and work in, about betrayal and the will to vengeance, but most of all it is about the resilience of friendship, and the transformative power of the imagination.

For more information visit www.wakefieldpress.com.au

Siblings

Brothers and sisters of children with special needs

Kate Strohm

Siblings tells what it is like to grow up with a sister or brother who has a disability or chronic illness. The siblings of children with special needs are often the overlooked ones in families struggling to cope.

Kate Strohm, an experienced health professional and journalist who has a sister with cerebral palsy, bravely shares the story of her journey from confusion and distress to greater understanding and acceptance. She also provides a forum for other siblings to describe their struggles with resentment, guilt, grief and isolation, their fears and also their joys.

Besides giving siblings a voice at last, Kate Strohm also provides strategies that siblings themselves, parents and practitioners can use to support brothers and sisters of children with special needs.

'This book should be read by anyone coming into contact with a family that includes a child with a disability.'

Professor Graham Vimpani

For more information visit www.wakefieldpress.com.au

One Common Enemy

The *Laconia* incident: A survivor's memoir

Jim McLoughlin with David Gibb

As a young Able Seaman in the Royal Navy during the Second World War, Jim McLoughlin was aboard the infamous HMS *Laconia* when it was torpedoed and sunk by a German U-boat. The tale of his survival is a heart-rending account of hope continually crushed by adversity, only to rise again. *One Common Enemy* includes Jim's account of the astonishing display of compassion by Werner Hartenstein, the fabled Commander of U-156 who undertook the most daring and celebrated rescue attempt of the war.

One Common Enemy is the story of a young man of incredible character and strength, obsessed with the sea, and thrown into the turmoil of war. Surviving was hard, but in the words of Jim, 'those who actually survive the terrors of war, remain prisoners of cruel memories for the rest of their days'.

For more information visit www.wakefieldpress.com.au

Wakefield Press is an independent publishing and
distribution company based in Adelaide, South Australia.
We love good stories and publish beautiful books.
To see our full range of titles, please visit our website at
www.wakefieldpress.com.au.

Wakefield Press thanks Fox Creek Wines
and Arts South Australia for their support.